Cape Town Calling

CAPE TOWN CALLING

From Mandela to Theroux
on the Mother City

Edited by Justin Fox

TAFELBERG

Tafelberg Publishers
a division of NB Publishers
40 Heerengracht, Cape Town, 8000
www.tafelberg.com
© in the selection 2007 author
© in individual extracts as listed on pp. 230–1

Set in Aldus 10.5 on 13 pt
Book design by William Dicey
Cover design by Anthea Forlee,
based on a photograph by Justin Fox

Printed and bound by Paarl Print,
Oosterland Street, Paarl, South Africa

First edition, first printing 2007
ISBN 10: 0-624-04297-9
ISBN 13: 978-0-62404297-6

Contents

Author's Note

The extracts in this anthology appear as they did in the original texts, without my trying to impose any consistency. I have retained variant spelling and punctuation, except in the case of the most obvious typos, which have not been accorded an overly officious '[*sic*]'. Where a passage has been left out, this is indicated with ellipses.

I'd like to thank those who have helped with the compilation, from my faithful readers Suzanne, Revel Jnr and Sarah to the staff at UCT Library, particularly Tanya in Rare Books. I'd also like to extend my gratitude to the authors and publishers for allowing me to reprint their work here. Lastly, the team at Tafelberg have been a tremendous support (anthologies inevitably become group efforts) and I'd like in particular to thank Comien, Anthea, Mandy, William, and of course Erika.

Introduction: Of Storms and Hope

JUSTIN FOX

Here's a Cape Town dilemma: I'm at my computer working on an introduction, but there's a hitch. And it's the age-old problem in this place of too much natural beauty. Outside it's a magnetic spring day. The mountain is a cutout, not a cloud between here and the horizon. Blue lines sweep out of the Atlantic and crash below my Mouille Point apartment. Why remain indoors? I should suit up and walk across the road to ride those green tubes, then maybe a flat white at Newport Deli. Perhaps this writing lark had best wait for tomorrow when the promised cold front will keep me inside. Then again, it might produce a decent swell ...

To surf or to write: the problem of Cape Town in a nutshell. There's all that comeliness and then there's its effect on the unfortunate urban victim who has little defence against its charms. (Of course these are essentially middle-class problems: a domestic worker trying to put bread on the table for five children is not going to be paralysed by the texture of October light on Lion's Head.) Most writers record the overwhelming force of beauty, of the presence of Nature at every turn in this place that is still (beyond Le Corbusier's wildest hopes) a garden city, where that garden is a combination of mountains, forests, vineyards, national parklands and quixotic ocean pressing from every side. It certainly makes for a compelling distraction from the business of living.

When asked to compile this book I must admit to a degree of unease. I've not had an uncomplicated or comfortable relationship with the city. In me there has been a tug-of-war between Cape Town's light and shadow. From an early age I became susceptible to the unique attractions of the natural world so incongruously found in the midst of a city. After school I'd join a gang of boys heading to Newlands

Forest or the lower slopes of Table Mountain to play until dark; every summer holiday I would spend on False Bay getting to know the coastline in anything that floated, as well as the flora and fauna of the peninsula's lower spine. This sort of imprinting is for life. There are certain smells, colours, folds in the land that I could never surrender, no matter where I might find myself.

And yet. And yet I too felt the melancholia and apathy so many writers have noted about the city. *Kaapstad: slaapstad*. I wanted, for long, to get out: Joburg, Africa, Europe, Pofadder, anywhere. But this restlessness, I've grown to understand, is also partly human nature, a need to test other pastures, to distrust the home that is handed to you – at least until you learn the value of roots. (In my family those roots are deep; my ancestors first stepped ashore on Woodstock Beach more than 300 years ago.) There were the dour dripping oaks of my childhood, a nursery school, junior school, high school and university all in the shadow of Devil's Peak, perpetuating a kind of claustrophobia that I felt I carried with me from one institution to the next. The dark political climate and strife beyond the railway line only reinforced the desire to leave.

Perched on the southern tip of Africa, far from the centre of anything, many writers have lamented the cultural backwardness, the oppression of living in a divided city. Even as Cape Town evolves, grows more cosmopolitan, holds its first Picasso exhibition, becomes an international convention hub, acquires its very own fashion week ... I still can't help feeling the old unease. Is it the parochialism and cliquishness that outsiders comment on, joking that only third-generation Capetonians are really accepted? Is it the self-satisfied airheads basking at Camps Bay cafés, flicking golden curls and agonising over which cocktail to order? Is it the smug self-sufficiency that comes with having so much beauty on your doorstep that you don't need to connect with your neighbour? Is it something to do with the schizophrenia of the city not being quite African, of holding onto Europe's apron strings, of not knowing who or what it really is? Or is it the crime, that ubiquitous topic of so much conversation and so little action, which makes this one of the most violent cities on earth?

But then again, Cape Town is an old lover. There are good days and bad days. Mostly, I think, I have made my peace. On the stormy days – perhaps a *Cape Times* report on gangland rape, or Sol Kerzner's promise of a Noddyland hotel for the Waterfront, will trigger my unfaithful-ness – Potchefstroom and Perth look suddenly greener. On the good days – maybe a school of Heaviside's dolphins playing outside my window, full-moonrise from Signal Hill or a spring morning so un-utterably blue it demands to be drunk, not written about – life here seems unrepeatable anywhere else in the world. As in all relationships, the dialogue is never over.

Some of the first writings about our claw of Africa talk of the Cape as Adamastor (variously manifested in the form of Table Mountain, Cape Point or the entire peninsula), a monster punished for his at-tempt to seduce Thetis the sea nymph. Adamastor is most memorably evoked in Luis Vaz de Camões' 16th-century epic poem, *The Lusiads*, in which the Portuguese bard treats the rounding of the Cape by Vasco da Gama as an allegorical encounter between man and a god-like figure. Getting past Adamastor is a rite of passage into a new world and the riches of the Indian Ocean. Exiled from the Pantheon of European gods, Adamastor rages at the bottom of the continent, a monster set to wreck the dreams of global conquest borne in sailing ships from the distant north. In Adamastor, Camões created a vehicle that suited generations of South African writers and poets who saw in this irascible figure much of the ambivalence they felt about the Cape and Africa. As such it has stood variously for amoral Nature, black subjugation, the clash between Europe and the Dark Continent, between new and old. Thus from its early representation in language the Cape has been figured in both positive and negative extremes, a place of danger as much as a symbol of beauty and hope.

Many grand notions and titles have over time attached themselves to this place: a paradise at the southern tip of Africa, the world's richest floral kingdom, a maritime fulcrum between West and East, a European outpost at the foot of the continent, the Tavern of the Seas. But the two names that are the most potent are also two of the earliest: the contradictory claims of this being both a Cape of Storms and a Cape of Good Hope. The tension between these ideas encapsulates many of the tensions of this city.

Legend has it that the first Portuguese navigator to round the southern tip of Africa, Bartolomeu Dias, named this stormy peninsula *Cabo das Tormentas*. However, King João II rejected Dias's name in favour of one that would be more inspirational for the Portuguese people: *Cabo da Boa Esperança*. The turning point for the Lusitanian caravels would spell untold riches in the East. But the dialectic between the two contending titles is as virile today in a city whose promise is limitless and whose socio-political storms act as a sea anchor.

Even the early settlers registered the dichotomies, overwhelmed as they were by the natural sublime and fearful of the wilderness and the Africans it held. Attracted to and feeling alienated from the landscape, they tried to find a language with which to snare it (a process that is ongoing). Some of the writing embraced the land while eliminating the indigenous inhabitants or rendering them as savage. Each generation of writers has faced the dilemma of representing an earthly paradise compromised. The very name 'Good Hope' implies a condition of becoming, not of being ... of a paradise deferred. Today it would be far too simplistic to view the city's Manichean metaphor in purely geographic or demographic terms as a wealthy peninsula of good hope and good fortune juxtaposed with a Cape Flats of stormy destitution. The city, as we shall see in the extracts that follow, is a melting pot of much more complicated joys and troubles.

Cape Town is a place with an embarrassment of natural riches clinging to a dramatic peninsula with a temperate, Mediterranean climate. Writers describe the land with a mixture of love, awe and, at times, dislocated paralysis. By contrast with this complex attraction, the negative is also frequently invoked, like the interminable gale-force southeasters, the miserably wet winters that flood the low-lying suburbs and a certain melancholia in which the landscape, it is argued, is complicit in.

The much vaunted beauty is also shot through with loss and disruption which every long-term Cape Town inhabitant registers. The palimpsests are everywhere. Our natural environment has been stripped of its large game: gone are the lions of Lion's Head, the hippos of Zeekoevlei, the leopards of Newlands. Palatial houses creep higher up the slopes while picturesque old suburbs like District Six have been bulldozed. The Khoisan were hunted to extinction, but their memory lives on in caves of rock art, defensive almond hedges planted by the settlers and in names like Rondebosch, no doubt the 'round bush' of a Khoikhoi kraal.

And the Cape has teeth. The sea, so enticing, freezes you on emersion. Kayaking in False Bay might see the back of your craft bitten off by a great white shark. Mediterranean-style outdoor living can be transformed to cursing pandemonium when the southeaster gets up. That beauty which is so beguiling, can turn on the unsuspecting in an instant.

Similarly the Cape is lauded as having a multicultural society that never fully accepted the Grand Apartheid handed down by Pretoria. It was, we were told, a liberal, tolerant city. A 'Tavern of the Seas', a meeting-place of nations. Cape Town's coloured population and culture are, in this light, viewed as a model for the creolisation of South African society, the perfect antidote to a racially divided past. But there's a political shadow that evokes a very different picture, one in which black South Africans feel alienated in Cape Town, where conservative white flight from the north has resulted in a bastion of conservatism and the only city in the country where the ANC is not in power. It's a place where racism has found a plethora of other forms in which to manifest itself, notably between coloured and Xhosa – a legacy of apartheid's divide-and-rule policies. Black Africans from elsewhere on the continent talk of Cape Town as a place of hatred and violence where xenophobia is so bad that foreigners fear for their lives in certain neighbourhoods. Even a recently arrived Transkeian, an *emaXhoseni*, is discriminated against by 'real' Capetonians (some of whom have been here only a few months longer).

There is much hope vested in Cape Town as being the goose that lays the golden tourism egg. Indeed the city's economy is increasingly geared towards the needs of visitors. The tourist industry is flourish-ing, creating many jobs and, in a sense, continuing the city's tradition of being an international meeting place. Local cuisines and cultural traditions, such as the Cape Minstrels, have experienced a boost and found their way onto the global tourist map. A Rip van Winkel waking from only a 20-year sleep (and many a voluntary exile returning on holiday from Sydney or San Diego is just such a character) would stand aghast at the changes. In another 20 years Cape Town might well be unrecognisable to us now. But many aspects of the old city are dying in the hand-over-fist scramble to turn us into a 'world destination'. From glamorous five-star hotels and film crews taking over streets or whole suburbs to the uninhibited development of various waterfronts in service of the tourist dollar. Building restrictions, heritage concerns or an adherence to the vernacular are given short shrift. The tourist and property boom speak of an obsession with today, and possibly tomorrow, but there's not much looking back in this place.

Apart from natural beauty, Cape Town still possesses some of the country's finest architecture and urban environments. There are Cape Dutch homesteads, elegant Victorian streets, 18th-century districts and charming cobbled lanes and squares. However the prevailing impression is darker. Most modern architecture has done little credit to our city and many suburbs, particularly in the north, deserve to be flattened (I'd like to see Fish Hoek on that list too). Worse, the majority of Capetonians live in sprawling shanty towns that stretch across the Cape Flats. Transforming their living environment, and making sure that what replaces it is not another urban excrescence, is perhaps the biggest challenge facing the city. Failure would see the demise of so much of what people have traditionally loved about Cape Town. History lies in those boxes of corrugated iron demanding to be remade.

Over the period during which the following extracts take place – more or less the last four decades – Cape Town has undergone a radical transformation. In the '60s it would have been possible to define, fairly accurately, what the city was. But in the intervening period its character and identity have changed dramatically. With an influx of immigrants from elsewhere in the country, the continent and abroad, with the end of apartheid and race-based town planning, the economic and property explosions, the invasion of foreign tourists, the effects of globalisation and the hosting of rugby, cricket and soccer World Cups, the city has been remade before our startled eyes.

If Cape Town exists in culture principally in the imaginations of those who live here, then it is nowadays as much a construct of Constantia housewives, Bo-Kaap tailors, Blue Train bergies and Bonteheuwel gangsters as it is of Congolese car guards, Chinese exchange students, English merchant bankers, German kitesurfers or Somali traders. The Cubist painting that is this anthology is a partial, narrow window onto the enormous, rapidly evolving portrait of our city.

The sleepy seaside town of my childhood is no more. But I do find bits of my Cape Town – ironically for a beach lover – in midwinter. When the tourist droves have left, the streets are rinsed with rain from the west and the sound of the *adhaan* hangs clear over the city from the mosques in Bo-Kaap. When a walk on Clifton beach is yours alone, among wrack tossed by a violent, frontal sea. When the Cape feels most like a ship battering its way into the Atlantic, the decks awash as the old grey hull ploughs southward. When the slopes of the mountain have their first green blush, patching over the scars of summer veld fires. When the nerve-fraying southeasters on False Bay have stilled and Adamastor's knuckles have become moist once again, the fynbos fragrant. When the chug of a Hout Bay fishing boat can be heard for miles and the whales are here to calve. It is in winter, for me, that the Cape is most itself. As a youngster I riled at the city's dead-season retreat into its harbour-dorp shell. Now I relish it.

Stephen Watson, poet and professor of English at the University of Cape Town, has frequently called for writers to remake this city in the incarnation of their imaginations. Recent decades have seen a partial addressing of his injunction. Cape Town lives passionately in poetry, especially in the work of Ingrid de Kok and Watson himself. In fiction too, the city has begun to take a modern shape, notably in Mike Nicol and Joanne Hitchens's crime-novel *Out to Score* and, teasingly, in a number of JM Coetzee's novels. But it is in the area of creative non-fiction, and travel writing in particular, that there has been a lack. This paucity saw the publication in 2006 of *A City Imagined*, edited by Watson, in which he invited a number of prominent writers to produce essays recreating the city that shaped them.

Watson's book prompted me to scroll back over recent decades to see what material was already in existence. It started as an entertaining literary exercise, but once the box was open, it wouldn't shut again easily. To limit my scope I concentrated solely on creative non-fiction (an anthology of Cape Town in fiction and poetry begs publication) that is 'modern' and deals predominantly with 'recent' texts. I took as a benchmark my own lifetime, thereby restricting my search to works that have appeared during, and focus predominantly on, the period between the late 1960s and the present.

The first five chapters of *Cape Town Calling* represent different sub-urbs or areas, while the last two deal with particular experiences of the city: prison life and the impressions of foreign travellers.

The first chapter looks at the City Bowl, site of the Dutch refreshment station established in 1652 and still the city's heart. The idea of a bowl is suggested by the encircling sandstone arms of Table Mountain that act as a backdrop and amphitheatre to the drama of the city. Although the initial extract by Steenkamp doffs its hat to Cape Town's early history, most of the pieces chosen reflect the political turmoil under apartheid and the birth process of the democratic city that followed. Where Uys and Kaplan describe various forms of anti-government protest, Johnson and Mandela focus on the euphoria and fear in the streets of Cape Town at the unbanning of the ANC and the release of political prisoners: momentous moments in South Africa's history as they are played out at City Hall. This thread culminates in Ndebele's meditation on 27 April 1994, the first time all South Africans were able to vote in a general election. It is interesting to note how Cape Town's raw materials – mountain, sea, wind – are remade and revisioned by each generation of writers, modifying old metaphors to suit the changing city. Thus through Ndebele's eyes we see craggy old Adamastor as a symbol of faith in the future, while Cameron's ascent of Platteklip Gorge is viewed in terms of a victorious struggle against AIDS.

Chapter Two considers District Six, a suburb at the foot of Table Mountain that was largely inhabited by poor coloured families. Although run-down, it had a charm and character all its own and was one of the liveliest areas of the city. In accordance with the Group Areas Act, parts of the District were declared 'whites only' in 1966 and zoned for demolition. In the ensuing years bulldozers flattened the area street by street and the inhabitants were 'relocated' to bleak suburbs on the Cape Flats. The extracts chosen show the many faces of the District: from the joy of family and community life played out on the stoeps and cobbled streets, to gang warfare and police raids. The tone is nostalgic mixed with anger and the voices are those of men and women across the racial spectrum.

Cape Town's affluent, formerly white suburbia has been the subject of much writing that has tried to represent the world of ennui and privilege that existed, and still exists, in many of the southern and northern suburbs. Coetzee's veiled autobiographical sketches and Kaplan's medical chronicle point to the uneasy interface between rav-aged black areas and safe white areas that abut each other along the old apartheid dividing lines. While Watson and Morris meditate on life in 'grey' (non-racial) Woodstock, sitting as it does on the edge of city, sea and mountain, Gordon plunges into the Bohemian and druggy student world of Observatory. By contrast, Bristow-Bovey has regularly found subjects for his satire in Cape Town's wealthier suburbs.

Many parts of the windswept, sandy Cape Flats – dealt with in the fourth chapter – became a dumping ground for people who had been evicted from white areas. In addition, the constant arrival of Xhosa men from the Eastern Cape seeking jobs filled a growing number of 'dormitory districts'. When they were joined by their families, they began creating 'illegal' shantytowns which have subsequently grown into Cape Town's largest suburbs. Where Jaffer and Ramphele recall the days of struggle and police brutality, the ensuing extracts focus on life on the post-apartheid flats where AIDS, TB, gangs, poverty and endemic crime threaten the fabric of society. As Johnson prophetically notes in a 1986 article recording the war zone that was Crossroads township: 'I fear the hideous human harvest in the children who have grown up with this limitless violence around them.'

As any visitor will learn soon after arriving in Cape Town, the city has two seaboards – Atlantic on the west and False Bay on the east – each with its own unique charms. False Bay with its warmer water, calmer sea and old-world atmosphere is presented as a very different kettle of snoek to the glamorous, nouveau-riche Atlantic side. Watson, Breytenbach, Nicol and Malan all describe the natural beauty of sea- and landscapes, and carefree life 'on the bay' where three of them have made their homes. Shifting focus to the western seaboard, Cope charts the transformation of Clifton from the beach shacks of his childhood to the apartment blocks of millionaires' row. By contrast, Morris looks at how a white community in Noordhoek comes to terms with having a township on its doorstep, a process similar to the one recorded by Nicol as he tries to adapt to the slummification of Muizenberg.

As Cape Town was a centre of struggle against apartheid and is today one of the world's crime capitals, many people have experienced this city from behind bars – the theme of the sixth chapter. Mandela, Kathrada and Breytenbach record prison life as a rite of passage, rungs on the ladder of personal and national liberation. By contrast, Steinberg looks at the underworld of prison gangs, whose influence reaches far beyond Pollsmoor's gates.

The final chapter takes a look at how foreign visitors – American, British, Australian, Kenyan and Burundian – have experienced Cape

Town. Reporting for the *New York Times* during the dark days of the 1980s, Lelyveld's take on the city is considerably more pessimistic than most post-1994 tourists'. But despite travellers pursuing such hedonistic pleasures as following the progress of the Rugby World Cup, or enjoying the city's riotous nightlife, there is an undercurrent of unease about the discrepancies between rich and poor. For those from other parts of Africa – such as Papa Chris – who seek asylum in this city, the welcome is as icy as the Atlantic that washes our doorstep.

That's more than enough time spent indoors. Let me go and dunk myself in all that debilitating beauty. It's four foot and hollow at Off the Wall. My board is waxed and the southeaster is not yet up ...

CITY BOWL

from Poor Man's Bioscope (1979)

WILLEM STEENKAMP

There is nothing like a slow stroll up Adderley Street if you are a man who likes to roll his tongue around the full fine flavour of our oldest city. Just about everything that has ever happened in Cape Town has run its course within sight or sound of the first of Van Riebeeck's streets. It is, if you will excuse my being a little fanciful, the main amphitheatre in the poor man's bioscope.

So be my guest and take a stroll up Adderley Street sometime. If you know where to look you will still be able to spot the scenery of a good many great shows of the past ... a building, a name, perhaps just the vibrations of an ancient sorrow or excitement. I cannot walk up Adderley Street (for some reason most people seem to walk *down* it instead of up, but I am ever contrary in my ways) without being reminded of a dozen things I have seen happen there, and a couple of dozen more that I would have liked to see.

He travels fastest who travels alone, they say, but unless you know your Cape Town pretty well it is worth while to take along a guide to lead you to the finest of the things to see and think about.

Or better still, take several; the poor man's bioscope has seen three centuries of shadow-play, and you cannot understand the end of any show unless you have seen the beginning as well.

For the first guide, let me recommend a gentleman with the unlikely name of Mr Wilberforce Bird, late Controller of Customs at the Cape. I regret to say that Mr Bird took his transfer to a rather more celestial department of the civil service at least a century ago, but he left behind him an encyclopaedic book entitled *The State of the Cape of Good Hope in 1822* which is as good a programme for our early show as I can think of.

Let us imagine, therefore, that it is a balmy spring day in 1823 or thereabouts, and you and I and Mr Bird are making our way up the

Heerengracht, which will not become Adderley Street for another 30 years or so.

To our left as we stroll along the dusty sidewalk is the Castle of Good Hope, the sea lapping at the roots of the outward bastions from which great muzzle-loading guns stare out to sea. They are in semi-retirement at the moment, because the last threat to the Cape came to an end with the final collapse of Napoleon Buonaparte (the Corsican Tyrant, let it be said, has just struck a final blow at the Cape by inconsiderately dying in exile on St Helena, thereby causing something of a recession among various local merchants who had made rather a good thing out of supplying the garrison which guarded him there).

In front of the Castle is the Grand Parade, a huge expanse of beaten earth which stretches westwards all the way up to the grim old Grand Barracks erected in the Dutch East India Company days. Fronting on the Parade, as Mr Bird points out, are two buildings which play an important role in the daily affairs of the Cape Colony. One is the customs house, an essential cog in the machinery of any seaport. The other is what he, like most Capetonians, refers to as the 'Tronk' ... the old Dutch East India Company's gaol, which was erected nearly 50 years ago.

A much more imposing building than the Tronk is the many-pillared Commercial Exchange, built by subscription during Lord Charles Somerset's rule at a time when the pockets of the Cape merchants were running over with money and their hearts with pleasant expectations of profits yet to come. Alas, they over-reached themselves and the Exchange is something of a white elephant just now.

So remarks the sharp-tongued Mr Bird. He concedes grudgingly that it is a fine building, but what is to become of it? There are rumours that it is to become a place of public entertainment or bought and turned into a church. In the interim the proprietors are pinning their hopes on the possibility that Cape Town will be declared a free port, but I fear they hope in vain.

We progress a little further up the Heerengracht and reach the Society House, from which issues one of the principal heart-beats of the city's social life. Like the Exchange, the Society House was erected by subscription shares; it has billiard and card rooms and a ball room in which 'assemblies' or subscription dances are held during the winter. It also has coffee rooms, where for dues of nine rix-dollars a quarter you may go to refresh your innards with a cup of coffee and improve your mind by paging through a small and dog-eared variety of old newspapers and pamphlets.

Mr Bird is pretty scathing in his comments about the poor attractions of the coffee rooms and the rapacity of the Society House's proprietors, but even he has to admit that the place has its attractions. For example, it is so wonderfully located in the centre of the Heerengracht. No matter where you are bound for – the Parade, the customs house, the government offices, the wharf – you are sure to pass it. As all roads are said to lead to Rome, so do they also pass the Society House; and between 11 o'clock in the morning and five o'clock in the afternoon almost everyone who is anyone in Cape Town is likely to pop in for a greater or lesser period of time. Physicians, lawyers, civil servants, officers from the garrison, wealthy merchants ... Some will hurry their way through a cup of coffee, others will settle down on the green benches in front of the Society House and spend hours gossiping or just watching the world go by.

One gathers from Mr Bird that a good many of the loafers on the green benches are what he calls 'Indians' ... yellow-eyed and arrogant gentlemen whose health has been so damaged by the fevers of that great sub-continent that they have been forced to transport their wasted carcasses to the Cape for months of convalescence and recuperation.

What do the gentlemen on the green benches gossip about? Mr Bird is acid in his comments. For one thing, he says, they are fond of what is called 'shaving'. The idea is to seize some topical talking-point, grossly embroider on it and then see how many people can be made to believe it. If you have been shaved, you can redeem yourself by seeing how many others you can shave in turn.

Mr Bird does not mind the shaving so much; what rouses him to savage contempt is the way the loungers on the green benches ogle any passing woman. 'Every female, who passes through this street to her visits or her occupation, runs the gauntlet of these acute Heerengracht observers', he says. 'The fashionable shop for ladies' dress unfortunately is situated at the very door of the Society House. Ill luck to the poor girl, who, as she turns the corner, discovers a newly created fracture in her stocking, between the shoe and the bottom of the petticoat. Nothing escapes the close investigation of these idlers, and although no word is said, the titter and the laugh draw forth a profusion of blushes.'

Mr Bird concludes that if every ailing expatriate's physician would prescribe a few hours' ball-throwing on the Parade 'he would confer a triple obligation, by giving occupation to the idle, restoring the hypochondriacal Indian to health, and removing a nuisance from the Heerengracht'.

All this talking has made us thirsty and we go into the Society House, running a gauntlet of stares from the green benches and knowing that in all likelihood the owners of the stares will shortly be dissecting us in the most detailed and libellous way. We enjoy a cup of good coffee (after all, the Dutch *know* how to make a satisfying brew, and the Cape has only been a British possession for some 16 years). As Mr Bird has warned us, however, the periodicals scattered about are nothing to write home about, and after thumbing through a battered old pamphlet entitled 'The Life and Adventures of Joshua Penny' we leave to continue with our walk.

As we emerge into the street Mr Bird makes an interesting observation. If this had been a town in England or Ireland, he says, there would have been a swarm of beggars clustering around the Society House's door; 'but here a beggar is unknown, save for one, who, on the Wynberg road, like Lazarus, lieth at the rich man's gate. Blind and old, he possibly may be led there by daily kindness, in order to enjoy the warmth of that sun, of whose blessed light he can no more hope to partake.'

Thus pondering the Mother City's paucity of mendicants, we stroll on, wending our way between the pedestrians of all colours and shapes and sizes, from knights of the Garter to sweating slaves laden like pack-donkeys, who pass us as they go about their business.

Mr Bird points out some of the other sights as we make our way to the top of the busy street. He shows us the handsome Dutch Reformed Church which future Capetonians will call the Groote Kerk. Next to it are the old slave quarters, he reminds us. These days the long white building houses such important men as the virtually omnipotent secretary of the colony and his three fiscals. It also contains the law courts, from which as we pass we can hear the advocates pleading their cases in a torrent of Dutch so eloquent that, as Mr Bird says with a sardonic grin, 'the mind is almost deceived into a belief that they are arguing for truth, and not for pay'.

Alas! Most of these impassioned voices are about to be choked to a whisper by a fiat from the Governor, the Earl of Caledon, who intends to ban the use of Dutch in the law courts; thus unwittingly laying an early brick in the melancholy edifice of rancour and distrust which will culminate, in eight decades' time, in the second and most terrible of the Anglo-Boer Wars.

But all that is still eight decades away, and all unknowing and un-caring we follow Mr Bird away from the Supreme Court towards the new colonial public library building in near-by Burg Street. Till very recently, we are given to understand, the library was housed in the Supreme Court building. However, the government has just given it this handsome home of its own. The new building is very well suited to its purpose, Mr Bird remarks. It has facilities for chemical experiments by scientifically-minded citizens, while there are two large reading-rooms in which those seeking a good read can enjoy such delights as the books from the well-known Dessinian collection.

The Dessinian collection, Mr Bird explains, was built up by a German named Joachim Nicolaus von Dessin, who came to the Cape around the middle of the 18th Century and rose to be secretary of the Orphan Chamber. A pleasant and tolerably well-educated man, Mr Von Dessin had been a great favourite with all during his lifetime, and in death performed a final service to humanity by not only willing his slaves their freedom but also by directing that his collection be turned into a library for Capetonians. His collection has since been greatly ex-panded, Mr Bird notes, but adds sadly that the one thing Mr Dessin could not bequeath along with his books was a sufficient quantity of people who wished to read them: 'Reading,' he says, 'is not an African passion ...'

Suddenly a car hoots loudly and anachronistically. We find that Mr Bird has vanished, and so has the Cape Town of 1823. Feeling a strange sense of loss, we re-trace our stroll of a century and a half ago. Anxiously we cast about for the sights Mr Bird was showing us only five minutes ago. The Mother City has changed so much: can there be any landmarks left to guide us on our way? Why, even the Heerengracht, or most of it, has changed its name to Adderley Street, in honour of an almost-forgotten British parliamentarian.

Praise be, the Castle is still there. It is as forbidding as ever, but considerably changed. Its battlements now sport rows of red bricks, and what remains of the artillery is now so smothered in paint that any old-time gunner would have died of the apoplexy in his efforts to force a smouldering slow match down the clogged touch-hole of any one of the pieces of ordnance. Indeed, no gun has fired a shot in anger on Cape soil since Mr Bird's countrymen put General Janssens (not to mention a certain ancestor of mine named Jan Zacharias Moolman) to flight at the Battle of Blaauwberg in 1806. The waves that used to slap at its outer bastions are long gone, forced to retreat by the land-filling operations that destroyed the lovely little fishing harbour of Rogge Bay and created what we modern-day Capetonians call the Foreshore.

The Grand Parade is still there, of course, and now and then it still shakes under the thumping feet of drilling soldiers. But it is a shadow of what it used to be. Urban expansion has taken great bites out of its former great size. Its western front now ends at Darling Street, and the Grand Barracks have gone and are commemorated only by a narrow street which bears their name. Ah, well ... At least Capetonians still flock to the morning markets there, and the palm trees stand as tall along Darling Street as they did when Mr Bird knew it by its older name of Keisergracht.

The Commercial Exchange is gone, too, although a mall named Exchange Place serves to remind us of the old Cape merchants' grandiose designs. The Society House is gone as well, green benches, dog-eared pamphlets and all; so have the 'Indians', not just from Cape Town but from India itself.

We note with some relief that the Dutch Reformed Church has survived, though radically rebuilt since Mr Bird knew it. Set into one wall is the tombstone of Baron Pieter van Rheede van Oudtshoorn, the last Dutch governor to be buried at the Cape. It has been a long time since any notable was stowed away in the Groote Kerk's vault, and only Baron Pieter's bones still lie there; all the other remains were exhumed and reinterred elsewhere during the widening of Bureau Street in the early 1960s.

We nod a friendly greeting to the statue of Andrew Murray, the Scots-Afrikaner divine, as we pass the Groote Kerk's east entrance, and then walk on. The road and sidewalks are metalled now, and the traffic on them is worse than ever. It is not quite the same to look at as before, of course. Knights of the Garter are scarce nowadays, and slaves have vanished forever, while the girls wear clothes so scanty and casual that any old-time Indian would have fainted away before the first snigger. Yet the essence of the scene has changed remarkably little. The old fashions and customs of 1822 may have gone into the discard, but the passers-by are as polyglot a mob as ever they were in Mr Bird's time and the girls are prettier than ever.

Ah! Now we can see the old slave quarters-turned-Supreme Court. It has not been a courthouse for many years, of course, and has altered position slightly as a result of road-widening operations in the 1950s, but the long white building is as gracious as ever. We note with some bewilderment, however, that from a flagpole on the Old Supreme Court's roof waves a large green flag on which we can make out a golden crescent and some Arabic letters.

Have the descendants of the Muslim slaves so cruelly exiled here by the Dutch staged a takeover? Well, no. The Old Supreme Court of a few years ago is now called the Cultural History Museum, and the flag is there to advertise an exhibit featuring the second and lesser of the two Malay Artillery Corps raised in the early 19th Century. These days the lawyers plead their clients' innocence in the new (comparatively speaking) Supreme Court in Keerom Street, just a couple of minutes' walk away, and while Dutch never recovered from the Earl of Caledon's blow its lineal descendant, Afrikaans, is much to be heard at the bar.

Now we are almost at the end of our journey. We walk up Government Avenue into the Gardens, take note of the Parliament buildings on our left and St George's Cathedral on our right, and arrive at the pillared steps of the South African Public Library in which the Dessinian collection has finally found a permanent home. Here there are no rooms for chemical experiments, but it would do Mr Bird's heart a power of good to see how the number of books has grown since 1822. If reading has not yet grown into an African passion, it is certainly a much more popular pastime.

Seized by a desire to browse through Mr Dessin's wonderful collection, we enter the library. We find that the Dessinian collection's priceless books are not to be casually picked off the shelves, but are guarded in the Africana reference room. There it is cool and quiet, as a library should be, and automatically we pitch our voices low as we return the librarian's greeting. What are we looking for? Oh ... For a moment we are at a loss. Actually, of course, we are there for no good reason except that Mr Bird was conducting us to the library when he was so abruptly banished from this century.

Then we remember that well-thumbed pamphlet we had been examining in the Society House 20 minutes and 150 years ago.

'"The Life and Adventures of Joshua Penny",' the librarian repeats after us.

'He was an American sailor who spent 14 months living in the caves of Table Mountain during the first British occupation,' we explain, hastily dredging up a few of the facts we remember from our hasty perusal of the pamphlet.

The librarian helps us to find the correct reference and asks us to wait. In a few minutes she is back with what looks like that very same copy we had handled in the Society House. Gently (for now it is very frail) we open it and begin to read ...

from Between the Devil and the Deep (2005)

PIETER-DIRK UYS

Life outside the theatre influenced our passion and forced us to have opinions and act on them. The country was being strangled by the Afrikaner Broederbond's successful recipe for white supremacy called apartheid. The world called it apart-height, which easily became apart-hate. The small bleats of protest coming from our stages were often tolerated as irritating noises-off. The real dramas of life often made us feel ashamed of our creativity behind the safety of our theatrical 'fourth wall'.

Cape Town tried to pretend that life was going on as usual. The city prided itself on a liberal attitude, and, even though the roots of apartheid were anchored in 'the fairest Cape in the whole circumference of the earth', it was convenient to blame Pretoria for the reality of our politics.

In 1973 a city theatre festival was announced, at which drama, music and art were encouraged. It would obviously be within the structures of the law – in other words, for whites only. Because The Space was unashamedly 'non-racial', it was breaking the law by allowing blacks and whites to sit together in the same theatre. We decided to take part in this festival by presenting a piece of street theatre. Obviously no one in the tower of power down in Wale Street was quite sure what that meant. So we were officially included in the programme.

'The Space will present Street Theatre in Greenmarket Square!'

The public was fascinated. The production in the Main Theatre at that time was a new Tennessee Williams drama called *Outcry*, starring Bill Flynn and Michele Maxwell. While Greenmarket Square had not yet been given over to the colourful stalls of a daily market as it is today (it was illegal for the races to practise such business together!), the small, square men's toilet in the centre of the space – also for whites only – provided a perfect stage for our piece. It was publicised that Bill Flynn and Michele Maxwell would be doing an extract from their play on that 'stage' on a Saturday morning at 11.30.

The city would be full of shoppers, and workers would have time to have a look. Bill and Michele were famous and popular. Friends of The Space were concerned. Our enemies were perplexed. We were inspired.

Guerrilla theatre had always held an attraction for us. Even though we were never on the barricades fighting the monsters of oppression, the images of the Hungarian uprising, the Czechoslovakian bloodbath and the East German underground's attempts to puncture the façade of totalitarian power showed what could be done with the pen and the word. The American youth revolution against the Vietnam War demonstrated the power of the guitar and the song.

Saturday dawned, and Bill and Michele set off for their challenging experience. There was no amplification to help them, and they would have to project their voices into the ether, competing with doves and traffic, police sirens and drunks. While this was attracting the attention of a waiting crowd, the real presentation began to take shape.

Space stage manager John Nankin arrived on the south side of the Square. He was dressed elegantly, and so were those with him. They were part of a wedding party. He was the groom. There was a mother in a huge hat, a father with a fashionable moustache. There were best friends as best men, and a small page boy. They got out of their fleet of glittering, expensive cars, all lent to us by members of The Space Club, who were watching from a distance with fingers crossed.

It was nothing new for wedding parties to have their official pictures taken on Greenmarket Square. In fact, it was the ideal spot, with the historic buildings surrounding the cobbled area and the magnificent sweep of Table Mountain creating a perfect backdrop for that all-important moment in the lives of two young people, now joined as one.

Meanwhile, on the north side of the Square, the bridal party arrived. The bride was Toti Ebrahim, an assistant stage manager and aspiring actress, looking glorious in a shimmering white bridal gown. As there was happily no south-easter blowing, her three bridesmaids could arrange the long chiffon train behind her, while the small flower girls held their little baskets of rose petals in their gloved hands. The bride's mother was Cathy Zeeman from the Space Canteen. Her father was Bill Curry.

The two parties saw each other across a now crowded Greenmarket Square. They waved. People smiled with sentimental enjoyment. Weddings always make someone cry.

The wedding photographers arrived, Brian Astbury in the lead, with assistants who were ready to set up for the ultimate photo without fuss. The fact that there were more photographers than usual did not seem much of an issue. Yet.

On the roof of the whites-only toilet, Bill and Michele were passionately performing the great American dramatist. The crowd around them were fascinated. Very little of the dialogue was heard. Very few actually understood what was being acted, but this was Theatre and different from their daily lives.

As the two parties of the wedding group slowly walked towards each other, there was a slight parting of the waves. The crowd, who were concentrating on Bill and Michele on the raised platform, started taking note of the bride and the groom.

She looked so lovely. He looked so handsome. What a perfect couple. But what was wrong here?

One by one the Capetonians in the multiracial crowd turned away from the official focus of their attention and stared at this everyday occurrence. A bridal couple and their families posing for a picture. It happened every weekend. Facing them, a handful of working photographers.

Then it clicked. As the cameras whirred, like a veldfire the ripple spread through the crowd.

The bride was coloured! The groom was white!

While actors from The Space were expected to be provocative and tap-dance on the crumbling edge of the cliff, their Tennessee Williams presentation was dull by comparison with this impossible sight. There was no way that a white man would be allowed to marry a coloured woman. If they attempted a relationship under cover of duvet and darkness, they would be arrested under the Immorality Act. The Mixed Marriages Act forbade them even to think of it, and the Group Areas Act made sure that, even if they managed to stay together, they were not allowed to live in the same place!

And yet, here they were, in the centre of the most public area of Cape Town, on a crowded Saturday morning? Holding hands? Smiling at the cameras? Kissing for a picture? He with her brown parents. She with his white father and mother. Black and brown mixing with white. Normally, delightfully, happily.

The reaction was nuclear!

White people took nervous steps away from the scene, coloured people pushed closer for a look, and blacks just stood and laughed. Fear and fascination mingled. The outrage of the normality of the moment far outweighed the simple fact that laws were being broken here and people would be arrested. On the stage the Tennessee Williams dialogue petered out as Bill and Michele stood transfixed by the happening.

My job was to be on the lookout for the police.

We had already seen some familiar slouches skirt the edges of the crowds. Now photographers arrived who were not from the *Cape Times*. They were not just photographing the wedding party, who smiled sweetly at each camera with no hint of concern. They were photographing members of the public.

The bubble of fun could not last.

We heard police sirens approach. Because of the dense crowd, the trucks couldn't reach the centre of attention. On a signal from Brian, with casual smiles and supposed discussions on where the reception would be held, the wedding party split in two, making their way back to their cars. This time they were all mixed together. The white father in animated conversation with the coloured mother, the white best man opening the car door for the smiling black bridesmaid.

We held our breath.

The people of Cape Town started applauding. The swell of sound engulfed the entire Square. Bill and Michele joined them. The security policemen posing as photographers found themselves engulfed by a crowd of well-wishers who made it hard for them to take their snaps.

And then it was over.

We all stood around and looked at one another. I recognised some members of The Space Club. A coloured couple just shook their heads and shrugged. She was crying. The man was too moved to say anything. White friends were talking in low voices. The local bergies, already drunk on cheap booze, were now intoxicated by that brief vision of heaven.

'A white groom and a hotnot bride? Sies!' the toothless old hag screamed, and danced a wedding jig. Gracie and Spider had been watching from the steps of the church. Mario Lanza applauded with a flourish. Yvonne Bryceland picked up some paper flowers that a bridesmaid had dropped. All these things had to be returned. They had lent us everything: the costumes, the cars, the flowers. Even the shoes. Members of The Space Club had understood what guerrilla theatre meant in Cape Town in 1973.

Simple theatre in the street, reflecting the impossible ...

The show was never over in Long Street.

Sitting in our kaftans on the verandah of our rented flat above the fish and chips shop, Maralin [van Reenen], Grethe Fox and I would look over at the balconies of Carnival Court and the activity among the residents. Those 'girlies' and their friends inspired my play *Karnaval*. I didn't have to use much imagination. I just had to look out of the window.

Karnaval was set in that very space in Long Street on a New Year's Eve in the mid-1970s. Auntie Dora is celebrating in her own lonely way. She advises the young girls who board in the building and hopes they will not overstep the mark. Meaning not having sex with coloured sailors for money! Like an old Medea who never had the children to kill, she represents an older generation exhausted by the demands of being special and white. Changes are coming. The sun will rise and bring another day. So enjoy the darkness of the night while it lasts.

I invited the residents of Carnival Court to a preview of the play in the Outer Space. We had built a set based on their home outside. The balconies with the broekie-lace surround, the washing line with the baby clothes dangling in the wind. Even the dartboard askew on the wall. Springbok Radio blaring from Auntie Dora's portable radio. There was no subtle attempt to pretend here.

Brian and I watched them come across Long Street. Dressed up for the theatre like no one did any more. Their hair had been done, their stockings were new. Auntie Dora had her teeth in, all of them! A special treat. I didn't want them to hear from others about *Karnaval* and think I had been making fun of them. I was quite prepared for their anger and hurt. Brian thought the tough with the boep on whom I based the character on stage, Boytjie, would donner me!

They came out of the play in tears.

'Ag, dearie me,' wept the old woman who had inspired Cornelia Stander's Auntie Dora. 'Those poor girlies. Haai, so tragic, maar ag, so brave. There by the grace of God go we!'

And they thanked Brian and hugged me, and I signed their programmes and they went back to their Long Street lives, without having seen any similarity with themselves on our stage. So much for theatre being the mirror of life. Maybe it was just a window.

The Publications Control Board thought it was obscene and blasphemous.

Karnaval was banned after ten performances. The censors were probably right when they saw my characters on the balcony, swearing, loving, laughing and living in Afrikaans. 'Ons mense is nie so nie!'

Our people are not like that.

from The Dressing Station (2001)

JONATHAN KAPLAN

A small group of students had marched through the centre of Cape Town that morning, carrying banners calling for an end to apartheid. By lunchtime they were ranged on the steps of the Anglican cathedral near the Parliament buildings, their banners aloft, when the police arrived. A stand-off ensued in the warm sunshine, with motorists steering carefully along the road between the opposing groups. Though the police seemed uncertain about taking action against the students in such a public place, riot squad reinforcements were gathering in the sidestreets, and student messengers were sent to the campus to ask for help.

I was drowsing over my lecture notes when there was a bustle in the corridor outside, and the sound of running feet. The door to the lecture hall opened with a crash. A face peered in and addressed us, ignoring the man at the podium.

'There's going to be trouble at St George's Cathedral; hundreds of cops and riot trucks. We need lots of people there; they can't arrest everyone.'

'Young man!' shouted the lecturer, but the messenger had already left to spread the word. A few of my friends stood up. I joined them. Perhaps ten, in that class of a hundred, made for the door. Some of our classmates hissed at us. The lecturer glowered, and a Catholic girl crossed herself. Outside it was clear that there had been a much better response from the liberal arts faculties, for all over campus students streamed out of the buildings and jostled for lifts, piling into cars and pickups and vw buses that roared off down to the highway that led to town.

We approached the cathedral from the rear, through public gardens unusually empty of sweepers and gardeners and nannies with their charges. From ahead came a thready chanting and a thumping sound that I couldn't identify. Rounding the building, we came to where the battle lines were drawn. A host of students, men and women, occupied the stone steps of the cathedral and the pavement in front of it. Across the street, drawn up in solid rows, stood a phalanx of riot police. Steady as a heartbeat, they struck their batons against the Perspex shields they carried. The crowd flinched at each resounding blow, shrinking back towards the cathedral steps. Then a police colonel stepped to the front of the line, sunlight blinking off the braid on his cap. In one hand he held a yellow megaphone.

'This is a prohibited gathering.' The metallic warp cut through the sudden silence. 'You have thirty seconds to disperse.'

He stood there in his dark uniform, the bright yellow cone raised to his mouth.

'It's Daffy Duck!' yelled a wag in the crowd, and a roar of laughter drowned out the colonel's next words. He turned to the police lines, raising an arm. There was a cracking sound and tear-gas canisters lofted skyward, trailing arcs of haze. They struck the street, squirting smoke as they rolled towards us. A student scooped one up and flung it back into the police ranks, where it fumed under their feet. Gagging and swearing, the riot cops reeled, then charged in a body, their long batons raised. The banner-holders in the front went down under a storm of blows and were dragged across the roadway to the waiting trucks. The rest of us fled up the cathedral steps, gas canisters churning white clouds under our feet. We kicked them off the top step and stared, horrified, at the melee below, where people screamed and choked in the rising smoke and knots of students cowered under flailing clubs.

Men and women leapt up the steps, their arms outstretched towards us, while red-faced cops grabbed at their clothes and hurled them down, kicking them as they fell. In front of me a grisly tugging match ensued as we dragged at the hands of a girl while a policeman continued to rain blows on her back and legs. There was a shouted command and she fell, sobbing, into our arms. The police line retreated, stair by stair, exposing a wasteland of blood-splashed stone and lost shoes. We stood at the top of the stairs between the open cathedral doors. My eyes streamed; the gas stung my lips and smarted where it found moisture on my sweating face. People retched and coughed. Some helped to pass our injured to the rear, and carry them inside the nave. Others screamed insults at the police, calling them slime and filth and Boer baboons.

A breeze turned the scraps of paper in the street, thinning the tear-gas haze. The noise of the city returned, and I could hear the voices of office workers watching us from the windows of the buildings opposite. Then the colonel's megaphone screeched again.

'You are all under arrest!'

From our step came ragged laughter and shouts of defiance.

'Come and get us, you fuckers!' screamed a girl in a torn coat, then fell silent. Fresh police files were wheeling into line in the street below and lock-up trucks were backing up, their mesh doors open. The colonel waved his swagger-stick; the cops charged and the students recoiled. Those who could fled back into the church, the press of bodies carrying me with it. Over their heads I could see the flash of falling batons and hear the crack as they made contact. A tear-gas canister was bowled through the opening and then the doors shut with a crash on the daylight outside. Some students sprinted down the aisles to escape through the transepts, but those doors too were slammed shut before they reached them. We were sealed inside. From the street came cries, and the sounds of beatings.

The gloomy nave seemed filled with people. Some sobbed, or dashed about frantically, their chests heaving. Others staggered where they stood, their hair matted from bleeding scalp wounds. The shock of confrontation had revealed us for what we were: a bunch of self-styled rebels without cohesion. Someone had clapped a cleaner's bucket over the tear-gas canister, but trails of smoke leaked along the floor around its edge. It was not only the gas that made our eyes burn. I collapsed on a pew and lit a cigarette, my hands trembling.

'Not a fastidious churchgoer, I see,' said a voice beside me. I looked up and recognized the speaker, a medical student in the year ahead of me. Stefan gazed around at the defeated mob and shook his head. 'Looks like Casualty on a Saturday night,' he said. 'Smoke up, and we'll do something constructive.'

This was my first taste of trauma, but Stefan seemed to know what to do. He stood on a pew and addressed the refugees, his voice cutting through the moans and whimpers.

'Let's get the injured seen to,' he said. 'Anyone got some clean cloth?'

A girl pulled a blouse from her bag and held it up. Someone else produced a white lab-coat, and a couple of handkerchiefs were handed forward.

'Bring all those who've been hurt here to the front,' said Stefan, and he began, with the help of a penknife, to tear the fabric into strips. A cavalcade of wounded were assisted from the shadows; limping, shoeless, with bloodied faces and lacerated heads. I looked at their ragged cuts and thought I might faint. I set to work nervously, folding the cloth into pads and holding them against gashed scalps to staunch the bleeding. Other volunteers came forward to help. Stefan appeared at my side.

'Reassure them,' he said softly. 'Tell them head wounds always bleed a lot, but they soon stop. Tell them it's going to be OK.'

Stefan had gathered the worst tear-gas victims at the font. Some, their faces scorched by the irritant gas, could hardly see between their swollen eyelids. He spoke to them gently as he bathed the blistered skin. 'Don't worry, it burns at first when the water reacts with the chemicals. It'll stop after a few seconds.' His voice worked like a tranquilliser, and I began to understand a little of what healing involved.

*

I had treated my first casualties, however minor, and embraced my first cause. 'The Siege of St George's' they called it in the papers the next morning, and those of us who had been there gained a brief notoriety. A few went on to make names for themselves as political activists. One of them was my friend Stefan. For a while I occupied a student squat with him and Neil and Nils; the Marxist-Lentilists, who shared an admiration for Albanian communism and a conviction that meat or fruit, or anything but the most rigorous of subsistence diets signified bourgeois softness and a betrayal of the oppressed masses. They shared their spartan meals with some coloured children who slept rough in the cemetery behind the house, and laughed when our possessions were regularly stolen – 'redistributed' – by the most enterprising among them.

I didn't really mind the absence of luxuries. I was short of money and augmenting my living allowance by working as a mechanic, rebuilding the engines of the vw buses and Beetles that were the most popular student transport. And my social life had improved. Our kitchen was always full of people talking socialism through the night. A number of them were young women, attracted to the aura of revolutionary virility that hung around the house. With a few gallon jugs of proletarian wine the gatherings became parties. Though I didn't pretend to be an activist, some of the girls would try to expand my political consciousness through slippery sex, augmented by potent buds of marijuana.

But I was becoming aware of the political aspects of studying medicine in South Africa, as one of the select minority who qualified. The ironies of this privilege became apparent when we started our clinical training. Our professors adhered to the exacting standards of the English medical schools from which most of them had graduated. They had been drawn to the University of Cape Town's Groote Schuur Hospital because it was an international centre of excellence; it was here that the world's first heart transplant had been performed in 1967, and overseas doctors considered themselves honoured to work in the department of cardiac surgery and other specialities. One day we too would enter that elect society of healers, and begin to make a difference to humanity. Our medical training was rigorous and complete, for what we had in abundant supply was 'clinical material': the disinherited and oppressed from the townships and bleak rural homelands ...

The white bodies tended to be tidier. There was a regular attrition among young men in that society, who went scuba diving and hang-gliding and rock climbing, or drove too fast on winding mountain roads. A few, beaten down by loneliness or the fear of failure, would hang themselves or take fatal overdoses. In the 'non-white' mortuary (here too the principle of racial segregation was observed) the corpses were less reposeful: dead from spear-thrust, gunshot and axe. Bodies were disembowelled, bled dry from multiple chop-wounds, or contracted and charred by fire. They came from a place beyond the frontier of our known lives, where other rules of death appeared to prevail.

What we felt about that place was a sort of horror. People slaughtered each other there in a malevolent frenzy. One day, on the autopsy table, lay the body of a young woman. She was exquisitely beautiful. Even the coarse line of undertaker's stitches that ran from her neck down between her breasts to her pubic hair could not diminish her perfection. She had bled to death; gang-raped and then despatched with a bottle kicked up her vagina that had shattered, slashing the arteries in her pelvis. The social theorists would explain such incidents as the product of economic despair, or rage at the impotence that apartheid had produced among the dispossessed. I felt dizzy, terrified at the thought of such contemptuous destruction. The only way to deal with that fear was to keep it at bay through clinical detachment, clinical study.

from Long Walk to Freedom (1995)

NELSON MANDELA

Cape Town was thirty-five miles to the southwest, but because of the unexpected crowds at the gate, the driver elected to take a different path to the city. We drove round to the back of the prison, and our convoy took small roads and byways into town. We drove through beautiful green vineyards and manicured farms, and I relished the scenery around me.

The countryside was lush and well cared for, but what surprised me was how many white families were standing beside the road to get a glimpse of our motorcade. They had heard on the radio that we were taking an alternative route. Some, perhaps a dozen even raised their clenched right fists in what had become the ANC power salute. This astonished me; I was tremendously encouraged by these few brave souls from a conservative farming area who expressed their solidarity. At one point I stopped and got out of the car to greet and thank one such white family and tell them how inspired I was by their support. It made me think that the South Africa I was returning to was far different from the one I had left.

As we entered the outskirts of the city, I could see people streaming towards the centre. The Reception Committee had organized a rally at the Grand Parade in Cape Town, a great open square that stretched out in front of the old City Hall. I would speak to the crowd from the balcony of that building, which overlooked the entire area. We had heard sketchy reports that a great sea of people had been waiting there since morning. The plan was for our motorcade to avoid the crowd and drive round to the back of City Hall, where I would quietly enter the building.

The drive to Cape Town took forty-five minutes, and as we neared the Grand Parade we could see an enormous crowd. The driver was meant to turn right and skirt its edges, but instead he inexplicably plunged straight into the sea of people. Immediately the crowd surged forward and enveloped the car. We inched forward for a minute or two but were then forced to stop by the sheer press of bodies. People began knocking on the window and then on the boot and the bonnet. Inside, it sounded like a massive hailstorm. Then people began to jump on the car in their excitement. Others began to shake it and at that moment I began to worry. I felt as though the crowd might very well kill us with their love.

The driver was even more anxious than Winnie and I, and he was clamouring to jump out of the car. I told him to stay calm and remain inside, that others from the cars behind us would come to our rescue. Allan Boesak and others began to attempt to clear a way for our vehicle and push the people off the car; but with little success. We sat inside – it would have been futile even to attempt to open the door, so many people were pressing on it for more than an hour, imprisoned by thousands of our own supporters. The time for the scheduled beginning of the speech had long passed.

Several dozen marshals eventually came to the rescue and managed slowly to clear an exit path. When we finally broke free, the driver set off at great speed in the opposite direction from the City Hall. 'Man, where are you going?' I asked him in some agitation. 'I don't know!' he said, his voice tense with anxiety. 'I've never experienced anything like this before,' he said, and then continued driving without any destination in mind.

When he began to calm down I gave him directions to the house of my friend and attorney Dullah Omar, who lived in the Indian area of the city. We could go there, I said, and relax for a few minutes. This appealed to him. Fortunately, Dullah and his family were home, but they were more than a bit surprised to see us. I was a free man for the first time in twenty-seven years, but instead of greeting me, they said with some concern, 'Aren't you meant to be at the Grand Parade?'

We were able to have some cold drinks at Dullah's, but we had only been there a few minutes when Archbishop Tutu telephoned. How he knew we were there I do not know. He was quite distressed, and said, 'Nelson, you must come back to the Grand Parade immediately. The people are growing restless. If you do not return straightaway, I cannot vouch for what will happen. I think there might be an uprising!' I said I would return at once.

Our problem was the driver: he was deeply reluctant to return to the Grand Parade. But I remonstrated with him and soon we were on our way back to City Hall. The building was surrounded by people on all sides, but it was not as dense at the back, and the driver managed to make his way through to the rear entrance. It was almost dusk when I was led up to the top floor of this stately building whose halls had always been filled with shuffling white functionaries. I walked out on to the balcony and saw a boundless sea of people cheering, holding flags and banners, clapping and laughing.

I raised my fist to the crowd, and the crowd responded with an enormous cheer. Those cheers fired me anew with the spirit of the struggle. '*Amandla!*' I called out. '*Ngawethu!*' they responded. '*iAf-rika!*' I yelled; '*Mayibuye!*' they answered. Finally, when the crowd had started to settle down, I took out my speech and then reached into my breast pocket for my glasses. They were not there; I had left them at Victor Verster. I knew Winnie's glasses had a similar prescription, and I borrowed hers.

Friends, comrades and fellow South Africans. I greet you all in the name of peace, democracy and freedom for all! I stand here before you not as a prophet but as a humble servant of you, the people. Your tireless and heroic sacrifices have made it possible for me to be here today. I therefore place the remaining years of my life in your hands.

The Day Mandela Came Home (1990)

SHAUN JOHNSON

It was, I suppose, what these epoch-making days are supposed to be like. There was triumph, tremendous heart-soaring triumph, as Nelson Mandela stood to address the largest crowd I have ever seen, thus ending his 27 years of imprisonment. But there was also tragedy as parts of the crowd ran amok, leaving some celebrants dead and many more injured, and stores with looted, broken windows.

A hundred thousand people is as good a crowd estimate as any. It was a huge, unforgettable gathering, too big for the National Reception Committee to control.

The crowd on Cape Town's Grand Parade started building up early in the morning, and was big by 3pm, the scheduled time for Mandela to walk out of Victor Verster prison in Paarl. It grew more volatile and unwieldy as the blazing hot afternoon wore on and the delays continued. By 4.30pm, with no clarity yet on whether Mandela had emerged from prison, youths went out of control. Fear gripped the outer edges of the crowd as teargas fumes filled the air, along with the chilling, incessant reports of firearms.

But on the Parade, the sea of people made for a breathtaking sight. Against the colonial backdrop of City Hall – draped in ANC colours – a blur of faces milled and crushed. Ambulances snaked in and out of the crowds as organizers using a wholly inadequate public address system pleaded for calm and order. By 4.50pm the organizers were clearly worried, castigating 'elements causing unnecessary problems for us', but the news that Mandela was on his way calmed matters briefly. Rally organizers shouted at the youths, but to little avail. One said dolefully: 'Mandela may be out, but these kids are unemployed.'

Just after 5.20pm the Mandela cavalcade roared into the city. A huge crowd ran wildly alongside his car as it wound through the streets, beating on the windows and chanting. A group of women jostled and pushed, desperate to see the leader. They wept and laughed simultaneously. The press of the crowd slowed the motorcade to jogging pace and Mandela, in the back seat with his wife Winnie, looked out at the mad crush. He was impassive, his fist raised stiffly in salute. With helicopters – some belonging to the police, others to television networks – swooping over the square, the scene had all the elements of imminent battle.

Suddenly Mandela's whereabouts could no longer be ascertained. Some said he was trapped in his car in front of City Hall, others said he was in the building. United Democratic Front patron Allan Boesak warned, desperately, that Mandela would not speak unless there was order. 'No, no, no comrades,' he screamed, 'the police are firing teargas. Do not provoke.'

With the sun beginning to lose its sting, and still no sign of Mandela, a chant went up from a small group on the eastern edge of the Parade: 'We want Nelson!'

'Comrades!' shouted an organizer from the podium. 'He has waited 27 years for his freedom. We have stood here for five or six hours. Where is our patience?'

Mandela eventually spoke just before 8pm, and the crowd quietened. He delivered a hardline speech. He had clearly decided that his first appearance was a time to reassure and mobilize his own followers, leaving overtures and initiatives aimed at his opponents for later. The speech was an opening thrust, carefully prepared and delivered strictly according to the text. In a strong, but strangely unemotional voice, Mandela said he stood before the gathering 'not as a prophet, but as a humble servant.

'I place the remaining years of my life in your hands,' he said to resounding cheers.

At the end of the long, historic day, supporters heeded the ANC leader's call to disperse with dignity, and left the Parade peacefully. Groups of youths dancing the toyi-toyi laughed and greeted groups of riot policemen and soldiers as they spread out into the night …

Elections, Mountains, and One Voter (1994)

NJABULO S NDEBELE

Some two years ago, a few days after my arrival in the Western Cape to begin work at the University of the Western Cape, I remember driving home after work on a hot afternoon. I stopped at the traffic lights at an intersection along Modderdam Road. As I turned my eyes this way and that as drivers are wont to do during that momentary boredom of waiting for the red light, my eyes rested on Table Mountain. At that moment I experienced an epiphany. I knew then one of the reasons that had me running away from Johannesburg after only one year. I was desperate to be surrounded once more, after years of exile in Lesotho, by mountains and their reassuring presence.

Those mountains have given me some inner strength and suggested to me the value of stability. In the many years of anxiety about whether one would ever see home again, the mountains of Lesotho offered solace and certitude. They seemed to offer the assurance that one day things would work out. So, during my stay in the Western Cape, I was to seek out, by reflex action, the Table Mountain each time I was outdoors. I was to see the mountain in all its moods: when it was covered or uncovered by mist and cloud and smoke, or when it braced itself against the winds and triumphed.

I do have a peculiar personal trait. It is that I tend to be at my calmest and most deliberate when some remarkable event has made everybody else excited. I can receive the most stunning news with the utmost composure. I used to worry that I may be one of the most insensitive of people in the world. I've learned, though, over the years, that it is not so. I would simply be experiencing, at those moments, that most incapacitating of feelings, when one is torn asunder by the play of the clearest understanding accompanied by a momentary inability to turn insight into words. In that situation I have thought it best to resort to silence, for any utterance may not escape hints of insincerity precisely at a time when I felt most sincere.

All this is to account for the fact that when I opened my eyes on the morning of the 27th April, 1994, I sensed immediately the weight of the historical day, but although I felt awed, I registered no ebullient excitement. I was sure of only one thing: I would, in my own time, wake up and find my way to a polling station to vote. I already knew that I would not vote at the polling station nearest to me, in Pinelands. I had been informed that voting would take place in the Dutch Reformed Church. I reacted instinctively against that venue. But not wanting to yield to reflex emotion, I entertained an intense inner debate. Something told me that voting at that church would represent a special moral triumph. It would display starkly the symbolism of change and reconciliation.

It was not to be. My historic sensitivities were too powerful. I shied away from that moment of transcendence, not sure that I would be able to live with yielding to it in the days, weeks, months and years ahead. I shied away from an heroic public gesture in preference for a neutral venue where I would participate in the most personal of public events: the election. After all, hadn't I made some powerful emotional concessions at midnight in the centre of Cape Town during the ceremony to lower the old flag and hoist the new one? It was a most joyful moment. As I watched the new flag go up, I felt, for the first time in my life, that this country was really mine. All along, it had been an idea I longed for. Something I had hated and loved all at once. Now the ambivalence was gone.

During that intense moment, my eyes happened upon two white policemen whose faces registered pain, bewilderment and resignation. They were watching the end of all that had given the deepest meaning to their lives. They seemed lost. Yet, there they were, in the call of duty, ensuring the protection of victorious celebrants. My heart went out to them. I confirmed something else at that very moment: how much I had actually been socialised into the values of the struggle. "It is not the people but the policies," we had grown to learn. It had been hard to make that distinction. But I was influenced by it. That is why it is no miracle that during this moment of triumph, the mass survivors of oppression feel no special bitterness. So there were my two white policemen: I gave them my compassion, they protected me.

That is partly why, as I headed for the Civic Centre in Cape Town at about 9:30, I didn't really feel bad about having decided not to cast my vote in the Dutch Reformed Church. It was at the Civic Centre that I would cast my vote. That in itself carried its own special symbolism. I would vote at a place to which everyone had a civic right. In there we were made equal by right and legal precept.

But the reason for going to the Civic Centre was not entirely altruistic. I had received a report that the lines there were short and moving fast. As it turned out, I spent only one hour.

As usual, on my way to the Civic Centre, I looked for Table Mountain. It was totally covered in low cloud. Why would the mountain hide from me on such a day? That was a distant thought in my mind, but I registered it.

Inside the Civic Centre was a quiet and dignified atmosphere. I experienced what millions of other people in working democracies had learned to take for granted: queueing in line to cast a vote is a leveller of human beings. There we were: students, clerks, secretaries, teachers, chief executive officers, journalists, casual labourers, actors, the unemployed, etc, all in a queue to do one thing. I talked to those close to me. Although we said very little about the election itself, we enjoyed the opportunity the election provided us to share some intimate experiences. We never exchanged names, but we will all remember that joyous hour, in which we queued to make history.

When the voting moment came, it was fast and disarmingly simple, but profoundly intense. I trembled as I unfolded my ballot paper. It was really happening. I was aware of the terrible fear of making a mistake. I would not be able to live with a mistake. I began to look for my face. My one and only face. Other faces were a blur as I looked for the one face that embodied all my hopes and, easing my trembling hand, I drew my x with the greatest care in the world. And it was done. When I proceeded to cast the provincial vote, I was already a seasoned voter.

As I left the Civic Centre to return home, I noticed that the queue was already going out of the building. So there were other voters who had taken their morning hours easy. Driving home, I looked at the mountain. It was still covered. When I went out to celebrate the triumph of voting at a friend's house, the mountain was still covered.

I was never to see it that day. But, again as usual, I was confident it was there. Perhaps it was reaffirming its old lesson on faith: on election day. That the future is there for us: we need to have faith in it, and in ourselves. And so I ended my day unemotionally, but deeply affirmed.

from Return to Paradise (1993)

BREYTEN BREYTENBACH

How alive the Mother City used to be before fascist political engineers and other black-shoed Broederbond planners destroyed it! I used to think of it as an Alexandria in the southern Atlantic. Odd characters washed up against the mountain-flank, extraordinary destinies were played out in the tavern of the seas. The cosmopolitan make-up of the city facilitated its sparkling artistic and political life – the Muslim Malay community with their *kramats* (holy burial tombs) of noble forebears dotted around the Peninsula; emancipated slave descendants from many parts of the world, with quicksilver wit; eccentric scions of old Afrikaner families of mixed origin; refugees from Central Europe; deserters from dim foreign pasts; black labourers and trade unionists and intellectuals; effete Britishers looking for sun and a tax-haven; brown families from St Helena; dispossessed barons and shady war criminals; painters with little goatees and doe eyes and funny accents walking like ducks; Portuguese greengrocers and Indian tailors and Chinese launderers; long-legged, barefoot beauties from upcountry farms; *dagga*-smokers and antique dealers and Trotskyites and mad versifiers and nudist nature lovers and magicians and textile workers and jazz musicians and degenerates and creators and ascetics and foreign sailors who came to District Six and missed their boats and hedonists and doom prophets and charlatans and black-suited fundamentalists and suicide artists and crayfish fanatics and gamblers and crazy middle-aged students from the Congo and *samoosa*-eaters.

There used to be jazz dives and night-clubs and theatres and art galleries serving sherry and wild parties and ferocious discussions and red-mouthed harbour whores without teeth and vendors blowing bugles to sell their snoek and amateur political saboteurs and single-minded mountaineers and a symphony orchestra and subversive publications and journalists with fleas and bars burning down and naked midnight swimming and crammed double-decker buses and a carnival lasting a week and cinemas showing American musicals and fat mammies with flowery *kopdoeke* (kerchiefs) selling flowers on the Parade and prim office-girls with tight squiggly bums walking on stiletto heels and sad deep-voiced choirs wearing red fezzes and blazers and pocket-picking *skollies* (hooligans) and bearded bums called *bergies* sleeping on the mountain with the baboons and boat-builders and cheeky newspaper-vendors and soap-box orators and ageless nymphs playing Shakespeare in the open air and proletarians breeding budgies in Afrikaner suburbs and ancient polished motorcars and tattoo parlours and yogis and academics wearing medieval gowns and cabbalists and boxers and tea-party addicts and down-and-outers and star-gazers and visiting gurus and kite-makers and oriental weddings and real bookshops and experts in anemometry and poets who contracted tuberculosis after producing one slim volume of eternity.

Then came the time of the bacon-arsed politicians with the hairy faces and the pig-thoughts, the short-back-and-sides bureaucrats, the police-men with dogs, the bulldozers, the entrepreneurs, the murder squads, the death laws, the grand schemes, the blood and the blight ...

It is only now, more than thirty years on – after the expulsions, displacements, imprisonments, censorship, repression, destruction, corruption, riots and resistance of the intervening years – that the first timid signs of a cosmopolitan cultural life are resurfacing in Cape Town.

Some of the exiles have returned; access to the harbour has been established with the opening of clubs, restaurants and theatres on the waterfront; surviving buskers make old music on the pavements; the National Gallery has re-opened; a sharp new weekly, *South*, is published; State culture is finally on the retreat; new voices have emerged ...

We wander through the Bo-Kaap streets, also traditionally known as the Malay Quarter or Slamse Buurt, and Schotsche Kloof. Present-day descendants of the original inhabitants prefer to call themselves Cape Muslims. Their ancestors were brought here as slaves, political exiles and convicts from Africa, Madagascar, Ceylon, India and the area today known as Indonesia. The arrivals were already followers of Islam and they shared a common tongue, Malay-Portuguese, the trading language used from Madagascar to China. In the way that the unwritten history and customs and attitudes of the vanished Khoi and San constitute an invisible presence in the make-up of South Afriquas, this disappeared language infused and became a core ele-ment of Afrikaans. Maybe Afrikaans could be seen as a new avatar of that supple lingo of seafarers, slaves and nomads – of people who constantly have to invent themselves.

The hills are steep, the houses neglected, some decayed. Most are a mixture of Cape Dutch and English Georgian styles. Many were gaily painted, the colours now faded. Sometimes one still sees, as a nearly forgotten memory, a façade with its typical curvilinear Baroque parapet, its *voorstoep*, the sash-windows, the elaborately carved front door with a separate top and bottom panel, the decorated fanlight above the door, the wrought-iron fittings. The oldest Cape mosque, the Auwal, is still in use.

When I was young and carefree the plaintive voice of the imam or muezzin floated down from the heights, and to my dream-being the startled fluttering of doves is associated with dawn. The pious Muslims living here were tailors, fishermen, cobblers and coopers.

In a wasteland we come across a *kramat*, the burial place of a saint. Actually three people are entombed there. Inside the small, white, dome-shaped structure a believer is chanting prayers, perhaps giving news to the dead. A man with a fez tells us this piece of land, over-looking the city bordered by the silvery surface-memory of the sea, used to be a Chinese cemetery. Untended graves disappeared in the soil. In the old days people still lived with the dimension of a future, but all time eventually becomes earth. Even up here, in backyards of dilapidated houses and on vacant lots under the poor shelter of scraggly trees and shrubs grown crooked in their endless resistance to the wind, squatters with babies and a dog and a tethered goat live. A mother washes herself in a pool of stagnant water. People sift through rubbish dumps.

from Witness to AIDS (2005)

EDWIN CAMERON

In December, just days after the meeting in Judge-President Friedman's chambers, my computer analyst sister Jeanie, her scientist husband Wim, and their two children joined me for a few days in Cape Town. After my original HIV diagnosis in 1986, I made a secret promise to myself – while they were young I would offer each year to take my niece Marlise and nephew Graham for a short pre-Christmas holiday in Cape Town. The beneficial delight in the beaches, long drives, silly vacation movies and chatter was, I always suspected, more wholly mine than theirs. The glorious Cape sun always blessed us with indolence. It was perfect rest. But each year we did one incontestably strenuous thing. We climbed Table Mountain.

Perhaps one of the best-known sights in the world, the sandstone massif dominates Table Bay. For hundreds of years, since Sir Francis Drake's voyage around the world, the view of it and the view from it have arrested travellers, justly evoking lyrical descriptions. The whole mountain is now a nature reserve, jealously guarded by Capetonians and the conservationists and researchers from all over the world who treasure and study and walk amidst its priceless floral and faunal heritage.

The mountain rises 1 000 metres above sea level, its sheer rock faces hundreds of metres high. From a distance, the famous 'table' front looks like a monolith of rock. It is not. The frontal rock is deeply split by a gorge that angles across and into its face. Platteklip Gorge is a particular hikers' favourite, and one of the best-known routes to the top. In the 1940s Churchill's ally, South African Prime Minister Jan Smuts, favoured it for his regular walks.

We decided to tackle Table Mountain. On International Human Rights Day, 1997, early on a startlingly sunny morning, we started the ascent. My brother-in-law, Wim, was not as keen as the rest of us. But with an accustomed family mix of infectious enthusiasm and browbeating coercion we persuaded him to join us. Little did we know how well-justified his reluctance was. Two days later he was diagnosed with acute appendicitis and had to be rushed into hospital for emergency surgery.

But at the time no hint of illness of any nature seemed to mar the day. The path up Platteklip Gorge begins at a fresh reservoir of mountain water. As we set out past it I wondered whether I would make it to the top. Just seven weeks before I had not been able to climb forty steps from the common room to my chambers. Now, cleared of the PCP and with the virus incapacitated by four weeks of effective antiretroviral therapy, I proposed to tackle more than eight hundred steps up the face of Table Mountain.

Jeanie and Wim stopped often to check on me. Was I making it?

Yes, I was. Not without effort. Not with any speed. But I was making it. Twice the path crosses the stream that feeds the reservoir below. Then it heads steeply into the gorge that splits the sandstone cliffs. I drank deeply, thirstily, from the stream each time. The proteas, ericas, disas and pelargoniums that line the path, magnificently casual in their beauty under the mild December sunshine, seemed to beckon me up and on.

As we reached the top we paused, relieved and exhilarated, before strolling to the cable station restaurant 500 metres away across the flat rock plateau. As so shortly before, the climb had made me breathless, panting and sweating. But this time it was with exuberant joy. I knew that I was well, could be well, would be well. I had been given a second chance. As I gasped in the mountain air, I also knew what a mountain of privilege had brought me there. There was much work to do.

from Sea-Mountain, Fire City (2001)

MIKE NICOL

At the end of 1997, now thoroughly restive, I returned to Cape Town, to the city that once I had been accused of dismissing with indifference. 'Some of the city's writers just happen to live here,' ran the criticism, 'this place is of little or no interest to them as a subject for their writing.' Then I was singled out for having noted on the jacket of a novel that I lived 'on a wind-blown peninsula in the South Atlantic' and not 'in Cape Town'.

The biographical blurb was tongue in cheek but as I tried to regain my old way of life I began to think my critic had a point. Although I had always written the city into my fiction, perhaps I hadn't been living in Cape Town. Perhaps I had yet to understand the meaning of that phrase; a sense of place. I remembered the poet, Stephen Watson's, argument that writers needed to make Cape Town 'a place in the mind' for if they didn't 'not even its inhabitants [could] live there imaginatively'. After the richness of Berlin that existed as much by the immediacy of its fictional characters and their imagined stories as by its reality, I understood what he was getting at. And as Cape

Town was South Africa's oldest city, something would be seriously wrong if there were no literature to give it a resonance beyond the spectacle of Table Mountain, the Waterfront, and the wild and windy heights of Cape Point. Without stories and poetic imagery, how could the city lay claim to the status? History wasn't enough, it had to be reimagined. So I started to look at Cape Town the way Berlin had taught me to read a city.

After three and a half centuries Cape Town as a site of memory is thick with tales and plots, although perhaps the tour guides have been quicker to capitalize on this than the writers. Daily in Church Square you can hear the couriers conjuring up the middle of the eighteenth century to groups of Germans, Dutch, Americans, and Japanese. They point to two of the city's first buildings – the Groote Kerk and directly opposite it the Slave Lodge, a unique institution where the Dutch East India Company kept its slaves – and evoke the city that is layered behind the one we see. They stand on the traffic island on which the 'slave tree' grew and under which slaves were auctioned, and those lives are made real again. They mention that at night in the mid-nineteenth century, after curfew, Church Square was deserted, scavenged by packs of dogs and even by hyenas.

The tourists look around and see a modern city at work. They are not far from Parliament, where the second popularly elected government is in power. Overhead the sky is deep blue, behind the office blocks Table Mountain looms through the salt haze. The cry of seagulls can be heard above the traffic. But, of course, beneath what can be seen the secret life continues.

The difficulty with imagining Cape Town is that it has never had one reality: from the start there were the Khoi, the Dutch company officials, and the slaves. They all gave different meaning to the growing town, and ever since the versions of Cape Town have multiplied.

As a port Cape Town has always taken in groups of people, but inevitably grudgingly, and always by insisting they assimilate into, rather than try to take over, the city. This grouchiness is part of the city's secret life, a defence because it is open to the world, and desirable. After all it is the sea that gave the Dutch East India Company access to the tip of a continent that even today is difficult to traverse overland, just as it was earth – cultivatable ground – that brought them ashore.

Unsurprisingly, Cape Town's first metaphor was one of succour as the Dutch East India Company's refreshment station provided fresh victuals for the ships sailing between Holland and the Company's dominions in Malaysia. Simultaneously, however, the metaphor of succour was rendered harshly ironic as the Khoi were dispossessed of their summer pasturage, and slaves were brought to service a settlement that must have represented suffering and unhappiness to them.

And then there is the summer wind – a trade wind, rather bleakly called the southeaster – that is indisputably another of Cape Town's shaping characteristics. Each year, from October to March, for weeks on end the wind rattles across the city covering every surface in a fine grit, fraying people's nerves until, like the city's oak leaves late in the season, they are brittle and cracked and burnt. After a long blow there is a tension to the city visible in the grimaces on people's faces as they push down Adderley Street against the wind.

Despite this unease, the wind is also called the Cape Doctor. Not because it carries medicinal properties but because in previous centuries it blew away the stench of sewage and rot that made the old town unbearable and was one of the reasons the middle classes moved out and over the ridge to Rondebosch and Wynberg. Today again, the southeaster is a doctor. When it doesn't blow the city is blanketed by a brown haze – a concoction of chemical emissions, diesel and petrol fumes, and smoke from the fires of the ever-growing number of people who don't have electricity – that could soon render Cape Town's air as noxious as that of Mexico City, Los Angeles, Athens, or Tokyo.

from Poor No More (1996)

TONY WEAVER

Street of Council workers whistling up the whores on the balconies of Carnival Court, the Blue Lodge, the Mountain View – the whores hike up their skirts and flash their fannies and scream "dyy, djy, djou piel issie groot genoeg vir my poes nie."

When the men hiss "ksssssk ksssssk", the whores scream back "whassamatter, has your face gotta puncture?"

The street where the sex changes and transvestites living above Norman James' electrical shop storm out, satin gowns swirling to stand hips astraddle on the white line screaming "come, come, let's fight it out right now, on the spot, moffie to moffie."

Where every Friday night the Bergies pack out their milk crates outside the home of the Bishop of the Lutheran Church, spread table cloths and arrange bunches of flowers salvaged from restaurant bins. Lighting candles in Rama tubs ready for the ritual suip session, Friday night drinking Blue Train, methylated spirits, filtered through bread to remove the purple dye. Drinking to forget.

No more.

The working class whores are gone, the broken down brothels converted to upmarket B&Bs and backpackers' lodges. The Bergies drifted to Buitenkant Street when the shopkeepers stopped selling meths.

The gentrification of Long Street has begun.

It is not a particularly long street, Long Street. One thousand, four hundred metres to be exact. You can stand at the top opposite the Long Street Baths and watch a tanker sailing across the bottom. The heart of Long Street is only 700 metres long, from Wale Street to Orange Street. There it becomes Kloof Street for the next 1 400 metres, but Kloof Street should really be called Upper Long Street.

From the bottom of Long Street to the top of Kloof Street, 2,8 km, there are 45 pubs, restaurants and backpacker lodges. In the 1 400 metres of Long Street alone, there are 24 …

Artist Brett Murray has lived on the street for ten years, his studio is in an alleyway just next to Clarke's Bookshop. "Around about 1988, '89, the street went through a bad period, a big lull. Carnival Court was sold and was empty, a whole bunch of residential blocks were closed down, before that I used to cruise the streets at night, walk down to the Base, before that to Scratch, then one night I got fucked up badly.

"I'd been playing pool at the Stag's Head. I was pretty pissed by the time I left and I walked back, then as I got to Long Street five guys grabbed me. Three held me, the other two fucked me up. One guy had a club, and he just kept smacking me. They started searching me and found my bank card, so then they really started moering me, demanding my PIN number. I only had R5 in the bank, so I told them the number, and the last thing I remember was this huge boot coming for my head. I woke up two hours later, they'd taken my jacket, my shoes, I had a bunch of teeth missing."

Now Brett's biggest problem is that the street is so safe you can't get parking at night anymore. He welcomes his new-found security but mourns the old days.

"The gentrification of Long Street means we are losing a lot of history. Residents are being evicted to make way for backpacker lodges, the corner greengrocers are closing down to make way for antique shops. When Carnival Court was still going, the whores were working class, now they all look like the women in the Coca Cola ads."

Back then, a fading whore was taking the sun on the balcony at Carnival Court, her skirts hiked up, when a punter walked by and gazed at her cellulite: "Hey, darling, your varicose veins are showing."

"Verricose veins, verricose veins? They's not verricose veins, they's wires pointing straight to my love button."

Across the road from Brett's studio, at Club Heaven, you and your partner can get half an hour in a threesome in a private room for R250. That's after you've watched the manic redhead who used to be a brunette shove a huge dildo up her vagina a few inches from your nose to the tune of "I hate men with small dicks".

Club Heaven and the four other visible sex clubs on Long Street are causing problems for the owner of Long Street's trendiest be-seen spot, The Lounge. Shaun Petre provides space where jollers can hang out without being hassled, where women alone can relax without feeling like they're in a singles club. The Lounge is a wonderful series of interconnected spaces, like an old student house in Obs or Gardens, there's almost always someone there you can connect with.

Shaun says "the problem with the sex clubs is that some clients can afford to watch the strip shows, and the porn movies, but they can't afford R300 for a fuck. So they get horny and come to the clubs and hassle the women. But we recognize them fast – let's face it, they don't look like our regular clients, so we ease them out the door."

The verandah at the Lounge, hanging out over Long Street with grand views in both directions, is one of the finest places to be in Cape Town. Long a favourite hangout for Cape Town alternative trendies, it is now one of the big backpacker haunts.

There are now seven backpacker lodges in Long Street, with more opening all the time. Sitting on the stoep at the Lounge, I asked British backpacker, David Cogan, what was so attractive about the street. "It is the most amazing place," he replied, "the street is so cosmopolitan and yet so African. There is always something happening, music, parties, during the day you can spend hours browsing in the shops, and at night there is always a, what's the local word? A jawl."

Big jols. This is jol city, and Long Street is where the jollers who are in the know hang out. David's friend, Liam, an Irishman, says "everybody in Cape Town seems to think the Waterfront is the place to go. Sure and all, it is pretty enough, but who wants to go and drink in a shopping mall, I can do that anywhere in the world."

I asked Brett Murray about one of the new clubs. "Who goes there?" He had to think about it. "Flash who think they are trendies. TV, advertising, modelling, marketing, BMWs, cellphones, the people who crush each other to death trying to get in front of the camera for a social page photographer, they wouldn't let me and you in there. It's sort of a singles bar for the rampantly heterosexual recent Capetonians who are old enough to remember sex without AIDS and stupid enough to fuck without condoms.

"They're mutton dressed as lamb smelling like fish." …

Cranfords, the legendary bookshop where you walked lightly in fear of toppling piles of dusty volumes perched precariously in towering stacks, closed down after a dispute between the owner, Irving Freeman, and the landlady. Six thousand cartons of books were sold off in job lots or pulped, a priceless heritage lost to South Africa.

Sadly, along with Cranford's (now an upmarket club by the same name), a host of other old name businesses have also gone. Palm Wine and Spirits was the nicest place in Cape Town to buy fine wine. The brothers Kearney, Tim and Michael, always dressed in yellow dusters, were two of the most courteous men on earth. Looking a bit like hairless versions of the Thompson Twins in Tintin, they exuded an Olde Worlde charm which was totally democratic in character.

A Bergie would walk in and hesitate between buying a bottle of Paarl Perle, Golden Virginia or Oom Tas, and the Kearney brothers would enter into a serious and polite discussion about the merits and demerits of the wine. The next customer might well be John Platter, and the discussion on rare cabernets would be equally learned and polite.

Give and Take Pawnbrokers, "the shop with the three golden balls", is gone, as are a bunch of small greengrocers, roti and curry places, and other Mom and Pop businesses.

But two of the oldest businesses on the street remain: Revelas Fisheries, and James Electrical. Norman James has traded from the same little shop for 45 years, and he yearns for the old days of Long Street, the days when Long Street was a village: "After District Six was destroyed, the whole character changed. There used to be lots of little Jewish and Indian family businesses, people were living here, the prostitutes were working class and so were our clients. This was one big family in those days.

"I remember the girls around here, they would come in to get something fixed, a toaster, a kettle, and they would say 'Mr James, I'll pay you tomorrow, there is a Japanese ship coming in tonight'."

Mr James has never been robbed. Once, thieves broke into his shop through the back, and left a note on the floor saying "sorry Mr James, wrong shop".

Mr Francisco da Silva owns Revelas Fisheries. Mr Da Silva still fires his ovens from an old wood-burning stove, just as he has for the last 30 years, on and off. He has lived through the rough and the smooth, he mourns the end of District Six and Chiappini Street and Loader Street and the departure of the Jewish traders who filled the street with life. "But it is coming much better now, this street, with these backpackers who are coming, it is giving much more life, more people, foreigners who are living on this street, they are crying when they leave. Just the other day, we had a German couple leaving after six months on the street, and they come to me and they say 'Mr Da Silva, we are crying, Long Street is the best street in the world'.

"The rough and the bad types they do not come here anymore, this is now a very safe street, but maybe it is not so exciting anymore, huh?"

Long Street is changing, and maybe, yes, it isn't that exciting anymore. Last year, Dear Michael died, the end of a Long Street era.

Dear Michael was a famous tramp, one of the few white tramps who regularly worked the city. You could smell Dear Michael a couple of parking meters away, a feral smell, a swamp smell rising from the night of the living dead. Dear Michael walked Long Street picking fleas from his beard, examining them against the light, then squashing them on the bonnets of smart cars.

Towards the end of last year, two months before he died of exposure in an alleyway off the street, Dear Michael collapsed. An ambulance arrived and refused to pick him up. They called a Cleansing Department rubbish truck whose men loaded Dear Michael and took him to the depot where they hosed him down before delivering him to Casualty.

Long Street.

Mutton dressed as lamb smelling like fish.

DISTRICT SIX

from 'Buckingham Palace', District Six (1987)

RICHARD RIVE

I remember the Big Days such as Christmas and New Year. But especially Christmas. Those were glad times and sad times before the official letters came in brown envelopes from the Board, before the inspectors came with their questions and forms, before the threats to be moved became real. The days before the minor diaspora. Those were the years when we believed that we in District Six would live there for ever, that if anyone moved it was because the rent had not been paid or the lights had been cut or they just felt like moving. Nobody ordered anyone else to move anywhere because of the colour of their skins. Moving in our vocabulary meant going to live in the next block or the next street or maybe shifting from Clifton Hill to Horsburg Lane.

We prepared for Christmas from the day or maybe the week before. Some say that people in the District prepared for Christmas from the Boxing Day before. I remember the air of expectation on Christmas Eve and then the reality of Christmas in District Six during the days before we were shifted to Hanover Park and Bonteheuwel and Manenberg. Sometimes today, especially during those Big Days, our eyes still travel over the mounds of rubble, beyond the man-made craters and the piles of dead soil to the celebration of Christmas past. We still remember.

My Christmas Day, when I was sweet fifteen and rapidly growing up, when I was at High School and wore long trousers for the first time, when I was in love and carefully cultivated my first moustache and practised making my voice deeper, always started the evening before. Elvis was king and we all wore curls on our forehead in imitation of Tony Curtis. As the first bells of St Mark's rang out an hour before midnight, we began dressing in order to attend mass. I tried hard to feel grown-up but was already sleepy, and the tolling reverberated through my drowsy head. The dark had rolled down Table Mountain and covered the streets and lanes and stoeps and houses. There was also the smell of rain in the air. The second tolling, half an hour later, was the signal for lamps to be blown out or lights to be switched off and keys turned to lock houses, as we began to mince our holier-than-thou way up Caledon Street to the incense-warm stone church on windy Clifton Hill. We smelt of Waynick's hire-purchase suits and pungent Christmas-present deodorants. My older brothers also smelt of cigarette smoke, and my one unmarried sister of a sweet and sickly eau-de-cologne called 'Passion at Midnight'. We solemnly made our way up the street avoiding puddles and ignoring invectives hurled at us by less holy Christmas Eve drunks bent on disturbing the peace.

While dressing at home, my eldest brother and I had been alone in the boys' room. He winked an eye at me and slipped over half a glass of whisky. He said it was only once a year and after all I had just written the Junior Certificate examination. I downed it in one gulp and felt my insides set on fire. Once in church I felt dizzy and nauseous. The drowsy atmosphere, the thick smell of incense, the roll of the organ music, all turned my stomach. Fortunately I was supported on either side by two grown-up brothers in their new, stiff, navy-blue suits. I was not able to listen to the long, soporific sermon but did pick up the preacher's references to the joy of Christmas. I realised that this was not intended for me. Half-dreaming I agonised about the wickedness of boys of fifteen, still at school, who drank whisky and then had the audacity to attend a church service. My stomach gave an extra turn. I was afraid of getting sick right there over my brothers' new navy-blue suits and disgracing the family. When they went up to take Holy Communion I was too miserable and ill to accompany them.

By the end of the service I was recovering rapidly. When we came out into the night it had rained slightly and a playful wind was gusting and mercifully blew the last fumes of whisky out of my head. Fatigue was now rapidly setting in and I walked back almost asleep, hooked into the arm of my sister supporting me. I crept into bed and was soon astride my cowboy stallion riding the range. It was springtime in the Rockies and my six-guns exploded between strums from my guitar. I was oblivious of the low hum of discussion around our dining-room table of my mother and sister, who were speaking in the kitchen while cooking, of the gossip about who was in church and who was not and why.

Christmas morning blazed bright and apricot yellow. The wind had dropped and the sun had chased the dark and drizzle back over

Table Mountain. The streets were still mirror-wet and the lamp-posts glistened proud and upright. Christmas Eve drunks were evaporating with the water puddles.

But in our home the family slept on as if dead, their new clothes neat on hangers in wardrobes or suspended against doors. I was the only one Awake, feeling wonderfully refreshed as I breathed in the cool, robust air.

The blare of a Christmas choir band burst into the morning and I rushed onto the stoep to watch. It was the 'Young Stars of the East' who trumpeted and strummed 'Christians, Awake' as if they meant it. The bandsmen wore white panama hats, white flannels and bright-red blazers with formidable badges on the breast pockets. Two men, one of whom was Last-Knight, our barber, proudly bore the banner aloft depicting a nativity scene under an enormous Star of the East, which proclaimed for all the world to read that the band was established in 1934 and had as its motto 'Per Ardua ad Astra', which made it seem like a local chapter of the Royal Air Force.

Mr Joseph Knight, the barber's correct name, was very dark-skinned and soon after he moved into the District, received the nickname of Last-Knight. His elder and even darker brother, Henry, helped out in the shop when it was full of customers or Joseph was away from work. On one such occasion when his brother was ill, Henry was running the shop. Alfie du Plooy had not had a haircut for three months and resembled a very shaggy St Bernard dog. His mother, who had a reputation as a shrew, sent him to have his hair cut. Mr Henry Knight took one look at his shaggy mane and sent him home with the cryptic message that if his mother thought that any decent barber would plough through that jungle of hair for one shilling, she had another guess coming. Mrs du Plooy marched on the shop with a howling Alfie in tow. Arms akimbo she stood in the doorway and, not finding Last-Knight there as she had expected, addressed his brother.

'If you don't cut my boy's hair right now for one shilling, I'll hit you that you'll look like the night before last.' The name stuck and the brothers were known from then onwards as Last-Knight and Knight-Before-Last. Now Last-Knight proudly bore the banner of the 'Young Stars of the East' behind a much older and less hirsute Alfie du Plooy as drum-major.

My family had by now woken up. I wished my mother and sister a merry Christmas and then my brothers, who seemed to be anything but merry. They had started their celebration immediately after the church service and were now suffering from massive hangovers. I cleaned my teeth and washed my arms and face in water my sister had warmed for me on the primus stove. When we were all ready we sat down to a breakfast of hot, egg-rich bread dotted with sesame seed which my mother could bake to perfection. These slices were smothered in thick layers of melting butter and slabs of sweetmilk cheese. My brothers merely pecked at them.

Then the presents. We had no Christmas tree so the presents were stacked up on the sideboard. I gave my mother a string of imitation pearls I had spent weeks selecting and months saving up for. My sister received a bottle of pungent perfume (not 'Passion at Midnight'), and my brothers, deodorants. I always gave my brothers deodorants, the same brand. Then I received my presents. My brothers, I think spitefully, also gave me deodorants, the same brand. The men in our family seemed obsessed with deodorants, and the air smelt sweet and sickly as we all tested ours. From aunts and uncles who believed in my scholastic potential, I received books about schoolboys in England, Tom Merry, Bob Cherry and the Boys of Greyfriars, as well as *Beano* and *Dandy* annuals. And a pocket knife which sprouted a multiplicity of blades and gadgets with a multiplicity of uses, even one for taking stones out of horses' hooves, if only we in District Six had had horses with hooves out of which I could take stones. And from my sister, a new wallet containing a crispy new five-pound note. My mother always gave me 'something useful that you can share with the family'. It could be a kettle or a wardrobe or a piece of linoleum. The family kept up the pretence for at least a few days and made a great play of saying in my presence, 'Boil some water in Richard's kettle,' or 'Hang it up in Richard's wardrobe,' or 'Doesn't Richard's lino match the curtains nicely?'

Then I carefully removed my new clothes from their hangers – the shirt, tie and suit, which was navy-blue. Maybe one could only get suits at Waynick's on hire-purchase if one chose navy-blue. Maybe every clothes shop in the District had a sale at the same time of navy-blue suits. I put on my new shoes, which were pinching, and feeling decidedly uncomfortable went out into the street to team up with Ronnie, Norman and Armien who were all wearing new navy-blue suits. On our way to morning service we stopped at Moodley's shop, which was open since he was not a Christian. Neither for that matter was Armien but he was our friend and went wherever we went even though he was a Muslim.

Moodley's shop was dark inside and smelt of curry-powder and turmeric. At the entrance one negotiated hessian bags rolled down at the top and lined to the brim with beans, peas and lentils. We fervently believed, and it formed the basis for much discussion among ourselves, that in spite of his advanced age, and frail and desiccated appearance, he still had enough energy for his three wives, all of whom he had bought in India. Two of them we had never seen and it was rumoured that he kept them in the storeroom at the back with the masala. The third served behind the counter. She was a pale, ghostlike creature with a dot painted on her forehead, her teeth stained brown from chewing betel. We could just make her out in the permanent twilight of the shop. In a fit of extravagance we bought twisty ice-creams, turkish delight and blackballs that stained our mouths when we sucked them.

The crowded congregation at morning service was stiff and starched. We sat stiff in our starched rows sucking discreetly and loosening the laces of our overtight shoes. Armien was with us. I usually sat in the front row, where I could see the porcelain effigies displaying the nativity scene. My mind would wander back to the Christmas plays at primary school, where I was usually cast as a sheep which shepherds watched. My sister and brothers had also in their time always been cast as sheep, and my mother had fatalistically accepted that with our limited acting ability she would always have to alter the sheep's costume for the new incumbent. Then after one glorious audition I broke with mediocrity and was promoted to being a shepherd watching his flocks by night. I watched either too enthusiastically or maybe too unenthusiastically, for the following year I was demoted to rejoin the flock. Fortunately my mother had kept the costume. Now at fifteen I was long past such childish things as nativity plays. When the collection plate came round I generously took sixpence out of my stiff new wallet and dropped it in loudly so that those around me could hear.

Then out into the sunlight to do the wishing rounds. First to wish my married sister and her husband in Bruce Street, where I received a present and cake and ginger-beer. Then to wish my aunt in Coronation Road, where I received a pound note and cake and ginger-beer. Then to wish my Standard Two teacher, with whom I still maintained contact, in Lavender Hill, where I received cake and ginger-beer. And then, because I could not face another slice of cake or glass of ginger-beer, I went home to the midday meal for which by now I had no appetite.

Everyone enjoyed the feast except me. The whole family was present. We wore paper caps and looked silly. We pulled paper crackers and looked even sillier. We found cheap trinkets inside them and pretended they were pieces of treasure. We read the platitudes on the strips of paper in the crackers and discussed them as gems of wisdom. Then, with the sun shining warm outside, we started with hot, mutton curry, then the pièce-de-résistance, a huge, roast leg of lamb done to a turn, crunchy sweet potatoes, green peas and yellow rice with raisins and cinnamon. Over the meat we poured thick, spicy gravy. Then, exhausted with eating and the heat, we still had a choice of fruit salad which we called 'angels food', rice pudding and trifle. The adults had wine and spirits with their meals and although I was offered a glass I wisely declined …

Dusk changed to dark, and dark was accompanied by the quiet of exhaustion. District Six rested from the hurry and bustle of yet another Christmas. Here and there the sounds of a band still wafted faintly on the tired night air. Somewhere Bing Crosby was singing 'I'm Dreaming of a White Christmas'. Many of the older people were happy that one of the Big Days was over. Now only Boxing Day and New Year remained. Others were too tired to care and just went on sitting breathing in the mountain air, fanning themselves and speculating softly about how many more Christmases they would be allowed to remain in District Six before someone in Pretoria ordered them to move.

I still clearly remember the characters and the incidents …

Ten years later. Five years before that, they had declared District Six a group area set aside for white occupation. Then the anger, frustration, protests and meetings. The destructive bulldozers and front-end loaders starting their punitive work, and my family embarking on its own minor diaspora.

We fanned out in many directions like the spokes of a cart wheel. Finally 207, like all the other houses in Buckingham Palace, was razed to the ground without anyone consulting us. My family was luckier than most. We left before the major demolitions started. We saw the writing on the wall which could no longer be ignored. Life was becoming far too cramped and claustrophobic for us. Everyone in the

District died a little when it was pulled down. Many died spiritually and emotionally. Some like my mother also died physically although she was fortunate not to be alive to see the wholesale destruction. For her there would not be the painful memories we would experience. We buried her from 207 Caledon Street, which was still standing, and then the cortege moved to St Mark's Church, which is now still standing. It then went by rail to Woltemade, where she was laid to rest in a cemetery set aside for our so-called ethnic group. To part is to die a little. We all died a little when we parted from the District.

Many were forced to move to small matchbox houses in large matchbox townships which with brutal and tactless irony were given names by the authorities such as Hanover Park and Lavender Hill to remind us of the past they had taken away from us. There was one essential difference between the old places and the new ones. District Six had a soul. Its centre held together till it was torn apart. Stained and tarnished as it was, it had a soul that held together. The new matchbox conglomerates on the desolate Cape Flats had no soul. The houses were soulless units piled together to form a disparate community that lacked cohesion.

My remaining sister married and left. Three of my brothers also married and left. One did not marry but also left. I left. None of us went in the same direction. By this time I was grown-up and qualified and went to board with a respectable, Christian family in Grassy Park who had never experienced uprooting the way I had. Although a relatively young man, I existed alone with my memories in my separate cocoon in my separate area set aside for my separate group. And I tried to forget the past but the voices caught up with me and crept into the house where I was hiding, moved along the carpeted passage into the lounge with its stereophonic set and then into the kitchen with its refrigerator and electric stove and finally spilled over into my secluded bed-sitting-room. And the voices whispered, 'They have done this terrible thing to you, to all of you. Go and see. They have taken your past away.'

So I went to see.

It was late one Saturday afternoon that I forced myself to go. I took the bus to Plumstead and then a train to Cape Town. I walked up to the District clambering over broken bricks and half-flattened foundations of houses once inhabited by people. And the ghosts of the past swirled around me in the growing dusk. I walked along what had been Hanover Street with a few left-over houses standing self-consciously on both sides. They resembled broken teeth with craters in between where the raw gums showed. I turned up into Tennant Street and then walked left along what had been Caledon Street. From that corner to St Mark's Church every building and landmark had been flattened: Handler's Drapery Store, Bernstein's Bottle Store, Buckingham Palace, Seven Steps. Only the church on Clifton Hill stood in stony defiance overlooking the destruction. I stood where the entrance to 207 had been, where the house had stood in which I was born and where I had been raised. From there I could look over the desolate landscape to the dazzling lights of Cape Town which stretched to Table Bay: the neon signs, the brightly lit shops, the streetlamps whose lights failed to reach the District. In my darkening landscape individual buildings stood out in neglected silhouette: Bloemhof Flats, the Zinzendorf Moravian Church, Aspeling Street Mosque and St Mark's, with the desolate winds and ghosts of the past moaning around them.

They had taken our past away and left the rubble. They had demolished our spirits and left broken bricks. They had destroyed our community and left dust and memories. And they had done all this for their own selfish and arrogant reasons. They had sought to regulate our present in order to control our future. And as I stood there I was overwhelmed by the enormity of it all. And I asked aloud, 'What men have the moral or political right to take away a people's past? How will they answer on that day when they have to account for this? For the past will not be forgotten.' The south-easter swept the voices of accusation and recrimination into all the houses into which the people had been driven, into the matchboxes of Hanover Park and the concrete slabs of Bonteheuwel and Manenberg. And the people on the bleak Flats whisper and remember what greed and intolerance have done to them. And they tell their children and their children's children because it must never be forgotten.

Few people were living in the few buildings and houses which still remained on the lunar landscape. Some of those who remained were people who would not move. Others were those who could not move.

And then I thought of the rowdy rumbustious weekends of my childhood and my youth and compared them with these bleak weekends those who remained are forced to endure.

On this Saturday of my pilgrimage, the evening lights shone bitterly in the left-over houses, leaving tiny pin-points of isolated neglect. The south-easter howled and wrapped itself around them as if in collusion with those other forces bent on blowing away the last remnants of this once vibrant community. Nobody now ventured out on Saturday evenings, because there was nowhere to go. Star Bioscope had burnt down a few years before and the British and National had long disappeared. There were no street-corners where youths lounged around lamp-posts, no shops, no shebeen. Going anywhere meant negotiating the dark, walking along bits of street and stumbling over rubble. Hanover Street had been reduced to a broken, macadamised pathway running nowhere over this raw and tortured landscape.

Sunday mornings the church bells of St Mark's still rang out defiantly, reverberating through the empty surroundings and calling to prayer the many who were no longer there. But the faithful heard the bells and came on foot, by bus, by train and by car. The peals reached Manenberg, Cathkin, Kensington and Retreat and people came for their weekly identification with their past. They made their ways over the rubble and stepped over the foundations of the houses they had formerly occupied. I joined in the morning service in the church which no longer had any choir stalls. The stained-glass windows depicting Matthew, Mark, Luke and John were cracked and there was no organ left to boom out the accompaniment to the responses.

I remember as a boy of eight going with my mother to present our huge family bible as a gift to the church. And I now wondered whether it was still there and I was afraid to look in case it had also gone. And I also remembered the brave show as the Church Lads Brigade marched up Caledon Street from their hall, with bugles blaring, drums beating and flags flying to fight the good fight. That was the one fight they could not win, and the Brigade, like other institutions, died with the District. And I also remembered how I used to sing in the church choir dressed in black cassock, white surplice and shiny, stiff and scratchy Eton collar. But now the stalls were empty of boys' voices fluting, and the dwindling congregation sang ragged and unaccompanied. And after the service most of the people left to return the many miles to their Cape Flats dinners and their District Six memories.

And Sunday afternoons the same feeling of desolation settled over everything. The few remaining families sought respite from their loneliness, the sameness of their lives and the ever-present threats of removal, and picked their way past Castle Bridge to bus-stops on Sir Lowry Road or made their way down to the station. And as they passed the Grand Parade they remembered the important protest meetings and the futile resolutions which were passed. I myself remember marching with placards through the streets of central Cape Town as part of a long protest procession; we passed groups of whites who jeered at us. I vividly remember one man in uniform who held up his rifle in one hand and bullets in the other, and I can still see the silent contempt on his face as I wondered why he hated us. Why did he want to shoot us? What made us his enemy? The south-easter gathered up my memories, my questions, my resentment and confusion and scattered them over the Flats into the houses and the concrete blocks with spidery staircases clinging to them.

And on Sunday evenings the sun set and threw the sombre land-scape into deep, menacing shadow. The lights flickered on in the few remaining houses, and from St Mark's came the thin, organless sounds of evensong. And then the hush of hopelessness descended and the quiet. Few children still played in the streets and fewer made their precarious ways over the scarred land. Their parents stayed indoors waiting for the notices to come, for the final axe to fall. And they closed their doors, shut their windows and drew down the blinds on their premature night and on the District that had died before its death.

from Sala Kahle, District Six (1998)

NOMVUYO NGCELWANE

Apart from us, there was another group who liked to use the stoep, and for something rather more serious than a hopscotch game! A group of young men from Richmond and Stuckeris Streets would come, especially on Fridays, to gamble with dice, or sometimes cards. Their arguments usually ended in a fight, and on one or two occasions people actually died from stab wounds.

I still remember one Friday evening. I was just on my way out to run an errand for my mother when the sight of two men dashing at each other with knives in their hands made me stop at the front door. Their group of friends had dispersed and were watching from a distance.

"*Gee my my geld! Gee my my geld!*" – Give me my money! – one was shouting.

"*Ek het dit gewen, dis nie joune nie,*" – I've won it, it's no longer yours – the other replied.

At this, the first man went berserk. He lashed out with his knife, tearing his opponent's shirt. The man staggered backwards a few steps, looked down at his shirt, then rushed forward. But he tripped over a stone and fell flat on his face. The man with the knife did not waste time. He moved in quickly and start stabbing his opponent.

"*Nee man, dis nie nodig nie!*" – No man, it's not necessary! – called someone, gingerly moving towards the two. But the man kept on stabbing.

There were a lot of screams and chaos, the women calling their children and trying to get them away from the scene. "Nomvuyo, come back inside and shut the door!" I heard my own mother calling. I ran inside, very frightened, and shut the front door.

I dashed upstairs to watch from the window. The man who had done the stabbing was nowhere to be seen. All I saw was the group, now surrounding the victim who was still lying on the ground. One guy knelt down, tried to turn him over and then screamed. "*Vra die babie om die ambulans te bel!*" – Tell the Muslim shopkeeper to phone for an ambulance!

By the time the ambulance arrived, the man was dead and the body was covered with a white sheet.

As gambling was strictly against the law, police vans would regularly stop near our building with the intention of arresting the young offenders. But these guys were like springbok. They would disperse at the sight of the van. Often leaving all the cash behind, they would disappear down the lanes or leap over some wall to safety.

We children were aware of this and were always on the alert. We often helped ourselves to the abandoned money, usually a heap of silver coins and even a couple of bank notes.

The adults in our building did not like these men hanging about our stoep because the *tsotsis* would sometimes knock young children out of their way when fleeing from the police, hurting them badly.

In the end the decision was taken that the stoep should be washed down every Friday afternoon after four o'clock, so it would be too wet to sit on.

We children took turns to scrub it with soap and water, and to our parents' delight the *tsotsis* resorted to gambling on the pavement at the corner of Cross and Richmond Streets each time they found the stoep wet ...

In those days, it was common to hold such parties [*stokvels*] on Sunday afternoons. This was in order to make it possible for women to attend who "slept in" as domestic workers during the week. The ladies would wear their Sunday best, and so would their male friends.

The house parties would end at ten o'clock at night so that the women who were off duty on Sunday afternoons, would be in time for the last buses back to their "sleep in" places of work.

There were a few popular venues for these *stokvels*, but the most popular was No. 22 Stone Street.

At this address, which was a ten-minute's walk from Cross Street, lived Tat'uBhungane who had a very big room and a piano. He stayed alone because his family was in the country. The Black residents of District Six hired the room for one pound ten shillings, from one o'clock in the afternoon until ten in the evening. This was far cheaper than hiring the local halls at Primrose and Ayre Street, for instance. The person the party was given in honour of had to hire a pianist – *maskhanda*, as they were called in Xhosa. There were a few young men who were used as *maskhandas*.

The best income at such a party was from the bar. Much as the law did not allow the selling of liquor and the running of shebeens, this happened in a big way. If there was to be a house party, the shebeen queens would stock up beforehand with bottles and bottles of beer and brandy. Africans were not allowed to buy liquor over the counter, but that did not have much effect on the shebeen queens. They simply sent Coloured boys to buy it for them. The "carry-boys", or "mailers" as they were also sometimes known, charged a small sum for each bottle purchased – a tickey (three-pence), per bottle.

Every now and then a carry-boy tried to cheat on the shebeen queen by running away with the money given to him to pay for the liquor. It was not easy to trace such a skellum and of course it was impossible to report the theft to the police as the whole liquor business was illegal to start with. Because the carry-boys knew very well that they could not be reprimanded, they would vanish for a couple of days and then reappear and roam around as if nothing had happened ...

The liquor was usually bought on Friday afternoons as the shebeen business was only good during the weekends. The Cross Street residents, like most other people in District Six, never consumed liquor during the week, and the police, who regularly raided the shebeens, chose Friday evenings to do so. Every Black child in District Six was aware of this and while playing in the streets on Fridays, they would be on the lookout for police vans. Whenever they spotted one, they would shout, "*Kubomvu! Kubomvu!*" – It's red! It's red! – red being the colour of danger. This was the signal to the residents that the police were on their way.

The police knew that they were being watched, so sometimes, instead of driving from Richmond Street into Cross Street, the obvious way to get there, they would drive down Dove Lane, and by the time the children saw them, it would be too late to shout, "*Kubomvu! Kubomvu!*" The ordinary residents of District Six never had telephones, but there was an excellent communications network operating throughout the area whenever there was a police raid. If the police raided in Cross Street, someone would quickly relay the message to Stuckeris Street to stash away any illegal stuff. From here, the news would be passed on to the "Strong Yard" in Roger Street, from where it went to Ashley, Caledon and William Street. By the time the *amaBhulu* got to these places, there would be no sign of liquor.

Sometimes, however, the police were too clever for the law-breakers. They would wear civvies, park their van far away and arrive on foot. Neither the children nor the older people would recognise them until they banged on the front or back door, as they always did. They never waited to be allowed in but forced the door open and moved from room to room, ransacking beds and wardrobes and leaving the place upside down. There was no respect for the people who lived there, they were only interested in the hidden liquor. Sometimes they did find a few bottles in a backyard, but nobody would own up, even if they threatened to arrest everybody, and in the end they left empty-handed because the owners' names were not written on the bottles.

There was one policeman who would always try to get us children to tell him where the liquor was. He was nicknamed "Rooikop" because he was a red head. But we would never tell, even though he would be walking right past the bottles safely tucked in stockings and hidden under the washing on the line …

Robberies were reported to the disciplinary committee by the victims and discussed at great length, and the spots where the robbers hung out were avoided. The Seven Steps leading off Hanover Street was the most notorious place for robberies. My father used to say that you are never safe until you have passed the Seven Steps.

"If you go past the Seven Steps in the evening without being harassed," he always said, "then you must know your ancestors are with you."

To avoid this place, the residents who travelled back from Langa by bus got off at Sir Lowry Road instead of Castle Bridge near the public toilets. From there they would walk up Stuckeris Street as far as Hanover Street, cross and continue up Richmond to Cross Street. This was not the shortest route, but it was the safest way after dark.

Once Mzwandile's brother, who was asthmatic, and Themba Memani, a young, energetic sportsman, came home from Langa by this route. It was Saturday and they caught a double-decker bus from Mowbray into town. On the lower deck, near the door of the bus, two White policemen were standing. At the Sir Lowry Road bus stop, Themba and his friend rang the bell and descended from the upper deck. The police, as usual, harassed them.

"*Maak gou*, kaffirs! Hurry up!"

The two did not argue but quickly got off the bus. Only when it had moved a few yards away, they started swearing at the police.

"*Wat sê julle*, kaffirs?" one policeman demanded.

"You heard, you white pig," Themba replied.

That was enough. The two policemen jumped off the bus and went for them.

"Wait for me, Themba! *Sukudishiya!* – Don't leave me behind!" shouted Mzwandile's brother.

"*Baleka*, man! Run, man! *Afikile amaBhulu*. The *Boere* are coming!" Themba called back.

Themba was faster than his friend, but Mzwandile's brother tried to keep up with him. He knew that if the police caught him, he would pay for the sins of his friend as well. As they could never catch Themba, who ran like the wind, Mzwandile's brother vowed to himself that they would not catch him either.

The poor fellow was overtaxing himself. He wheezed and panted but still could not shake off the two policemen. As the road went up-hill, the police drew nearer. Just when they were about to grab hold of him, a group of Coloured men started shouting, "Hey! *Los hom, los hom uit!* Leave him alone!"

The police, sensing trouble, turned back.

When they reached Cross Street, Mzwandile's brother and Themba Memani were so tired that they could hardly talk. Only later did they tell the story and praise the Coloured men for saving their skins.

Bhenya, another resident, was, however, less fortunate. It was the same weekend, and he had gone to BoKaap on foot to visit friends. Because he knew that he would be coming back late and would be passing the Seven Steps, he had taken along his sjambok as protection. On his way back, Bhenya saw a group of young men sitting on the Seven Steps, as he had feared. He decided to carry on regardless.

When he drew nearer, one of the skollies got up.

"*Het djy 'n metsjie?* Do you have a match?" he asked.

This, of course, was an old trick. As soon as Bhenya put his hand in his pocket for the match, the man grabbed the sjambok and started whipping him.

At first, Bhenya faced his opponent as if he was going to fight back.

"*Slaan hom!* Beat him!" encouraged the skollie's friends.

The skollie got in a few good swipes while Bhenya tried to get hold of the whip. The skollie only pushed him away and whipped harder. Bhenya could not stand the pain. He turned around and started run-ning. The group of young men roared with laughter.

"*Ja hom! Ja hom!* Chase him! Chase him!" they shouted.

Bhenya ran for his life all the way back home. Whoever had used his own sjambok on him had done a good job because his back was covered with nasty purple welts.

Word about Bhenya's whipping immediately went round District Six. To some, it was a joke because Bhenya had been warned time and again by his relatives not to carry the sjambok around.

"If you have to carry something, let it be a walking stick rather," they had begged him. "A sjambok is too dangerous."

Bhenya had ignored the advice and paid the price.

from The House in Tyne Street (1996)

LINDA FORTUNE

There were four cinemas in District Six, all within walking distance of each other.

The Avalon was the most select and here the more modern films were shown. It was always a pleasure to go and watch a film at the Avalon because no ruffians or "bad elements" were allowed in. It was especially famous for showing Indian films with subtitles. The whole of the Avalon would be booked out by our primary school if a special film was shown, and I saw Mother India, The Ten Commandments, Boot Polish, The Good Earth, Ben Hur, The Big Fisherman and many more great films there with my best friend Jane.

The entrance to the Star bioscope was in Hanover Street, right opposite the fish market. The side entrance was opposite St Mark's Church in Clifton Street. To watch a film from upstairs in the Star was alright, but one had to be brave to go in and take a seat downstairs.

Doctor Zhivago, starring Omar Sharif, was showing and I wanted to see it very badly. I had left school by then and was working. I didn't want to go alone to the Star, so I asked my mom if she would go with me, but she refused, saying, "You know I never go to places like that because the smoking gives me asthma."

Ron was going out and Shirley had to study. It was the last time that Doctor Zhivago was going to be shown and I had no option but to ask my dad – I even offered to pay for his ticket! He never went to the cinema as he preferred to read books, so I was very surprised when he agreed to accompany me.

When we arrived at the Star, the upstairs seats were all booked out. Only two seats were still available downstairs and they were right in front.

"What shall we do?" I asked my dad.

"We may as well buy the tickets and stay to watch the film."

It was unbearable sitting right in front. The smell of the dagga being smoked at the back drifted down there and the people around us were making a lot of noise, some using obscene language.

I tried very hard to concentrate on the film. I was getting more and more scared of sitting there and wanted to tell my dad that we should leave, but he seemed to be enjoying himself. I consoled myself with the thought that no harm would come to us while he was there, especially as the surroundings did not seem to bother him much. I tried to relax, but it was impossible not to feel uncomfortable: fleas or bugs had started to bite my legs!

The film eventually did end and it was a relief to be outside in the fresh night air again.

On the way home Dad said, "I never again want to hear that any of my children, including you, wish to go to the Star. Even if you can get seats upstairs. The place has changed so much over the years, I had no idea that the patrons could now do just as they pleased."

Maybe it was a good thing after all that we went that night, though, because the Star burnt down soon afterwards ...

In Hanover Street there were many old buildings, some of them without any electricity. Different kinds of people lived in these buildings – "select" people, average families, and gangsters all lived next to each other, and all hung their washing from the balconies. There was no other place. Couples who got married moved in with their families and new babies were born and grew up here. The elderly passed away and younger people took their places. People of all colours and creeds lived side by side. Sometimes a fight would break out, but when it was settled, things would just go back to normal. Here and there a brilliant child would manage to study in these conditions. He or she would finish school and end up being someone of importance. Everyone in District Six would respect such a person.

One building in particular always interested me: Hanover Building opposite the Rose & Crown Bar. This building was very tall and it had the most beautiful stucco around the top. The balconies looked so daintily odd against the stark ugliness of the surrounding cardboard and corrugated sheeting structures and the washing lines with their eternal washing hanging out to dry in the breeze. Buses, cars, horses and carts, bicycles and people all buzzed past in the street below.

I spent quite a lot of time opposite Hanover Building because my father spent quite a lot of time inside the Rose & Crown, and my mother always sent me to go and call him if there was someone to see him. I hated this.

Because I was a girl I was not allowed to go into the bar, so I had to wait outside and ask the first man on his way into the bar to please tell my father that his daughter Penny was outside waiting for him. Dad always took his time to come out.

It was while I had to wait for him that I used to look at Hanover Building. By now it was well known that District Six was going to be declared a white area. I felt sad to think that this beautiful old building, together with so many well-constructed homes, would soon be demolished.

If my dad took particularly long to make his appearance, the guys that walked past the bar would pass comments about my standing there, and so, to take my mind off an unpleasant situation, I stood there and daydreamed.

If this building stood in Sea Point it would be looked at in a different light, I would think. If only the landlord could revamp and clean it!

I had hundreds of ideas of what could be done. I was only a teenager then and would imagine that I was a tourist taking photographs of this lovely, renovated place to show my friends back home in England or whatever. If only the City Council or someone would see the beauty in this building and repair it! Or maybe the tenants could be asked to hang their washing in the backyard instead of over the balconies. It would already look so much better. Why couldn't they rather put up window boxes and fill them with geraniums or petunias like in Austria?

In my imagination I saw all kinds of wonderful possibilities for the building. At the entrance one could place two large flower pots ... oh, I used to think, Hanover Street would be so attractive if it was cleaned up. All the skollies and loafers would automatically improve themselves and tourists would come from all over the world to see how we all lived together peacefully in District Six. New Year would be the best of all times! The Cape Coons' Carnival with its brightly coloured satins, umbrellas, painted faces, singsongs and the general feeling of wellbeing and fun would swing through District Six, down to Adderley Street and Green Point, and everyone would be enjoying themselves.

For our row of semi-detached cottages in Tyne Street I pictured white walls, yellow shutters, doors and window frames, and tall flowering shrubs in big white pots on either side of the front doors – with shiny brass door handles and letterbox covers.

I would step out of my dream the moment my dad appeared from the Rose & Crown, and then the two of us would walk home hand in hand.

"Dad," I said one day, "I'm getting too big now to be standing outside a bar waiting for you. You must tell Mom to send one of the boys to fetch you. But," I added, "the problem can be solved if you stay away from that place."

"Look, Penny," he said, "I like going there sometimes. That's where one picks up all kinds of information."

With that I couldn't argue. Dad probably first heard about the government's plans for District Six in the Rose & Crown.

from Acid Alex (2005)

AL LOVEJOY

Eric Jackson was in Hostel 2 with me and was already in the gangs in Cape Town. He was a Mongrel. I began to learn what that was all about. He told me Nienaber was right about the need for me to *raak wys* and get *gedagtes* but there was more – I had to learn *respek* and *disipliene*. These were hallmarks of an *indota* – a blooded ouen. Until I learnt what they meant I would always be a laaitie on this side of the fence. I could have all the pluk and all the gedagte I wanted but if I didn't know how to be *stambula* I would never be a successful *skelm*. If I wanted to get into a gang the ouens would have to know they could rely on me. I would have to do what I had to do, keep my bek shut and be willing to do anything to learn how to do it better.

Wally moved down from Joburg and he and Swallow built a house in Table View in Cape Town. He gave me a Holiday Permission and even paid for my train ticket.

Why? I don't know. It was during the holidays that my new life away from school started.

Eric's girlfriend Tania lived in Buitenkant Street, Gardens, and that was where we hung out. The nearest merchant was a coloured woman called Mams who lived in Canterbury Flats, District Six.

I became very close friends with both her sons.

Mams had married a man of white and coloured blood, and her two sons, though both had features of coloured men, had dark and very light skin respectively. They were Joseph and Whitey. Joseph was a Bun Boy and Whitey was a Mongrel. I hung out with one or the other and they were completely different in other ways too. Joseph only drank and Whitey mostly only smoked.

I mean, Whitey did drink but not a lot. I used to get back from clubbing with Eric, who would fuck off to doss at Tania's pozzie. Then I would go find Whitey at his mochie's spot. His mochie worked for a white woman as her char and her husband was a Captain in the boere. Whitey's mochie had a tiny room just outside the kitchen door. I would knock, Whitey would ask who it was and I would tune him – Yster, or my new nickname among them, Schoolboy shortened to Skollie. He would drag out a mattress with a blanket and a pillow, we'd make a quick pipe and doss. If it was still early enough and I could phone, Mams and Joseph would come fetch me. Him and five or so of his Bun Boy couplings would escort me into The District so I could sleep in my own bed. In the mornings when Whitey and I got up, we would take a stroll down to Milly's in Buitenkant Street. We'd buy two pies and if we had enough money we'd buy a litre of lurk. Lurk is the name for *skoon wit wyn*. Then we'd slip into the alley behind Milly's and down it. If it was still not a good day – we'd go down to Mams.

Mams was incidentally one of the biggest merchants in The District.

One day, about five years before, Joseph had gone down to the station to try and snatch a purse or some move because they were living on the bones of their arses. He spied a white man on the station with a briefcase and snatched it. He got away, and when he opened it – he found fifty grand. The shock was so much that he went straight home to Mams, gave it to her and asked her to give him a little something so that he could go for a dop. He told me he knew that if he touched a single note he would have fucked it up.

When me and Whitey arrived at Mams, she would walk into the room and upon seeing us would start marching around the flat *skelling*. She used to *skel* me too, which was cool because I knew all that yelling, hollering and cursing was just her way of showing love and affection. Making sure we had respect while we stood very meekly, not quite grinning out loud, and two bottles of lurk would appear on the table. Then she went off *skelling* somewhere else. Her husband, also called Whitey, always sat at the table listening to his radio and having a dop of his own. He would wink. And grin. Then she'd come back and suddenly there would be two rand-baalle, *skel, skel, skel*, until finally she'd give us two buttons with a smile – BUT – she'd first make us breakfast, which we *had* to eat, before we got goofed, or she'd *really* get befuck.

We smoked on the balcony. That's where my bed was. I used to get completely fucked and pass out on my kooi. As I sank slowly into my float, the sounds of The District would come echoing up all around me. Children shrieking at play, hawkers touting, voices raised in argument over the never-ending dice game in the courtyard. The clatter and ringing of bicycles, women yelling gossip to each other across balconies, a hundred radios blaring out tinny distorted music, the sounds of babies crying. A living kaleidoscope of sounds running around vibrantly in my mind against the backdrop and distant hum of Cape Town's city centre.

Skollie had never felt so at home.

Skollie was home.

Buttons were the pills we smoked in bottlenecks. Their medical name was Mandrax and the active chemical ingredient was methaqualone. According to the ouens, they had been legal up until a few years before. They fell under the sedative hypnotic category of drugs. I remember smoking my first one as clearly as the first time I had sex with Laura.

It was a hell of a lot better than fucking her, but buttons would eventually break everything in my life – not just my heart and not just once either.

We always used to smoke up on the little soccer field on the District Six side of the bridge across from the Gardens Centre off Buitenkant Street. That little soccer field has many memories. My first white pipe was one night when we were on our way to the Avalon Hotel to go and suip. Eric, his girlfriend Tania, Gavin and me.

There was some serious ritual involved too. The Mandrax tablet is pure white and rounded. The one side is split with a line and has the letters RL in cursive script. On the other side is the Mx legend with its tiny underline. It has to be crushed carefully into a fine white powder, using the shiny side of a folded square piece of heavy brown paper.

This is very important. Eric told me stories of okes getting stabbed in the face with bottlenecks for fucking up on a button pipe. Once it has been crushed into a completely flat pancake half-moon in the paper, zol that's already been cleaned and mixed is carefully sprinkled onto it. Then it is folded, turned over and more zol is sprinkled on the other side. The powder is carefully worked into the zol until it coats the *boom* completely. Then a very clean pipe with a girrick and a backstop is taken and a little bit of cleaned zol is put into it. The white zol is added and then more cleaned zol is placed on top and tamped down. This is called topstop. The way to smoke a white pipe is to just hit it once as hard as possible and hold it. And hold it. And hold it.

And rush off your tits.

It starts almost immediately. All your senses short-circuit and explode from the middle of your brain, overwhelming everything everywhere. Your body quickly melts away into senseless nothingness as you go hurtling deep into the brilliant pure white sea of rush. Every single fucking time.

There were a lot of gangs in The District. The worst of them in Canterbury and Bloemhof Flats were the Jesters, who were a coloureds-only gang that killed whiteys and darkies whenever possible. They were Hollanders – murderers. So were a lot of the Scorpions. I could only walk home with a gang escort – it was very dangerous if I didn't.

Cape Town was riddled with gangs.

On the other side were the marrobaners, who were the Mongrels and the Born Free Kids. There were also the Bun Boys, Yakkies, Sexy Boys, Funky Junkies, Coral Kids, Americans and Young Americans (all various *nommers* [numbers: prison gangs]) but they were all smaller in number and had less of a presence in that area. Cape Town's gangs were scattered in pockets all over the city because of politics. Uncle Guvvie moved people all over as it pleased him and this meant that the gangs broke up and rebuilt themselves from smaller cells. Mostly in the coloured and grey areas. The biggest gangs citywide were the Scorpions and the Mongrels. The Mongrels were a mixed gang of blacks, whites, coloureds – both ouens and kinders (who were known as *jostermeide*). There were so many more other gangs but I'm not going to go into all of them now.

I became a Mongrel, that is all that matters. I also entered into a lifelong relationship with the descendants of *emancipated* slaves, cast-offs, wandering white pricks and pure black men – the so-called coloured population of South Africa. For a great many years I spent more time in townships and ghettos than I did inside the white laager of the Group Areas Act, although the only reason I mention this is because of all the kak the gattas gave me for crossing the wire. Their poes. I fucking hate politics. Later on I'll tell you about the kak I had at the hands of coloured boere.

Eric told me the ideology behind the gangs came from prison. It started back at the turn of the last century in a black prison up in the Transvaal. Twenty-eight men banded together and swore an oath to stick together against Uncle Guvvie, the gattas, and everyone else – to the death. They created a place in the world for themselves and called it *nChonalanga*. This place had no borders. It owned no real estate. You belonged there by believing in it and by being able to open your mouth and identify yourself and where you stood inside that world as an indota – a man. As the years went on, rival gangs like the Big Fives started, until eventually it evolved into the modern South African prison gang system.

In prison the nongies (the 28s) are responsible for discipline and most of the smuggling. They are also the largest of the gangs and are separated from the other gangs because they practise sodomy. They rule the prison's nights and their motto is *Sondaf Ag-en-twintig*. They salute by stretching their hand out like a pistol with two barrels across their hearts.

The marrobaners (the 26s) are the thieves. They live for kroon and they steal to get it. They rob, thieve, connive, scale, sluk, skêbeng and schnaai their way into anything not nailed down. The only golden and much broken rule is never to sluk a brother. Their motto is *Son'd op Sesen-twintig* – duime.

The Hollanders (27s) are killers. Theirs is a badge more than a gang and is worn on both sides of the sun. You become a 27 by killing someone.

A Vyf is a piemp.

A Dertig is a grubby, *someone always after food*.

And so on.

On the outside it became blurred. An ou might be a nongie in the

mang without being an auntie or a *pop* because he might smokkel for
the brothers of *sondaf* to make his bene sterk – but on the outside he
would be *sondop* and marrobaan to make a way.

I took to this way of life like a duck to water.

Merry Sport of Minstrelsy (2005)

TOM EATON

The Cape Town minstrels have a special place in the hearts of Capetonians. I think it's somewhere near the aortal valve. The doctors say
it's too dangerous to operate, so there they stay.

They were once called Coons, but mercifully the vast lies that are
racial stereotyping are a thing of the past. After ten years of democracy we are free to call the Cape minstrels what they are: tone-deaf
sequined horrors of sartorial ghastliness, spangled harpies hell-bent
on dragging an entire city into their annual quagmire of mindless,
pointless, endless jollity. I don't like the minstrels.

But that's okay, because they don't like me. That's because I'm a
white piece of shit. Or was it a piece of white shit? I forget: the day
was hot, the traffic intersection was busy, and the men who dubbed me
thus had terribly few teeth. But certainly albino faeces was involved,
after the pair of merry minstrels asked me at a traffic light to sponsor
them R10 for transport, and I declined.

For a moment one wondered what Scandinavian tourists would
think of such an exhortation, especially having just read in their
guidebook that the Cape Malays (found between Cape Cobras and
Cape Wangai Orangutans) are cheeky but warm-hearted.

However there was no need for concern. Dental catastrophe and
its mesmerizing effects on human speech would have left our valued
visitors certain that two men in polystyrene boaters and cardboard
spats had just bestowed upon them the Peace of Weitsit.

Still, one had to wonder how much dung was flung when the minstrels' request for R10 million from the Western Cape government
was turned down. In the end they had to settle for a measly two million, and complained bitterly to SABC's Charl Pauw that they'd had to

spend "millions to give the citizens of Cape Town a free show". Them plastic ukuleles don't come cheap.

But more hardships were to come. With January 2 falling on Sunday this year, they were forced to take Monday off work to give the citizens of Cape Town the abovementioned free show. You just can't expect artists to work like this.

A burning sense of self-righteous entitlement; an entrenched belief that frivolous self-gratification qualifies as a spectacle worth watching; an aggressive assertion of partying as culture; horrible music; ugly uniforms; the smell of slightly burnt boerewors rolls hanging over the baking asphalt: has the minstrels' parade finally become a fully-fledged South African sport?

It's always been competitive: teams are judged on apparel, musical skill, the length of their tongues and whether or not their backer is a major Cape Flats crime lord. But surely it is time for the organizers (if such a word is applicable to an event that generally unfolds like a fire in a kindergarten) to realize the fiscal possibilities of selling themselves and their grand traditions to someone like SuperSport?

I for one would be fascinated to watch the single-string banjo duel for men over 65, in which competitors improvise up to three varia-tions on a short musical phrase ("Tjakkalang tjakkalang tjakkalay"). Synchronised parasol dropping; the 10km aimless meander; endurance waiting (where the hell are those busses?); all are no less watchable than golf or swimming or a root canal performed in a Rawalpindi meat-market with a 19th-century hand bore. With television money behind it, the parade could even expand to include real minstrels, people able to hold not only a genuine note, but hold it at the same instant as those around them.

Sport is culture, and eventually, as the fetish of inclusiveness takes hold, culture will be sport. It's a small step from Olympic curling to Olympic knitting, and a smaller one to Olympic hat-tipping and gold-tooth-flashing. Will the 2040 Games, held in Zumaville (formerly Benoni), see a Cape contingent go head to head with a posse of Swiss yodelers? If the minstrel organizers get organized, yes. Will I be there? I'd rather eat ground glass. Tjakkalang.

SUBURBIA

from Boyhood (1997)

J M COETZEE

In Reunion Park they had paid twelve pounds a month for their house. The house his father has rented in Plumstead costs twenty-five pounds. It lies at the very limit of Plumstead, facing an expanse of sand and wattle bush where only a week after their arrival the police find a dead baby in a brown paper packet. A half-hour walk in the other direction lies Plumstead railway station. The house itself is newly built, like all the houses in Evremonde Road, with picture windows and parquet floors. The doors are warped, the locks do not lock, there is a pile of rubble in the back yard.

Next door live a couple newly arrived from England. The man is forever washing his car; the woman, wearing red shorts and sunglasses, spends her days in a deckchair, tanning her long white legs.

The immediate task is to find schools for him and his brother. Cape Town is not like Worcester, where all the boys went to the boys' school and all the girls to the girls' school. In Cape Town there are schools to choose among. But to get into a good school you need contacts, and they have few contacts.

Through the influence of his mother's brother Lance they get an interview at Rondebosch Boys' High. Dressed neatly in his shorts and shirt and tie and navy-blue blazer with the Worcester Boys' Primary badge on the breast pocket, he sits with his mother on a bench outside the headmaster's office. When their turn comes they are ushered into a wood-panelled room full of photographs of rugby and cricket teams. The headmaster's questions are all addressed to his mother: where they live, what his father does. Then comes the moment he has been waiting for. From her handbag she produces the report that proves he was first in class and that ought therefore to open all doors to him.

The headmaster puts on his reading-glasses. 'So you came first in your class,' he says. 'Good, good! But you won't find it so easy here.'

He had hoped to be tested: to be asked the date of the battle of Blood River, or, even better, to be given some mental arithmetic. But that is all, the interview is over. 'I can make no promises,' says the headmaster. 'His name will go down on the waiting-list, then we must hope for a withdrawal.'

His name goes down on the waiting-lists of three schools, without success. Coming first in Worcester is evidently not good enough for Cape Town.

The last resort is the Catholic school, St Joseph's. St Joseph's has no waiting-list: they will take anyone prepared to pay their fees, which for non-Catholics are twelve pounds a quarter.

What is being brought home to them, to him and his mother, is that in Cape Town different classes of people attend different schools. St Joseph's caters for, if not the lowest class, then the second-lowest. Her failure to get him into a better school leaves his mother bitter but does not upset him. He is not sure what class they belong to, where they fit in. For the present he is content merely to get by. The threat of being sent to an Afrikaans school and consigned to an Afrikaans life has receded – that is all that matters. He can relax. He does not even have to go on pretending to be a Catholic.

The real English do not go to a school like St Joseph's. But on the streets of Rondebosch, on their way to and from their own schools, he can see them every day, can admire their straight blond hair and golden skins, their clothes that are never too small or too large, their quiet confidence. They josh each other (a word he knows from the public-school stories he has read) in an easy way, without the raucousness and clumsiness he is used to. He has no aspiration to join them, but he watches and tries to learn.

The boys from Diocesan College, who are the most English of all and do not condescend even to play rugby or cricket against St Joseph's, live in select areas that, being far from the railway line, he hears of but never sees: Bishopscourt, Fernwood, Constantia. They have sisters who go to schools like Herschel and St Cyprian's, whom they genially watch over and protect. In Worcester he had rarely laid eyes on a girl: his friends seemed always to have brothers, not sisters. Now he glimpses for the first time the sisters of the English, so golden-blonde, so beautiful, that he cannot believe they are of this earth.

from Youth (2002)

J M COETZEE

To bring in more money, he takes on a second afternoon of tutoring in the Mathematics Department. The first-year students who attend the tutorial are free to bring in questions on applied mathematics as well as pure mathematics. With only a single year of applied mathematics to his credit, he is barely ahead of the students he is supposed to be assisting: each week he has to spend hours on preparation.

Wrapped up though he is in his private worries, he cannot fail to see that the country around him is in turmoil. The pass laws to which Africans and Africans alone are subjected are being tightened even further, and protests are breaking out everywhere. In the Transvaal the police fire shots into a crowd, then, in their mad way, go on firing into the backs of fleeing men, women and children. From beginning to end the business sickens him: the laws themselves; the bully-boy police; the government, stridently defending the murderers and denouncing the dead; and the press, too frightened to come out and say what anyone with eyes in his head can see.

After the carnage of Sharpeville nothing is as it was before. Even in the pacific Cape there are strikes and marches. Wherever a march takes place there are policemen with guns hovering around the edges, waiting for an excuse to shoot.

It all comes to a head one afternoon while he is on tutorial duty. The tutorial room is quiet; he is patrolling from desk to desk, checking how students are getting on with the assigned exercises, trying to help those in difficulty. Suddenly the door swings open. One of the senior lecturers strides in and raps on the table. 'May I have your attention!' he calls out. There is a nervous crack in his voice; his face is flushed. 'Please put down your pens and give me your attention! There is at this moment a workers' march taking place along De Waal Drive. For reasons of safety, I am asked to announce that no one is being allowed to leave the campus, until further notice. I repeat: no one is being allowed to leave. This is an order issued by the police. Are there any questions?'

There is one question at least, but this is not the right time to voice it: What is the country coming to when one cannot run a mathematics tutorial in peace? As for the police order, he does not believe for a moment that the police are sealing off the campus for the sake of the students. They are sealing it off so that students from this notorious hotbed of leftism will not join the march, that is all.

There is no hope of continuing with the mathematics tutorial. Around the room there is a buzz of conversation; students are already packing their bags and exiting, eager to see what is up.

He follows the crowd to the embankment above De Waal Drive. All traffic has been halted. The marchers are coming up Woolsack Road in a thick snake, ten, twenty abreast, then turning north on to the motorway. They are men, most of them, in drab clothing – overalls, army surplus coats, woollen caps – some carrying sticks, all walking swiftly, silently. There is no end to the column in sight. If he were the police, he would be frightened.

'It's PAC,' says a Coloured student nearby. His eyes glisten, he has an intent look. Is he right? How does he know? Are there signs one ought to recognize? The PAC is not like the ANC. It is more ominous. *Africa for the Africans!* says the PAC. *Drive the whites into the sea!*

Thousands upon thousands, the column of men winds its way up the hill. It does not look like an army, but that is what it is, an army called into being of a sudden out of the wastelands of the Cape Flats. Once they reach the city, what will they do? Whatever it is, there are not enough policemen in the land to stop them, not enough bullets to kill them.

When he was twelve he was herded into a bus full of schoolchildren and driven to Adderley Street, where they were given paper orange-white-and-blue flags and told to wave them as the parade of floats passed by (Jan van Riebeeck and his wife in sober burgher dress; Voortrekkers with muskets; portly Paul Kruger). Three hundred years of history, three hundred years of Christian civilization at the tip of Africa, said the politicians in their speeches: to the Lord let us give thanks. Now, before his eyes, the Lord is withdrawing his protective hand. In the shadow of the mountain he is watching history being unmade.

In the hush around him, among these neat, well-dressed products of Rondebosch Boys High School and the Diocesan College, these youths who half an hour ago were busy calculating angles of vector and dreaming of careers as civil engineers, he can feel the same shock of dismay. They were expecting to enjoy a show, to snicker at a pro-cession of garden boys, not to behold this grim host. The afternoon is ruined for them; all they want now is to go home, have a Coke and a sandwich, forget what has passed.

And he? He is no different. *Will the ships still be sailing tomorrow?* – that is his one thought. *I must get out before it is too late!*

The next day, when it is all over and the marchers have gone home, the newspapers find ways of talking about it. *Giving vent to pent-up anger,* they call it. *One of many protest marches country-wide in the wake of Sharpeville. Defused,* they say, *by the good sense (for once) of the police and the co-operation of march leaders. The government,* they say, *would be well advised to sit up and take note.* So they tame the event, making it less than what it was. He is not deceived. The merest whistle, and from the shacks and barracks of the Cape Flats the same army of men will spring up, stronger than before, more numerous. Armed too, with guns from China. What hope is there of standing against them when you do not believe in what you are standing for?

There is the matter of the Defence Force. When he left school they were conscripting only one white boy in three for military training. He was lucky enough not to be balloted. Now all that is changing. There are new rules. At any time he can find a call-up notice in his letterbox: *You are required to present yourself at the Castle at 9 a.m. on such-and-such a date. Bring only toilet items.*

Voortrekkerhoogte, somewhere in the Transvaal, is the training camp he has heard the most about. It is where they send conscripts from the Cape, far from home, to break them. In a week he could find himself behind barbed wire in Voortrekkerhoogte, sharing a tent with thuggish Afrikaners, eating bully-beef out of cans, listening to Johnnie Ray on Springbok Radio. He would not be able to endure it; he would slash his wrists. There is only one course open: to flee. But how can he flee without taking his degree? It would be like departing on a long journey, a life's journey, with no clothes, no money, no (the comparison comes more reluctantly) weapon.

from The Dressing Station (2001)

JONATHAN KAPLAN

Conradie was an old army hospital, now converted to civilian use. It included a spinal unit, general medical and surgical wards, a paediatric department and a small neurosurgery unit. Long barrack wards with wide verandas lay among a grid of paths, along which raced the wheelchairs of the paraplegics. Khaki-clad convicts from a local jail mowed the grass and dressed the regimented flower-beds, while prison officers supervised the work from the shade, pointing with their thermos flasks. As a district hospital with a reputation for roughness, it was avoided by the academic high-flyers, who preferred the ambience of the university teaching hospital. It was here that I came to take up the post of surgical house-officer, shortly after graduating from medical school.

Conradie Hospital lay in an unusual position. On one side stretched the expansive avenues and bungalow homes of Pinelands, a white suburb of watered lawns where civil servants retired to bully their servants. The Cape Flats began on the other, a mosaic of concrete cube-houses and potholed roads that zoned the grey beach-sand into 'townships' – Mitchell's Plain for 'coloureds'; Nyanga, Langa and Gugulethu for blacks – and between them stunted jungles of scrub willow that hid the tracks and shanties of squatter settlements thrown up by migrants from the hinterland. The hospital served all races, after a fashion, with its patients delivered in racially specific ambulances to its segregated casualty departments.

It was often busy. The odd solid citizen from Pinelands, with diabetes or an asthma attack, would arrive in 'white' Casualty, expecting instant service from the single medical officer on night duty. Across the hall, on the 'black' side, victims of assaults, traffic accidents and incomplete abortions would turn up through the evening, filling the benches in the waiting room. Now and then a turf-fight would rage between coloured gangs, and the corridor would be flanked with trolleys from which slashed Gypsy Jokers and Manhattans, their jail-tattoos smeared with blood, screamed threats at one another while the walking wounded grappled in the reception area, feet sliding on the blood-slick floor. Those too embattled to have their injuries tended would be separated by the cops, cruel but impartial, who would club the casualties back into line. 'Listen to the doctor,' they'd order. 'You cunts can carry on killing each other outside when he's finished.' On my second night on duty a big-bellied sergeant, mug of tea at his elbow, showed me how to put a drain into the chest of a stab-victim with a collapsed lung. He liked to hang around the department chatting up the nursing sisters and sometimes pitched in as an extra medic, cobbling together ragged machete wounds with big, efficient sutures.

In South Africa that passed for normal hospital life. Its even tenor was about to be disrupted. Unrest had been simmering in the black townships around Cape Town, and the authorities now decided to suppress it with vigour. One morning I drove to work past convoys of police trucks on their way to Langa, Nyanga and Gugulethu, their windscreens blanked with steel mesh. They were led by a file of Casspirs: armoured vehicles, high and long and almost sleek, like racing coffins, their great lugged tyres raising the occupants above their surroundings. The cabs were framed by slabs of bullet-proof glass that also formed slits above a row of gunports along each side. They looked capable of driving right through township shacks, but over the course of that baking, windless day the confrontation which they portended seemed to have fizzled out. A contingent of riot police lounging at the hospital gates announced that the 'troublemakers' had been dispersed, a few arrested. Nevertheless the hospital staff remained on edge, and by 4 p.m. all those who could had left to make sure 'that everything was all right at home'. I stayed because I was the medical officer on duty that night.

By sunset the Casualty department would usually be starting to fill with the evening's harvest. It remained empty. I stood outside in the dusk, feeling the overheated stillness of the day give way to a wind blowing steadily from the east. With it came a smell of woodsmoke and the crackle of shots, rising and falling like an approaching brushfire. A helicopter clattered overhead, and then another, heading for the townships. A column of smoke rose against the darkening sky. From the distance came the sound of sirens. I thought I knew what was coming. I recalled the stories of war service I had been hearing since I was a child.

The first ambulance swung onto the tarmac outside Casualty. Another was just behind it, and another, and a snake of flashing lights that stretched back down the road. It was suddenly clear that those stories – and my training – hadn't prepared me for anything on this scale. I fled into the building from which startled nurses were beginning to emerge, pushing bed-trolleys.

'Call the switchboard!' I yelled to the receptionist. 'Tell them to page every doctor they can. We're going to be flooded!'

from A Writer's Diary (1997)

STEPHEN WATSON

1 January 1996
Driving from Observatory towards Woodstock, along the Main Road, evening coming on, the same sky of years before opening out, wide, bland, lucid but faded over the city bowl, over the renewed emptiness of the Atlantic itself opening into the west.

Our infinite again, here in Cape Town. But, as before, as in all those years before, always a hair's breadth away from nothingness, an utter vacancy.

And your obsession with this particular summer sky, in your child-hood as now, was always because it had the colour of eternity – or what, to you, was to become the colour of eternity.

The sky at the end of the street again …

8 February 1996 ·
Keep in mind, always, the motivation that prompted you first to write: those climbs, often beginning before dawn, with your father when you were still a boy. For instance, coming out of the cloud ceiling onto the summit of Devil's Peak, there to see that ceiling of cumulus below us, white in the early morning sun, and filling up the 30-mile trough between the Table Mountain massif and the Hottentots Holland.

In other words, it was beauty (even if a child's perception of it) that first led you to words.

Later, there were other things, scarcely beautiful at all. But it began, you might say, in beauty. And therefore it will be, as the Navajo say, "finished in beauty."

Or not at all …

4 March 1996
This is the time of year, now between seasons, when the southeasters start fading and southwest wind brings sea-mists on certain mornings.

By mid-morning the peaks swim through the mist, the sky behind them a purer blue. There is a heavy sparkle to the air as the moisture burns off.

Afternoons of great heat but, as always in March, the sense of coolness just behind the horizon – that lining of coolness to the oven of the sky, the day, given by the slowly turning year.

And then the skies of these evenings, with their clear foreheads …

9 March 1996
That unbelievable pre-autumn light on the massif of the Back Table this morning, after the first real northwest front has moved over the Cape during the night: the shadows of cumulus crossing the outcrops of freshened rock and the pine-plantations on the intermediate slopes, the flanks rich in fynbos, and the leucadendrons, lit by their new growth, just above.

I remembered these plantations, as if moulded to the slopes, and the outline of the mountain itself as I must have seen it once, in childhood.

And now, on this Sunday morning in Constantia, the quality of these clouds, the white of the cumulus almost silver, and the line of them blowing across the Peninsula, towards Cape Hangklip, the blue of the sky now doubly blue in the new coolness that last night's front has brought – all of this recalled "The Mountain Light at Kromrivier."

It reminded me, as well, that one of the rare pleasures permitted writers are those moments when the world seems to be imitating words they have already written, not vice versa …

19 September 1996
This changing city.

What strikes me most of all is how rapidly the very feel of Cape Town is altering. Its sole mother tongue now the tourist dollar, it has been made over to cater for the needs of that particular industry: waterfronts, shopping malls, restaurants, timeshares. In next to no time the place has been re-stylised, as if reality itself were no more than a species of hair-do, this city its latest, vogue boutique.

Not far into the next century I suspect that Cape Town, a city remarkable for having a mountain in the middle of it, will have managed to relegate even its natural environment to a kind of sideshow freak show. For the moment, though, as one half of it takes on the patina, the glaze of a giant Club Med, one sees clearly why the feel of the place has changed. More and more, it has become a city which specialises in marrying fantastically sophisticated surfaces (technologically-speaking) and utterly childish values.

And, strange to say, it is precisely this combination which defines the very texture – which is to say, the feel – of contemporary amorality.

From week to week the newspapers carry the usual flapdoodle about restaurants and wines, as if it were a sign of the city's coming of age, even cause for self-congratulation, that one can now eat as variously, profusely, and expensively here, as almost anywhere else on the planet. But not so long ago there was a tradition that maintained that such displays of complacent ostentation, especially in the midst of poverty and destitution, were not only acts of human thoughtlessness, but were sins and that they remained sins.

One of the chief effects of 1994, it sometimes seems, is to have granted a permanent vacation to the consciences of those who might once, back in the apartheid era, have felt a residual shame that they possessed everything while others had next to nothing. And so one hears not a murmur of such things. Even to raise the issue would be regarded nowadays as a kind of childish puritanism; or envy masquerading as high-mindedness. For we live in a cultural moment, now virtually global, in which even to speak of morality is to somehow sound moralistic.

21 September 1996

The cold southerlies have begun early this year. Already, at my desk at daybreak, the sky has that diluted blue, the added emptiness of its pale tones, which will be its defining feature all through the summer ahead. In fact, as its winter colouring pales with the coming of summer, so the sky seems to retreat, to grow that much more empty as a result. Thus that season always arrives in this part of the world carrying with it a sense of emptiness, as if it were the season of precisely this, far more than heat and light ...

4 December 1996
The summer city: with the first bout of heat it inherits that slightly blurred appearance that human faces take on when they are intent upon the pursuit of pleasure – a kind of paradoxical, predatory sleepiness.

5 December 1996
Weekday mornings of early summer when, soon after breakfast, the wind gets up in the yard, starts strengthening in whole suburbs of washing, and the cloud on the mountain is blowing in bright sunlight, yet misting grey on the slopes at the same time, shadowing the sandstone boulders.

These mornings of old men, pensioners, unsteady in the wind.

7 December 1996
There are days when, again, Cape Town has about it a quality of evanescence; when there is something remote and lonely, far-sunken about the place.

At the Waterfront this morning: around me, in the semi-emptiness of the early Sunday morning, the wind still operating its vacant carousel, playing tag with last night's refuse. The houses stuck still more baldly to the treeless streets, to the big hill behind the harbour. And the baldness of this city in the wind.

And now these afternoons with the sea, both white-capped and almost blackened by the southeaster gale, more and more bitter; the troughs between the waves running with a dirtied, soapy green; the light itself de-materialised by that backing of dullness as the first wisps of cloud start damming against the Back Table – it is then that even the buildings seem thinned out, all lives as castaway, cast off, as those of the homeless in transit through the streets.

In this wind, Cape Town becomes once more a city adrift, as if in exile from itself …

19 December 1996
Parties of hikers, families, coming down the last stretch of the jeeptrack, through tall forest plantations, towards the car park at Constantia Nek.

It is a Sunday evening: children are "pine-needle sliding" (as we used to call it) on lengths of waxed hardboard, into the north wind blowing through the saddle. They careen down the pine-needles that mattress these mountain slopes, then skid out onto the jeep-track, poplar and plane leaves flying about them.

But soon the dusk is quiet. So much so that the far barking of a dog in the valley below the Nek takes a bite out of the silence, each tooth-mark distinct along its perimeter.

The last party runs the final stretch of the track; they're no more than a short drive from their homes. Already the lights are shining in the clear dusk. The summer moon will soon sail clear of the spur of trees to the west.

Yes, whatever else, the city in which people can still do this, see this.

A Suburb of Contrasts and Change (1998)

MICHAEL A V MORRIS

To talk of Woodstock as a neighbourhood, as if it were a community of closely shared things, is false. Only on the map does it have any legitimate claim to neighbourliness on that scale.

The map's intimate geometry is incapable of expressing the richer street-by-street variations that animate this dense spread of housing, shops and factories between the railway lines and the lower slopes of Devil's Peak. It is a rather enigmatic and probably much misunderstood segment of the city, and it changes by the year.

In common with communities on the fringe of any big city, the contrasts enrich it, but make it a place that requires some negotiating, a sense of caution, of being awake to its true character, not least to appreciate it for what it is. It seems trite to say there's vitality here precisely because of the edgy presence of threat. Yet these things are taken in with the air you breathe. A fatal Sunday evening gang shooting a few weeks ago, two blocks from our house, already seems to have been subsumed into the general fabric of Woodstock life.

Nevertheless, you take nothing for granted: the city and almost all it entails is somehow bound up in Woodstock's nature.

You'll sense a change in the weather when the plaintive tooting of the whistle buoys off the end of the harbour – or the gruffer intermittent blare of the fog horn at the Greenpoint lighthouse – comes up from the sea with the dock's ripe smells, of brine and tar and fish, in the seeping mist that smudges the street lights and weighs the brooding sky down.

You can tell a wind change by the faint, comforting wailing of a muezzin reciting the Athaan, the call to prayer, in the gloom before sunrise. You know by their outraged yells that the staggering, aggrieved bergies, cackling over misfortunes too blurred to fathom, are heading home to their makeshift shelter under the freeway, or to the local shebeen, or just huddling out of the rain in the lanes behind the houses, rooting through the black bags.

The one or two pairs of crowned plovers that settle on the nearby soccer field at night are markers of a sort, too, but of less clear events. When you hear their sharp shrieks whip past in the wind at midnight, you know they've flapped up into the dark because someone's on the field. But the next day, the evidence is beguiling: a glittering of smashed glass, and discarded bottle necks, used or unused, suggests one thing; spent condoms, slimy and mockingly flaccid, another. Or new graffiti, angry and often unsettling for being indecipherable.

And there's gunfire. Although, to be honest, there's sometimes misguided paranoia about this. On the first night of the recent Waterfront fireworks extravaganza, I spent all of five minutes trying to identify the implausible weaponry, until, from our front door, the dazzle of the higher displays cascaded above the rooftops.

Always, though, when the sun's shimmering on the bay, and you hear the shouts of children on the street, it's a wholesome place to be.

Woodstock was established in the late 19th century on land once occupied by small farms and market gardens. Development grew off Victoria and Albert roads, the old routes that linked Cape Town with surrounding rural areas.

By 1885, the street pattern was established, and within 30 years, most of the large sections of land had been built on, chiefly working class housing, mostly semis and terraces. The street names run like a tabula of imperial essences: Kipling, Roberts, Chamberlain, Salisbury, Regent, Devon, Tennyson, Kitchener, Swift, Dryden. You could go on … more poets, generals and far, green shires.

But, like neighbouring District Six, it was tolerant enough to have people of different races living together. A 1993 City Council document on buildings in the neighbourhood notes: 'Compared to so many other urban communities which were affected by the Group Areas Act ... communities and families (in Woodstock) have been able to sustain some sense of social and cultural continuity.'

This is both true and untrue.

Kutbodien Parker, the graciously taciturn custodian of the upper Parker's Cafe on the corner of Palmerston and Roodebloem roads, remembers the days when he helped his father, Serfodien, deliver groceries as far afield as Sea Point and Lakeside.

He could be forgiven for thinking of these as the good old days, before supermarkets ... and the heartless intrusion of racist politics.

Old man Parker, who came to South Africa in 1906, built the shop and the two houses on each side of it in 1936. Kutbodien – who was born two blocks down, in Chamberlain Street, though spent his first 16 years in Bombay – started working in the shop while still at school in Salt River, in 1958. His generous recollection is that the people, 'mostly working class white people, were very nice, friendly and very pleasant'.

But the apartheid bureaucracy's tolerance of the Parkers as resident shopkeepers ended in 1981, when Serfodien Parker died. 'They refused to allow the property to be transferred into my name,' Mr Parker recalls. 'They forced us to sell. I was very angry, but what can you do?'

The government bought the properties for R42 000, and Mr Parker and his family moved to Rylands Estate. Just 10 years later, when the iniquitous law fell away, Mr Parker bought the properties back ... for a staggering R320 000.

Today, the old building is endearing for being worn and patched. The metallic, apocalyptic clamour of bulky console games that youngsters hunch over masterfully, is oddly jarring in a store so redolent of a kindlier time.

The Parkers' three sons and two daughters are pursuing professional careers – teaching, law, pharmacy, business, banking – and Kutbodien, now 57, is making plans to sell up and retire. They will remain in Rylands where 'it's quiet, and we have our friends'. When the shop closes, a landmark will go.

Across the road, though, a new landmark has firmly established itself.

Don Pedro restaurant looked like an ill-conceived venture when Kommetjie surfer Sean O'Connor launched it in 1991, working the flea market during the day to keep the restaurant going at night. It was unpretentious without trying to be, and soon became the meeting place of the Left, of unionists and academics, writers, journalists, artists, and of assorted local characters who felt at home there. It was a place for serious talk.

In pre-1994 days, 'it was a dark, smoky place, with people in union caps sitting round devising political strategy,' Sean recalls. The clientele has changed in recent years, with the 'trendy set' having discovered it, but 'we still get the old people coming in,' Sean says, 'talking about the struggle, the days of cohesion … they say that's gone now.'

Shady characters drift in too, sometimes. 'A drug dealer came by for supper one evening. He looked round appraisingly, then said: You should sell coke on the side. Half the people in this place buy their coke from us.'

In all these things – the drug trade, the closing of landmark cafes, the changing clientele of rad-chic establishments (and the wistful nostalgia for the struggle years), the mounting property prices – there are portents of the changes reshaping Woodstock.

Of all the factors, the economics of property is the key one. Estate agent Chris Ormrod notes that in the past few years, Woodstock 'has been absorbing the spill-over from the city bowl. It is no longer a market mainly for first-time buyers'. The prices – and the customers, including ad agencies and film companies – match the demand.

But Woodstock will probably always retain the resilient contrasts that make it so engagingly unpredictable.

from The Agony of Ecstasy (2004)

OLIVIA GORDON

Mandy … Mandy was a revelation. People who take ecstasy say that everyone almost falls in love with their mentor, the first person who introduces them to the drug. Mandy was that person who won my admiration and gratitude. To me, Mandy was ecstasy. The first time I met her was the night I arrived in Cape Town. Cara took me to a rave in the Three Arts theatre in the suburb of Plumstead. It was to be a low-key night; no drugs. I did not take drugs when I was out with Cara because she was too wary of their dangers to take anything. She was a party person without needing them. Before the rave she took me to a pre-party at a boy's flat. It was the first time I met Cape Town's e-people at close quarters.

As we walked into the living room I saw a turntable playing incredibly clean-sounding house. The beats were perfect: sharp and discrete. The TV had cartoons showing with the sound muted. About twenty e-kids were sitting up in nice armchairs and a boy who seemed to personify the whole scene was moving almost professionally from person to person, shaking their hands and welcoming them to the party. It was clinically polite. You could not fault it – these people believed in manners and love and good things. The room was full of élan. But it was also intimidating and lacked any genuine warmth. They were all so flawlessly good look-ing, these boys with their baggy combat trousers and bare or meshed vest-covered, tanned and honed chests. The girls looked like Barbie dolls with lollipops and plastic hairgrips. They, too, were frighteningly poised and toned. Not one bit like the British kids you'd see on a Saturday night back home. There was not a black face among them, but this was usual in this elite circle of a victorious race, although they were in no way racist since they all believed in equality, freedom and the New South Africa. One of the girls was Mandy. Tall, white, slender, languid, tanned: a privileged Stellenbosch girl. She had bobbed mousey hair that looked wild yet utilitarian. She drawled in a drugged-out voice, 'Wooooww. Raaaaaaaaad.' *Rad* was her word and later mine. She pronounced the word with such range of pitch and melody and utter expressiveness it sounded like she was having an orgasm. Her eyes would scrunch together and then open in wonder as she spoke it, like a child ...

January and February ticked by and I moved into a room in a house on Ivy Street, under the bridge that links downtrodden Mowbray with boho Observatory. The family I lodged with were your aver-age hippie Obs people. Suzie, a plump reflexologist with long curly blonde hair, her husband River, a shaggy-haired dopey guy with John Lennon glasses, their cute little boy Fred and a couple of dogs, Stanley and Brewster. I hid away from them, telling them nothing of my devilish outlook on life, and they must have taken me for an unfriendly, stuck-up kind of girl who rather than deigning to speak to them simply borrowed their Shirley MacLaine books and forgot to return them. These quasi-spiritual books, supplemented by a diet of back issues of *Odyssey*, the local eco-friendly magazine, afforded me little enlightenment; however they were all I could find, once sequestered in that little house.

Obs was a world of people who not only believed in fairies and angels but wore tie-dyed t-shirts depicting the little 'love-miracles'. It was a world where you might find a grey-haired man of a distinguished age pretending to be a lion outside the Spar supermarket: 'I am a lion! Rooooaaaaaaar!', rearing up on his 'hind' legs. These men were frequently surrounded by young girls who hung on their every word. The old men hung out in their tents at raves playing didgeridoos, flicking their long beards, were the ones handing out the tabs of acid and ecstasy, not to mention the 'candy flips' that were half ecstasy, half acid. Back on Lower Main Road, the centre of Obs, you might pass half a dozen beggars on every block. Most of them had been living on those streets for years and were tolerated and partially fed by the kind-hearted yuppie-hippie restaurateurs. Everyone knew everyone. The deeper you got into the 'scene', the more 'hectic' it became and the more like a 1960s California microcosm bizarrely lost in space and time at the bottom of Africa.

Operation Copulation (2003)

DARREL BRISTOW-BOVEY

There are many ways to spice up a flagging marriage but I wouldn't have thought that visiting Brackenfell was one of them. Brackenfell, in case you've never had the pleasure of driving past it at high speed while murmuring a spell to ward off evil spirits, is a dismal suburb in the north of Cape Town. Until recently, the best thing you could say about Brackenfell is that it's neither Salt River nor Woodstock. Actually, that is still the best thing you can say about it. That is no longer, however, the most interesting thing you can say about Brackenfell, because recently Brackenfell was announced as being the lucky beneficiary of Cape Town's newest and boldest marketing initiative.

When it comes to marketing, you have to take your hat off to Cape Town, and not merely to shoo it away. Cape Town is more ready and willing to sell itself than any large town you've ever met. Cape Town is the Hansie Cronjé of seaside settlements.

It doesn't miss a trick: the last time I arrived at Cape Town airport I was handed a book of coupons, redeemable against the price of my next visit.

Above all, Cape Town's strategy is broad. In recent times, it has sold itself internationally as the only place to be if you are (a) a homosexual sex tourist, (b) interested in sleeping with under-aged girls, (c) an admirer of Earl Spencer, (d) a money launderer or (e) a real-estate speculator. Or, indeed, any combination of the above. But the Brackenfell venture is a stroke of uncommon genius.

Brackenfell is the proposed site of a new multi-million-rand lodge, to be built in anticipation of a surge in swingers' tours. It will offer adult entertainment, on-call sex therapists and communal spa-baths. What is a swingers' tour, you ask, trembling? According to a recent report, one Robin Pike is advertising Cape Town as the ideal destination for international wife-swapping safaris. Allegedly, up to 100 British and German couples each month are queuing to come south and make whoopee with someone else's spouse. Projected revenue is more than R60 million a year, which explains why the scheme has been given the thumbs-up from Satour and the Ministry of Tourism.

I must confess the idea startles me. The notion that our husbands and wives are a marketable natural resource will take some getting used to. The realisation that the Big 5 now includes Mrs Katz from down the hall, frankly, leaves me dizzy. The obvious obstacle to the scheme is that old South African bugaboo – racial intolerance. Having canvassed the fellows down at the Chalk 'n Cue, I can sadly report that many a lad who would do his patriotic duty in the cause of tourism with Mr and Mrs Hamburg or the Von Stuttgarts would draw the line at his own better half in the clutches of an Englishman.

Still, there appear to be enough takers for the proposition to be viable: Johannesburg apparently has 6000 registered swingers, Cape Town a stately 2000 and Durban, ever keen to get in on the action, boasts a game 1000. Personally, I suspect that Johannesburg has a good deal more than 6000 but most of them don't realise they're swinging. They just think they work for an advertising agency.

There are obvious questions: How does one go about registering as a swinger? Must you pay a subscription fee? Is there a board of swinging directors? What constitutes a quorum at a swingers' AGM? And who provides the refreshments afterwards? Above all, what are the benefits of being a registered swinger? Discounts on bulk purchases of paper towels and red-tinted light bulbs upon presentation of a valid membership card? Special family rates at participating love shacks and motels? Frequent-flyer miles? There is so much to think about.

Even more boggling to the mind is the question of what scheme Cape Town will dream up to top this one. Brazil has already cornered the market in organ transplant tourism, and Indonesia has surely had the last word in hostage chic. In the marketing stakes, cities are like sharks. When they stop moving, they die. Just ask Tripoli, or Vladivostok – all the open marriages in the world won't save them now.

THE FLATS

from The Number (2004)

JONNY STEINBERG

Magadien was among the first generation of teenagers who lived their lives in the half-moon streets and tenement blocks of the post-removals Cape Flats. A mere 15 minutes' drive from the heart of District Six, the new housing estates of Cape Town's hinter-world constituted a different planet. The drearily symmetrical tenement blocks rising from the sand dunes, the distant blue outcroppings of the Peninsula's mountain range, the nameless public spaces filled with strangers: it was the sort of place one comes to in the depths of a troubled sleep. Indeed, Magadien was a guinea pig of the most far-reaching project of spatial engineering in the Western Cape's history, and a casualty of its catastrophic failure.

In pre-removals Cape Town, the boundaries dividing black and white, rich and poor, were porous and haphazard. Tens of thousands of the city's coloured and African populations lived their lives at the foot of Table Mountain, crammed into dense pockets of the inner city and the suburbs. There was the old neighbourhood of District Six, just inland from the harbour, and the Malay district of Bo Kaap, on the slopes of Signal Hill. Beyond these two ghettos, Cape Town's racial demographics were more complicated. The band of suburbs stretching south of the city – from Woodstock to Retreat – was largely white, but pockets of coloureds, some middle-class, others much poorer, were scattered throughout. In suburbs like Plumstead, it was not unusual to find a white middle-class block, with its prim hedges and pretty gardens, adjacent to a coloured working-class street, densely packed, lined with hawkers and shebeens.

Above the inner city, on the slopes of Table Mountain, middle-class coloured families lived in the suburbs of Vredehoek, Oranjezicht and Gardens. Many were involved in the messy, complicated business of passing for white.

Out in the city's hinterland, the Cape Flats, a vast expanse of scrub-land and sand dunes that flanks the city's south-eastern perimeter, hosted a motley collection of outsiders. There was scattered farmland, but the sand dunes and the beach scrub was good for neither grazing nor cultivation. There were recent and older immigrants from the countryside, both African and coloured, banging on the city's doors with more or less success: a peri-urban underclass. And then there was the spill-over from the inner city, the poorest of Cape Town's poor, ejected from the cramped quarters of neighbourhoods like District Six.

It is often said that it took the madness of apartheid, and thus, by implication, the madness of the Afrikaners, to re-engineer Cape Town. It is often English-speaking writers who say these things. In fact, plans to reinvent the city began a decade before the National Party came to power. And the wellsprings of inspiration were to be found not in the obstinacy of a parochial nationalism, but in the giddiness of European modernism; remanufactured Cape Town sprang from the imaginations of cosmopolitans and futurists – English-speakers, all of them.

In the late 1930s, the radical modernism of Le Corbusier was the rage among South Africa's more erudite urban planners. There were circles in which his new book, *The City of Tomorrow and its Planning*, was something of a bible. 'The city of today is dying,' Le Corbusier wrote, 'because it is not constructed geometrically. To build on a clear site is to replace the "accidental" layout of the ground, the only one that exists today, by a formal layout. Otherwise, nothing can save us.' Forty pages on, he declared that 'surgery must be applied to the city centre. Physic must be used elsewhere. We must use the knife …'

Le Corbusier's South African disciples took out their knives in 1940. The Cape Town city council began planning its Foreshore Project: a grand overhaul of the inner city, the pinnacle of which was to be the construction of a Monumental Approach to Cape Town – a boulevard so wide it would 'take five minutes to cross it in a stiff south-easter' – stretching from the harbour into the heart of the city. The Approach was to be lined with sky-scraping office blocks, welcoming the visitor to South Africa's shores with a dizzying spectacle of the modern. Among the confidential papers in the city council's sketches were plans for three slum clearance projects: District Six, the Malay Quarters and the Dock areas.

The Foreshore Project ended in disaster, but that is another story for another time. The point is that plans to move coloureds from the inner city had long been in the air by the time the apartheid state got to work. If the reinvention of Cape Town had taken place along pure Le Corbusian principles, coloureds would have found themselves in 'vertical cells': tall residential buildings ringing the outskirts of the inner city. But plans seldom travel well, especially to the colonies, where the questions of fear and control are bound to shape the organisation of people and space. White South Africa was not about to build spanking new homes for coloureds in the heart of the city. So, instead, the fate of Cape Town's coloureds was inspired by another modernist idea, that of the Garden City; the coloureds were to be moved to 'the countryside'.

The Garden City was the invention of late-nineteenth-century England, a society which, like mid-twentieth-century South Africa, was wondering what to do with its workers and its industry. The idea was to move both from the city into self-contained satellite towns on the urban periphery. Young working-class lads and lasses were to grow up in quaint, quasi-rural 'clusters', surrounded by lush meadows, vast stretches of common land, and farms.

Mutilated in ways both comic and chilling, this is the idea that animated the building of the cluster-like townships on the Cape Flats. Flying over the Flats on the descent into Cape Town International Airport, you can see the clusters in all their glory: concentric layers of streets, turned in upon themselves, forming tight, hermetic circles, each surrounded by a barren wilderness of no-man's-land.

With some imagination, you can just make out some of the benign intentions behind the original Garden City idea. The notion of the inward-looking cluster was meant to foster a village-like sense of community. Yet driving through Manenberg, or Heideveld or Hanover Park, one feels as if one has been locked into a maze, as if the ghetto is a dense universe. The idea of buttressing the clusters with greenbelts was intended to create open spaces in which the cluster-children would spend their afternoons. But the 'greenbelts' of the Cape Flats are intraversable scrublands; the kids are locked inside the labyrinth.

From the aeroplane window, you see six-lane highways linking the Flats to the city; in theory, the satellite towns are 15 minutes from downtown. But this is premised on the universality of the family car; the working-class families of the Flats have no cars. Moving in and out of the satellites is a costly expedition.

Most important of all, perhaps, the Flats neighbourhoods were built on the premise that coloureds lived their lives in nuclear families. Indeed, it was a conceit of modernism that the nuclear family was synonymous with the twentieth century, that other forms of kinship were the residues of more primitive times. Yet the coloureds of the inner city had lived their lives in extended families. You saw from Magadien's earliest recollections how the boundaries of the Mekkas' world traced a jagged, invisible circle around Hanover Street: between granny's house, Jackie Oakers's barber shop; St Mark's Cathedral where Annie's brother sang in the choir. The extended family was not just a source of emotional support: it was the structure through which people like the Mekkas negotiated their way into Cape Town's economy.

And so, between 1966 and the early 1980s, tens of thousands of people were wrenched from their lives in the inner city and dumped in the satellites on the edge of town. Extended families were dispersed to all four corners of the Flats, and everybody shared their cramped streets with strangers. The more well-to-do moved into districts of square, free-standing houses: Surrey Estate, Ravensmead, Uitsig. The poor made their new lives on the crescent-shaped streets and in the squat residential buildings of places like Valhalla Park, Bonteheuwel, Manenberg and Heideveld.

The Mekkas found themselves in 12 Daphne Court, Heideveld, a short, wide tenement block surrounded by two others just like it. Together, the three structures formed the walls of an open courtyard. One stepped from one's front door into a common space shared by dozens of families.

The Mekkas' extended family, which had once lived within a small radius around their Cowley Street home, was scattered across Cape Town. The city was a mirage of lights on the evening horizon. In Heideveld itself, life was lived in a sharp dualism between the very private and the very public: within the curtained windows of their cramped flat, and in the courtyards formed by the tenement blocks. There was nothing in between.

And so townships like Heideveld became crowded, public worlds of strangers, effectively severed from the rest of the universe. If the people of the inner city built their lives around extended family networks, the people of the Flats, thrown into an alien world, were to organise their lives around their immediate neighbours. The whole of life was lived in the tenement courtyards, and each courtyard became a world.

The new neighbourhoods of the Cape Flats were to become deeply insular. Each block came to constitute a territory, its defenders possessive of insiders, aggressive to outsiders. 'The boy from across the road married Annie's sister,' Magadien tells me when he describes the Hanover Park neighbourhood where the Mekkas finally settled. 'And the next-door neighbour married my cousin. My sister is married to Brian van Rooi, who lived at the end of the block. My older daughter is Brian's niece. Few people left our block. And few new people arrived. We have lived our lives together for the last 40 years.'

And yet the people from just three or four blocks away were like foreigners. A few hundred metres from his house, Magadien would find himself in a world of strangers, sometimes indifferent, often hostile. The ghettos of the Flats were divided into hundreds of micro-turfs, each given life by a micro-identity. It was not only about who married whom. It extended to who did business with whom, how one earned a living, and, perhaps most important of all, the politics of the street gangs, which drew entire communities into their wars.

from Our Generation (2003)

ZUBEIDA JAFFER

It's early Saturday morning and I leave Ruschka at home because I sense that today is going to be hard. Reaching Bonteheuwel, a sprawling township on the Cape Flats, takes less than twenty minutes from my home in Wynberg. I park my car on the sandy sidewalk and walk towards the small council house belonging to Ivy Kriel. Activists are dotted all along the fence in front of the house and in the small barren space meant for a garden, now filled with plastic chairs. I pass through them, nodding a silent greeting which they return. Those who are speaking to one another are whispering.

I join the line of family members as they slowly file past the body. Ashley Kriel is lying flat on his back in the coffin in the middle of the tiny room. There is barely space to move. And then I see his face. I look but cannot see. Yet, I do see. His forehead is swollen. His eyes are closed. A deep gash leaping out of his forehead has been stitched up by the coroner. The dark curls are brushed back. In that split second, my eyes blur and I feel my knees bending. A sharp pain shoots through my chest. A comrade hoists me up under my arms, steadying me. I am helped up the narrow steps to a bedroom upstairs where I find Ashley's sister Melanie. We are both crying.

I know that I had to look at him some time. I was reluctant because I wanted to remember him as I knew him. But it would have been strange for me not to be part of the family ritual. Melanie, unlike her sister Michelle, is unable to function. While twenty-four-year-old Michelle is in the kitchen below helping visitors to the family home, her sister, sedated the night before, cannot stop crying.

It was Michelle who had called me a week ago at UWC and given me the news: "Zubeida, the police have shot Ashley. They took me to see his body in the morgue this afternoon. Please tell everybody." I became icy cold. As if a winter chill had descended on my office. I cut out, suppressing all emotions.

"Where is your mother? Don't worry, I'll be there as soon as I can."

I had left work immediately, thinking about the need to form a funeral committee, finding lawyers to investigate the killing, raising the money to help the family. There was no time to deal with emotions. Organising often became a way of coping with horrors that we dealt with daily. We had to be strong for the family, for the community, hiding how completely shattered we were.

I was aware that Ashley had left the country about a year after his final school exams. Some had tried to dissuade him but he was angry. He and his friends in Bonteheuwel were shot at with birdshot and beaten whenever they tried to organise meetings at their school. He wanted to be equipped to fight back and had decided the only way was to be armed himself. He left the country at the end of 1985 and joined the military wing of the ANC, Umkhonto we Sizwe.

I regret now that I looked at his face this morning. Unknown to many of us, he was sent back after being trained and had been living at a house in Hazendal, a small working class, Coloured suburb near Athlone. I would have preferred remembering him as I knew him.

I used to watch him closely when he arose to address the crowds at meetings of the United Democratic Front. I was never quite sure whether it was his political rhetoric or his personal charisma that set the crowd off. "Viva Ashley, Viva! Long live, long live!"

Igama lama Ashley Kriel, malibongwe.
Igama lama Ashley Kriel, malibongwe.
(The name of Ashley Kriel, let it be praised.
The name of Ashley Kriel, let it be praised.)

He had this way of raising his arm alongside his ear when he shouted: "Amandla!" (Power!) To which the crowd responded tumultuously: "Ngawethu!" (To the people!) All speakers ended their speeches with these words. But not all raised their right arm as Ashley did. Some right arms were pushed forward diagonally with their fists clenched. Other arms were bent at the elbow at a kind of right angle to the shoulder. Ashley's arm was always straight in the air with four fingers clenched in a fist and the thumb extended, the ANC's power salute.

The extension of his arm elongated his body, giving him a new kind of height which added a further dimension to his defiant words. I could see the young women comrades in the audience tantalised by his charm. Although the sexual appeal would have been dominant amongst the women, he had his male admirers too. The combination of personal charm and political commitment made him a youth leader of great attraction.

He was the Che Guevara of the Cape Flats. Long, tapered face with a mop of curly black hair. A lean, slender body dressed in khaki shirt and black beret. We were all proud, very proud of him.

When Ashley came to ask if he could stay with me for his final school year, I was happy to have him. We were able to provide him with comfortable study space so that he could do the best he was able.

In a different time, he may have been the local Don Juan. But he grew into his teens just when the schools' protest erupted in the Western Cape. With the formation of the United Democratic Front (UDF), one of our veteran youth organisers, Cecyl Esau, was quick to identify Ashley as the one who could help bring the youth of his township together to form a branch of the Cape Youth Congress.

While all of us who had organised and mobilised people against apartheid developed a special relationship during those years, it did not always mature into full-blown love. Ashley was one of the few who evoked that unreserved emotion. He was loved not only by his family but also by many of us who saw in him the embodiment of all our hopes. He was young, from an impoverished background, but held his own on public platforms with veteran leaders such as Alan Boesak and Oscar Mpetha.

The previous week, as part of the funeral committee, it had been one of my jobs to piece together the scant information that we had about the circumstances surrounding his death. Mourning in that crowded little house where his body lay, I relived the painful night when I sat down to prepare a fact file for the press.

I have waited for Ruschka to sleep so that I can be undisturbed as I compile my notes into a coherent whole. When the night is mine, the words come easily and I stop only intermittently when two of the metal arms of the typewriter with letters e and r get entangled. With my forefinger, I lightly unhook the one arm from the other. They slide into place on the keyboard and I resume my typing:

Ashley Kriel was alone when he died. Salma Ismail, the schoolteacher with whom he boarded, was at work. Her younger brother Imtiaz Ismail had taken their vacuum cleaner for repairs. They knew Ashley as "James".

In a prepared statement this week, police said he died from a bullet fired from his own weapon during a scuffle with two policemen who had tried to disarm and arrest him at the Athlone house.

The statement does not explain why Ashley was wearing handcuffs as claimed by Imtiaz Ismail who returned from his errand about 1.30 p.m.

Imtiaz's witness is as follows:
"As I pulled into the driveway, three or four plain-clothes policemen told me to stop. I switched off the car. They told me and the friend with me to stand with our hands against the car and they searched us.

"I then walked around the back of the house with the policeman following me. I saw James lying on his side. There was blood on his forehead. His arms were stretched out in front of him and he was wearing handcuffs.

"The police were looking for more handcuffs but could not find any. They took the handcuffs off James and put them on me.

"I asked the one policeman what was wrong with James and he told me: 'Hy is doodgeskiet omdat hy 'n terroris is.' (He was shot dead because he was a terrorist.)"

I blot out Ashley's face as I write and write, finally signing off the sheet as issued by the Ashley Kriel Funeral Committee.

The next day, we hand out the fact sheet to journalists at a press conference with an addendum: "The above information will be used by the *Weekly Mail* this week. Journalists are free to make use of any information since it is not possible to bring family members and others together here at this press conference."

A further information sheet has all the details of the funeral programme for the following day. We could not have imagined how complex our funeral plans were to become.

I pull myself together and help Melanie move down the steps so that she can follow her brother's coffin out of the house. His body is placed inside the waiting hearse. We get into our cars and slowly file into line so that the procession can move in an orderly fashion towards the New Apostolic Church.

It is a dark grey winter's day, as if the skies reflect the sombreness of the mourners. We hope it will not rain and deter people from gathering on the sports field as planned.

At the church, we see the armoured vehicles parked all around. Casspirs with armed men peering from their open doors greet fearful mourners as they file into the church. Many of us are accustomed to this display of force but for the average member of the New Apostolic Church, this is not something they generally encounter when they attend Sunday services.

I can see the fear on people's faces. They are quiet and very nervous. The proceedings are brief. Ashley's uncle speaks. The priest makes some general biblical commentary, his blandness offensive to the activists.

I scan the pews: women in their black dresses or suits with black hats or lace scarves. Men with their hats in their hands resting on the laps of their black pants.

They are part of a conservative religious community and they love Ivy. She had listened to the deacons as best she could when they explained the detail of the service. She knew they were not excited about welcoming the many khaki-clad youth who were determined to demonstrate wearing the volunteer uniform of the ANC.

She cared deeply for her son but she never cared for his involvement in politics. She never quite understood it. And now it had brought about his death, justifying her opposition to his involvement. He was the one she had relied on when she became ill. He was the one whom she had hoped would care for her when she became old.

She has a weak heart and when she could not work, when Ashley was fourteen, she reluctantly allowed him to go out in the middle of the night to sell the local daily Afrikaans newspaper, *Die Burger*. She and her daughters waited for him at 5 a.m. to take the few cents he earned for the day to buy bread. Then she would make him as comfortable as possible for his short sleep before he had to wake up again and ready himself for school.

The crowd surges towards the door at the end of the service, then suddenly retreats.

"What's going on?" I ask.

Before anybody can answer, I smell it – the pungent ammonia stinging the air floating through the open church door. "Oh my God, they are shooting!" shouts a mourner.

The armed men stationed outside the church shoot rounds of teargas at the pallbearers as they descend the steps. The activists take over and run with the coffin all the way to a second church to get it away from the gas overpowering the mourners.

As I pass through the door and out into the hazy daylight, I see the coffin dancing grimly on the shoulders of the young men moving rapidly down the streets. I cringe, thinking of Ashley's battered body bashing up against the coffin sides as different waves of comrades pass the casket on like a baton in a relay and run with it as fast as they can.

There is little point in trying to get to my car. Some churchgoers are in a hurry to get home as quickly as they can. The only way many of us can maintain our dignity is to walk through the mass of armed men circling the church and follow the body on foot. Fleetingly, I imagine that today is the day I will die. Ruschka will be looked after. I do not have to worry. I have always wondered when it will come, but today all the elements are in place. A helicopter hovers directly above us in the overcast sky. Rows of yellow riot vehicles are backed up by masked men who train their automatic weapons on us. All along the road, sharpshooters are crouched on the rooftops of the small Bonteheuwel dwellings, prepared for retaliatory action from the ANC's military wing, Umkhonto we Sizwe (MK). We know such an offensive would never come on the streets of Bonteheuwel, crowded with civilians. The commander-in-chief, Chris Hani, would never sanction such action. There is talk that he had taken a special liking to Ashley and that he had personally given the go-ahead for him to be sent back into the country. In these times, it is not always possible to distinguish between speculation and fact.

I gather from the police reaction that they too must have believed that Chris had a direct interest in this fatality. Although I have never met him, I feel he is the one person we can rely on to fight back against the might of the apartheid military machine. Yet it would have made no sense for MK to plan anything at the funeral to endanger ordinary people. Public demonstrations or funerals are seldom occasions for military activity. They are used rather for mobilisation of communities and their radicalisation, providing fertile soil for underground military activities.

Arriving at the Anglican Church, the funeral committee quickly realises that any plans to move the funeral onto the field would be too dangerous. We confer with Archbishop Desmond Tutu, the Reverend Alan Boesak and Moulana Faried Essack and decide to merge the programme planned for the field and the one for the church. The church service becomes a mass rally and the mass rally becomes a church service.

Out comes the ANC flag to be draped over the coffin. Hymns merge into freedom songs and freedom songs into hymns. Tears become laughter and laughter becomes tears.

from Steering by the Stars (2002)

MAMPHELA RAMPHELE

Bulelwa's is a story of resilience and success. I remember her visiting me at home years after I first met her, an attractive, self-assured twenty-year-old woman with a bounce in her step as she approached to embrace me. She had an infectious laugh on her slightly moon-shaped face with keen black eyes which danced each time a smile welled up within her. A full smile or a laugh exposed her uneven teeth and a suggestion that a visit to the dentist was long overdue.

Bulelwa had a strong sense of her own worth. She oozed self-confidence, humour, and a sheer enjoyment of life. She was lovely and at ease in any style of clothing: long African traditional outfits or modern tailor-made outfits from boutiques in suburbia.

These were features that made her stand out in 1991 when I first met her and she was fourteen years old. She was engaging. She was not daunted by the prospect of walking up Table Mountain for the first time with strangers as guides. Nor did the idea of sleeping in a hut on the mountain open to the elements dampen her enthusiasm. She was articulate in both Xhosa (her mother tongue) and English.

Her adolescent body was filling out in 1991 but she was quite comfortable with it. She was curious about the new people she met and did not shy away from asking detailed questions about my background and motivation for getting involved with young people in New Crossroads. She was encouraged to hear that I had come from humble circumstances and yet had never doubted that I could achieve whatever realistic goals I set for myself. We bonded from that point onward.

'You are my role model, I know I will make it,' she said ...

Bulelwa was born in KTC in 1977. Her family moved to New Crossroads when she was five years old. Like most of the residents of New Crossroads, her childhood was continually disrupted. This disruption was caused not only by the everyday difficulties of living under apartheid, and the associated violence and upheavals characteristic of many townships in the 1980s, but equally by the difficulties of living in poverty with its related instability and uncertainty.

Bulelwa's self-confidence and determination to succeed against all odds was a family characteristic. Her mother, Mrs Leseka, was born in Cape Town towards the end of the 1940s. She grew up in the shacks at Athlone (before it had been upgraded into a coloured township) because her parents were unable to get a house in the townships set aside for Africans. Life was made more difficult by the Coloured Labour Preference Policy and jobs could only be come by if there were no coloured labourers available. Like many others, her family had to endure intolerable levels of overcrowding and scant social services. To exacerbate matters Mrs Leseka's father was also responsible for supporting his brothers and sisters in the Transkei. Given his low wages, his daughter's education was sacrificed in favour of the survival of the extended family.

MRS LESEKA: I was a member of the Methodist church in Langa. We used to sing in choirs. One day I saw people coming to my home. My father told me that these people wanted me to marry their son. My father had no objections if I wanted to marry. Because I was already grown up, I agreed. So in 1973 I married this man. He was from the Transkei. We lived in KTC.

While we were staying in KTC I went to the township superintendent's office in Nyanga looking for a house because, in 1981, New Crossroads was already built. I had problems at the office because Basonti kept telling me that there were no houses. He said, 'I do not even want to put you on a waiting list because there are no houses. There are none.'

I woke up one day and said I would not go and see Basonti this time. I wanted to see the senior superintendent. I was referred to a certain Mr Du Toit. I explained everything to him. At that time my husband was in hospital because he had an accident while he was at work. I didn't want my husband to come back to a shack from the hospital because the doctors told me that he wouldn't be able to walk again. He was paralysed from the waist downwards. I explained everything to Du Toit: that my husband was still in hospital, there were no toilets, there was no water. Mr Du Toit said I should come the following morning.

The following morning Mr Du Toit instructed Basonti to give me the keys. Mr Du Toit gave me the house number in New Crossroads where I should go. Basonti didn't give me the keys. He just said he would meet me at the house. I waited there from ten o'clock in the morning until two o'clock without a sign of Basonti. Basonti came after two o'clock. Instead of opening the house and inspecting it before giving me the keys, Basonti got out of the car and threw the keys at the door, without saying a word. He then went back to the car. I just took the keys and said, 'Thank God'. If I hadn't gone to Du Toit I would not have got the keys that day. I was so excited when I got that house.

For Bulelwa the move to New Crossroads offered a period of relative stability. By 1981 there were four children in the Leseka family – Bulelwa, her two elder twin sisters, Rose and Fika, and her younger sister, Pumla. Bulelwa's mother would collect her husband's wages for him while he was in hospital and used this income to support the family.

When Bulelwa's father was discharged from the hospital he came to live with the family in their new house in New Crossroads. Shortly afterwards his company sent him a letter informing him that as he would be unable to work any more they would send his pension money. Bulelwa's father consulted a lawyer in Athlone about his case and managed to secure a sum of R11 000 from the pension fund and an additional monthly disability grant of R200. The lawyer also agreed to fight for a lump-sum payment from the Third Party insurance involved in the accident.

Bulelwa remembered the time after her father's accident as an idyllic period in her childhood when there was always enough food and money for the children. With the lump sum from the pension fund Bulelwa's parents opened a spaza shop at the house where they sold cool drinks and groceries. Mrs Leseka also bought a second-hand truck to transport the grocery stock. Bulelwa was five years old. Their home exuded warmth and pleasant smells of food and fresh flowers. Yet Bulelwa said little about her father. He did not appear to have been a formative influence in her life.

The idyllic life came to an abrupt end two years later when her father decided to leave them. The wound inflicted by that decision was still raw in Bulelwa when I first met her.

I can only speculate about the reason for Mr Leseka's desertion of his wife and children. Bulelwa did not think that her father had any reason to leave the family. He might well have been experiencing pressure from his parents and other family to share his newly found 'wealth' with them. Mr Leseka might have felt resentful that his wife was 'profiting' from his misfortune. It does seem odd that Mrs Leseka had no idea of the extent of her husband's dissatisfaction with their marriage ...

On occasions Bulelwa expressed resentment about her father's new house, new wife and lack of support in spite of his material well-being. The pain of this neglect was excruciating for the children.

In spite of this traumatic family fracture, Bulelwa's mother worked hard to provide her children with a loving home and a good education. It was fortunate that her parents had earlier moved into a house in the same street not far from her own. The two households were run jointly after this trauma. They shared the joys and cares of life. Bulelwa spent most of her remaining childhood living in her grandparents' house helping them with chores in their old age. They in turn gave support to their daughter and her children.

Bulelwa did well at school. When we met she was in Grade 9 at Guguletu Comprehensive School – at the time one of the few schools functioning well. She liked the teachers who encouraged her to work hard. They read, wrote and spoke English as part of the teachers' strategy to prepare them for life with English as the main language of communication. The school also offered computer skills training, encouraged debating forums and educational trips.

BULELWA: When our friends come they sit with us in the lounge and my mother lets us use her house freely. She would ask to be excused unless she doesn't know the friends. If she doesn't know them, we would introduce them. After introducing them she would waste no time in making snacks and serving us.

Then she would go back to her bedroom. She told us that she understands the need for young people to have friends. She also had friends when she was growing up. She preferred boyfriends to girlfriends.

When it comes to friends my mother tries her best to satisfy us. If they come at night she prefers them to come inside the house. If they stand outside at night and send neighbouring children to call us she doesn't like it because she doesn't know whether they are our friends or strangers. She prefers that visitors should come in so that she can see who they are. There are many dangers at night. One can get hurt outside. It is best for our friends to come in. She says if friends do not want to come in, mothers become suspicious. Our friends know what our mother likes and dislikes.

My best friends are my sisters and cousins because where we stay there are fights over little things. My sisters and I decided to be our own best friends. We don't talk to any other children in our street. We do not know the reason for this estrangement. Other people come to try and ask us what is happening. Other children say we are putting ourselves above others because many of the things children in our street do, we don't do. We don't go to many of the places they go to. We do not smoke. We do not drink. So they have separated themselves from us. In fact we are not hurt, *asi hetisheki,* because at home we are many. We are four girls. So we are all friends. If one of us has a problem – like we do have teenage problems – we help one another to overcome those problems before we go to our mother.

Bulelwa's decision not to go outside the family was for her the best way of coping with her circumstances. Good peer relations and whatever support she could derive from such relationships had to be sacrificed. Success demanded that she distinguished herself from the destructive lifestyles prevalent among her peers. The cost was alienation from her peers because success in places like New Crossroads, where the majority of people are unable to succeed, is seen as a threat to community solidarity.

The closeness between the Leseka sisters was not surprising. They realised how important it was to derive strength from one another in the face of a hostile neighbourhood and their mother's limited material and emotional resources.

Bulelwa's life came under increasing strain both at school and at home. The continual disruptions to schooling in the run-up to South Africa's first election in 1994 began to erode teaching and learning even in good schools like Guguletu Comprehensive High School.

As part of the project I arranged positions in schools outside the township for those among the group of sixteen who wanted to move. Bulelwa and five others moved to Rhodes High in Mowbray at the beginning of 1994. Because it was connected to the train, bus and taxi routes it was accessible to township pupils.

Rhodes High was started in the 1940s as a traditional working-class school for white children. Like similar schools elsewhere in the country it opened its doors to all children in the early 1990s. The headmaster of the school was supportive of the new arrivals and did his best to ease their adjustment. But there was a huge gap between the New Crossroads pupils and their new peers. Their school experience had not prepared them for the discipline of regular classes and homework, the need for extra reading and self-motivation. Their reading, writing and mathematical skills were far below those expected of their age and class level. English was taken seriously as the medium of instruction unlike in township schools where teachers were often not competent users of the language. Bulelwa coped best of them all with the new challenges ...

By 1995 Bulelwa's family was in severe financial trouble. Bulelwa often found herself without money to get to school and was frequently absent. One of her teachers noted in her report that her frequent absenteeism was having a negative impact on her progress. The death of her grandmother in 1993 had deprived the family not only of a loved one, but also of an essential old-age pension which made a difference to the family's income.

Bulelwa managed to get a part-time job at the New Crossroads Youth Centre where she worked after school each day. The money was sufficient to cover her transport costs for the week and enabled her to attend school. The Youth Centre also gave her R50 as a once-off grant to buy books and a school uniform.

Then one afternoon she arrived at the Youth Centre in tears. She explained that she could not possibly justify keeping her money for school when there was no food in her home. Her mother was pressurising her to contribute this money to the household. Mrs Leseka had also being trying to persuade Bulelwa to transfer to Stembele Matiso High School in New Crossroads, which would solve the transport problem. Both knew that the education that Bulelwa would receive at the local high school was vastly inferior to that at Rhodes. But for Mrs Leseka, desperate to provide for her five children, this seemed a necessary sacrifice to enable the family to keep afloat.

Bulelwa knew all too well that a good education could be her only ticket out of the poverty of New Crossroads. Staying at a good school meant making a 'selfish' decision at the expense of her family's well-being, and against her mother's wishes. Not making this 'selfish' decision could cost her a brighter future. The long-term benefits of being in a better position to improve the family's welfare would also have to be foregone.

At the time a researcher on the project went to visit Mrs Leseka to talk to her about Bulelwa's dilemma, hoping to convince her of the importance of keeping Bulelwa at a good school. The researcher arrived to find that the Leseka's household furniture had just been taken away because Mrs Leseka had been unable to keep up the hire-purchase payments. The family had not only lost the furniture, but the total investment of the payments made up to that point. It was obviously not a good time to talk about Bulelwa's schooling. Bulelwa had to fight the battle alone.

In spite of all these obstacles Bulelwa persevered. She read widely, had a good command of written and spoken English, planned ahead and worked diligently to achieve her goals. She was determined to make the best of life and her leadership qualities came into their own at different levels. She continued to work at the Youth Centre as part of our Child-to-Child programmes. She read to younger children. She told them stories which amused them and nurtured their curiosity. She in turn received financial and moral support from the Youth Centre. She also built on the Wilderness Leadership School trail experiences to promote an Environmental Awareness Programme at the Youth Centre. The programme encouraged young people to explore the natural treasures in and around Cape Town. She became a volunteer of the Pride of Table Mountain Project which took township youth onto the mountain every weekend.

Bulelwa graduated from high school at the end of 1996. In 1997 she obtained a commercial education diploma from Damelin correspondence college financed by a bursary from the Italian embassy which she had negotiated on her own. Her first job was at one of South Africa's largest insurance companies.

Bulelwa did not consider studying full time after high school graduation as it was too expensive. She also opted out of doing a university degree.

'There's a problem I see with going to university,' she told me.

'Studying for four years and then not being able to get a job and being stuck at home with a degree would be a risk. I don't want to spend a lot of money studying and then when it comes to searching for a job I face problems. I want to study while I work so that I can get experience.'

Bulelwa's personal life was also successful. She married in 1997 – a double wedding held in Port Elizabeth with one of her sister's marrying her husband's brother. A case of the sisters' solidarity stretching into their romantic lives.

from Notes on the Cape Town Skollie (2005)

SUREN PILLAY

A few years ago I found myself amongst some youths who were familiar to me. I did not at first recognize them because their faces were covered by the chequered scarves that we associate now with the Palestinians. It was in a community called Rylands, one of the two group areas designated by the apartheid state for so-called 'Indians' in Cape Town at that time. It was also the neighbourhood I grew up in. The last time I had seen youths covering their faces in this manner, in this neighbourhood, had been about ten years ago. And that time I happened to be one of them. It was the school boycotts of 1985. And we used the scarves to protect our faces from identification by the police as we set up barricades of burning car tyres in the street. And when we hurled petrol bombs at the ubiquitous canary yellow police vehicles which surrounded our schools. But I get ahead of myself.

This time the youths I met were participating in a march organized by a newly formed group which called itself PAGAD – People Against Gangsterism and Drugs. It was a group formed by local community leaders, particularly teachers, who were fed up with the proliferation of gang violence and drug use and trade on the Cape Flats. Their unhappiness was framed within a particular religious-moral discourse. They were overwhelmingly Muslim and it was to Islamic scripture and symbolism that they turned in order to articulate their desire to, in their words, 'rid the community' of gangs and drugs. The strategy was to call public meetings, at the end of which a march would proceed to the house of a drug dealer, who would then be given a 24 hour ultimatum to cease engaging in the practice of drug sales. Or he or she would face the consequences. Most people covered their faces during these marches for fear of retribution from the drug dealers and the gangs they were a part of. Some did it no doubt because, and I say this without facetiousness, the drug dealers might recognize them as past clientele.

This movement grew rapidly but went largely unnoticed by the mainstream press in Cape Town in 1995. Unnoticed until one of these marches, a march to the house of Cape Town's most feared and power-ful gang leaders, became spectacular. The Staggie twins, Rashied and Rashaad, were leaders of the Hard Living Kids, the HLS, as they are known on the Cape Flats. By the mid-nineties a turf war was unfold-ing between the Hard Livings and the other big gang on the Cape Flats, the 'Americans'. As the marchers stood outside the house, one of the twins, Rashaad, arrived in his SUV. He drove into the thick of the crowd, jumped out of the vehicle and started jesting at them. A scuffle broke out, and then in the darkness of it all, shots rang out. When the crowd that surrounded Rashaad moved back in panic, he remained standing, shocked and with blood oozing from a gunshot wound. Within seconds more shots penetrated his body and he fell into the gutter. In a flash a petrol-bomb was flung at this limp body which burst into flames upon impact. In a surreal moment Staggie then stood erect and briefly walked, arms flailing, shrouded in flames, before col-lapsing finally onto the tarred road. I can describe this event in detail because it was recorded and photographed by the press contingent that was there. The image of the flame-shrouded Rashaad Staggie's final steps played over and over on the local news in the days thereafter. PAGAD was no longer just an organization that those of us from the Cape Flats knew about. It was now a national security concern, more so than the issues they sought to address.

My concern at that time was with the representation of PAGAD in academia and in the media. Even though this was long before the post 9/11 hysteria, all kinds of Orientalist phobias about PAGAD were circulating, like it being instigated by Iranians, which I felt were prob-lematic. In the months that followed I went to the PAGAD marches, spoke with members and attended their meetings. That's when I realized that I knew some of the youth involved. More particularly, those who were part of what they called the G-Force, a group whose identity was very guarded because they were armed and were most likely involved in the spate of pipe-bombings that ensued during this time. I had been to school with some and knew others from around the neighbourhood. A number of key gang leaders were killed in drive-by shootings, all after having been warned by a PAGAD march. When I asked some of them why they were resorting to violence they said that they felt that the new South Africa was not protecting them sufficiently and that they had to take the law into their own hands. Of course, the state could not allow its monopoly over the legitimate use of force to be threatened, as a good Weberian would remind them, and PAGAD itself quickly became criminalized.

from Sea-Mountain, Fire City (2001)

MIKE NICOL

I worked on a second assignment for the *Cape Times'* One City, Many Cultures initiative. This time I was asked to report on the city's health. Once I'd gone through statistics that revealed one of the highest rates of murder, rape, assault, and child abuse in the country, and been told that alcohol was a factor in almost all violent crime and in the alarming number of car accidents that killed and maimed thousands of people each year, a psychological portrait of a deeply disturbed city began to develop. A city in trauma. But if any one factor emerged as a metaphor for this trauma it was a disease that had been a scourge of the city for three centuries – tuberculosis. TB.

According to the statistics, Cape Town had the unhappy distinction of being the TB capital of the world, and it had been for a long time. Why this should be wasn't understood, or even a question worth asking by those, like Mariette Williams, who literally devoted their lives to the TB Care Association, a non-governmental agency that worked closely with the Cape Town city council. Her office was in Manenberg.

In a preliminary phone call she suggested that we meet outside the Philippi police station. She made this arrangement firmly in the tone of voice I suspected she might use with a difficult patient. I had been trying to make a more complicated set of arrangements because I was worried about my car. Not once had I mentioned this concern but Mariette knew the unease of strangers about the slum of Manenberg. She knew Manenberg existed for many – myself included – like an intimation of the apocalypse, an out-take from the movie *Blade Runner*.

'It's quiet at the moment,' she reassured me, 'your car will be alright.'

We met as stipulated and I followed her the short distance to the Manenberg Clinic. A short distance but far enough to separate one reality from another. It was nine o'clock in the morning but already there were groups of men everywhere: lounging outside backyard gates, standing on the corners, leaning against posts. An old man sitting on an upturned plastic bottle container talked animatedly to a passer-by. There was something timeless in the cameo: a young man listening to an old man's story. The streets were active, noisy with running children and dogs and women, their hair in curlers beneath doeks, watching and smoking. Yet the streets also looked as they appear after a riot: littered with stones and half-bricks and smashed bottles and oddments of clothing.

The clinic was surrounded by a high fence of concrete poles and an automatic gate. The street was visible between the poles but gangsters couldn't run in during their wars and use the clinic as part of the battleground, which happened before the fence was erected. During the worst of the gang wars in 1998 the clinic was forced to shut for three months but reopened in small offices on the other side of Manenberg. These were inconvenient and cramped but this was an emergency and at least the clinic was up and running. 'We were proud of that,' said Mariette. 'Let's just hope it doesn't happen again.'

We went inside and she found a small backroom where we could talk. Somewhere in the clinic a baby whined unceasingly.

Mariette was a University of Cape Town graduate. She was born and raised in the city. She was committed to her work and she talked honestly and bluntly about it and the conditions under which she had to work. She said if she told me her salary, I'd laugh. She admitted to occasionally being resentful that it was so low but then she chuckled and said: 'That's NGO work, that's the reality.' The thing was she couldn't imagine being or doing anything else. For Mariette this was an exciting, relevant job. To use a war metaphor: a matter of being in the front line of what she called the 'TB-HIV onslaught.'

With an incidence of five hundred and sixty people per hundred thousand, TB thrived among the poverty-stricken where living conditions were overcrowded and people's diet was haphazard and the stress of unemployment, lack of money, and alcoholism ground into the daily life. On a map of Cape Town great parts of the city would be shaded by these conditions. Also TB was what Mariette and her colleagues called an 'opportunistic disease' – an airborne bacteria ready to hook into the lungs of anyone whose immune system might be ailing. Anyone, say, who was HIV positive. A statistic had it that forty percent of those with HIV could develop TB.

This was of great concern to the people monitoring the city's health. They spoke of TB now manifesting itself in the white population where it had been virtually unknown for decades. They talked, as Mariette did, of an onslaught.

'Consider,' said Mariette, 'as you walk down St George's Mall, forty percent of the people you pass probably will have been infected with TB.'

Which was why TB had been declared a health emergency in the city and a treatment strategy developed by the World Health Organisation instituted in an attempt to contain the risk. The nature of TB was such that it required six months of dedicated treatment. Six months of daily medication. If the medication was stopped after a few weeks or months the complications that set in were alarming, both for the patient and for society. Within a few months they would become ill again but by now the TB bacillus would have mutated and the original medicine was no longer effective. The cost of treating a patient with drug resistant TB was R35 000, against a cost of R3 500 for the 'ordinary' version of the disease. And patients who were drug resistant transmitted a TB strain that was drug resistant, in other words, a strain that was expensive and difficult to cure.

'There are just two simple statistics we have to remember,' said Mariette. 'The first is that eighty percent of TB patients only go to a clinic long after they've contracted the disease. The second is that one person can infect twenty others through contact in the street, train, taxi, and café.'

A top priority for Mariette was to make sure people took their medicine. This was where the WHO programme was having some success. Under this strategy volunteers from a particular community became 'care supporters' and saw to it that TB patients took their pills daily. After a five-day training workshop the supporters took over the function that would normally be the responsibility of a nurse at a clinic. But because there weren't enough nurses, let alone enough clinics, having 'care supporters' in the immediate community meant there was a greater chance of sufferers staying the course.

In Manenberg there were one hundred and forty patients and twenty care supporters with a maximum of ten clients each. It was part of Mariette's job to supply the back-up to these care supporters. Which was no easy task at the best of times, and nothing short of impossible during the periodic gang wars.

'I'm not a fearful person,' she told me, 'but about a year ago while I was sitting in this very office I heard shooting. These were serious guns and that was the first time I felt scared. Nowadays I phone ahead to find out what's happening here. And when I'm here, I'm careful. I watch what's going on in the street, I drive with the windows up, I keep the doors locked, that sort of thing. When it's quiet or there are flashy cars driving around you know there's going to be trouble.

'I'll tell you one thing, the care supporters helped us enormously through the gang wars. Even under those desperate conditions we had a really good compliance rate. People would wait until the shooting died down then duck out and run to the care supporters. I think it's because a strong relationship develops between the patient and the care supporter who lives here, who knows what's going on, so that even during the worst times people will do their utmost to get their medicines. The only thing that sometimes concerns me is that if I get shot there has to be some contingency plan. And I don't mean get shot in that I'm being targeted, but that I get caught in the crossfire.'

Mariette said this as if she's said nothing particularly out of the ordinary. How many people, I wondered, had that consideration at the back of their minds as they went about their daily jobs? It was a measure of her personality that she quickly added: 'Can you imagine what it's like to live here under these conditions?'

We left the clinic and drove to a care supporter called Anne, who lived in a quiet side street where the fences on either side were of corrugated iron. Anne supported seven patients. She was short and open-faced with a ready smile but also, I suspected, a will of iron. Each week she went to the clinic to fetch the medicine for her patients and every day they came to her home to receive their tablets. For this Anne received a token gratuity of R40 per patient. 'The money helps,' she laughed, 'of course, yes, but I'm not doing this for the money. I'm doing this because I want to help people.'

One of her patients was Isah, thirty-eight years old and unemployed. He'd been diagnosed with TB shortly after losing his job.

'My dream is to be healthy again,' he said. 'I want to get a job when the treatment's finished so that I can support my family. In the end it's up to you to look after your own life, not so!'

Mariette took the long way back to the clinic. We passed a row of burnt-out shops where the owners refused to pay protection money to the gangs and were closed down and then looted. We passed huge graffiti that was dark and evil and the one featured the gangster icon, Tupac Shakur. We passed a dog in a gutter that Mariette said had been lying there for two days. It was still twitching.

'There is a malaise here,' said Mariette. 'As if this whole community is suffering from depression. I've worked in Guguletu and it's not like this.' She was frustrated, desperately wanting things to change but now knowing how to go about it.

I remembered Isah's words: 'Manenberg is mos, well, Manenberg. You get robbed with a knife at your throat just getting bread. It's disgusting. It's not the way to live.'

from High Traffic (2005)

GABEBA BADEROON

That night I was wearing a red scarf. A wounded colour, the blood invisible, the heart not beating.

From Devil's Peak and the University's redbrick buildings held together with ivy, I drive downhill into the afternoon heat, and at the robots turn right toward Claremont. My mother's family used to live in Claremont in a narrow house just behind what is now the curved glass and brick Cavendish Square. When you walked in the front door of their house you could see down a long passage right into the garden in the back.

Growing up in Athlone, I'd heard stories of their impossible neighbourhood, with its mixing of religions, occupations and colours, and the glacial social distance between Upper and Lower Claremont, below the railway line. I'd listened to my mother's eldest sister, Auntie Faranaaz, tell of the one store in the area, where they shopped for flour and beans, dished from large bins into brown paper bags, about a time before there were brand names for salt and bread, and the long war years when milk and meat were rationed.

The sound of the bilal – the word for the athaan in Cape Town, taken from the name of the slave who called believers to prayer in the first Muslim community in Mecca – could be heard from two directions, the Main Road and Stegman Road mosques. My grandmother was a seamstress and my grandfather worked in a photographer's studio – their house was hung with exquisite curtains and colourized black and white portraits of the five children. My mother was the youngest, the only one to take the bus in reverse of the route I'd just driven along the Main Road to the University. In the class of 1958 at medical school she was the only black woman.

The men of the neighbourhood worked in schools, factories and the building trade. On Saturday afternoons, many of them gathered round a table in my grandparents' garage to play dominoes with a wooden set that my grandfather had made himself. Each game ended with a shout and the loud slap of the final piece on the table.

Their neighbourhood was abolished when it was declared 'white' in 1968. My mother and her family were removed from the area and sent down Old Lansdowne Road to build only the second house in a wild place named Pinati Estate. I was born a year later, so I knew the Square as a white mall where eventually we would go to watch movies, but sometimes when she picked us up at Cavendish Square, I have seen my mother cry quietly in the parking lot.

At Stanhope Bridge, I take a left perpendicularly away from the mountain toward the suburb of Lansdowne to buy floorboards for my mother's bedroom. In the flat bowl in the lee of the mountain I travel through my mother's memories. As I drive down Old Lansdowne Road, the geography of the city becomes more functional – the closer I get, the more frequent are the businesses in the building trade, many of them decades-old markers on this road. A large yellow sign for Target Tiles marks the road till the gold-domed mosque of Islamia College. I stop when a uniformed prefect blows a whistle at the pedestrian crossing and children in long white robes, their heads covered with white koefiyyas and scarves, walk in laughing lines across the street at Express Electrical.

My whole family is sustained by the building trade – my brother is a tiler, my uncles are plumbers, plasterers and building contractors, my father was a carpenter – so I know about the secret equality of the city's dispersed architecture. There is unexpected beauty in the houses in poorer areas, adorned with mouldings on their modest windows and exquisite cornices on their ceilings – the match of any building in town – because they have been built by the same people.

To get to the bridge from Old Lansdowne Road I curve past Artistic Aluminium with its confluence of aesthetics and construction. Along the road near the black part of Lansdowne, men and women push shopping-trolleys piled high with metal and wood gathered from building sites and the piles put at the kerb on the days when municipal workers in their orange uniforms collect the garbage. Balancing their loads of discarded goods, they move slowly up the bridge and even more carefully on the decline toward Pearce's Scrap next to the red robot.

Once I enter New Lansdowne Road, the businesses change to a mixture of dentists' rooms and halaal fast-food shops that cater to workers at the factories nearby. Near the oblique intersection of Lansdowne and Vlei Roads, the turret of Mohammadeyah Mosque hovers above a scalloped, second-storey wall. At street level, just before the startling combination of first-name familiarity and precision at Ernie's Ferrous Metals, I turn the corner and arrive at Lansdowne Boards.

It is my third visit and, as usual, it involves a wait. I am more interested in the place this time, not absenting myself by thinking that I haven't finished Tatamkhulu Afrika's *The Innocents*, but look again at the large glossy tiles on the floor that caught my attention last time because they handle foot traffic well.

Traffic is an important concept here. For our floorboards, my brother Immie and I had to choose between 6mm and 8mm laminates, the latter for high traffic areas like doorways or lobbies. We went for 6mm ones – cheaper by hundreds of rands – but Lansdowne Boards were out of stock so we took the higher traffic boards, even though my mother's bedroom is a quiet place, mostly a place to pray …

While my ID book is checked and I wait for my credit card to be approved, I look toward the back of the shop. In the section behind me is the Collections area, where a vast reserve of wood and composite products is stored. The composites have awkward composite names too – novoboard, supawood, lifeseal formica – and have a low-gloss neatness that in the dim light looks more finished than the slim, bare, wood planks with their splintered, angled edges. Next to the square shelves at the back of the shop is a huge set of open doors where deliveries are received. A pile of pallets stacked in the opening catches the afternoon light. My eyes drop and I realize suddenly from the places where the paint has worn that the tiles on the floor are *trompe l'oeil* ones. Even the grouting between the tiles has been painted on the cement.

While a man takes my floorboards from an open box in the Collections area, the thin skirting planks catch my eye. Since we are close to finishing the flooring, I go back to the counter and order the skirting and quadrants that will neaten the edges of the boards where they meet the wall and wardrobe. Ims has given the room's dimensions to the man behind the counter, who retrieves the information from the computer under Imaan, a misspelling of Imran's name, but 'Imaan' means 'faith', so the mistake is not too bad.

In addition to the floorboards, I end up with seven lengths of skirting, and two of quadrants. The man who takes all of this to the car is accompanied by a helper no older than nineteen. 'Sit dit hier', he says lightly. 'Nei, nie so nie, sit dit soes 'n visstok. 'n Mens kan sien jou pa vat jou nie vis nie.' He rolls down the back window of my car halfway and lays the thin wood on it at an angle that won't pose a hazard to other cars. 'Pass that to me, please, Miss', he says. I hand him the flexible sun visor and he folds it under the wood to protect the window.

I drive back to the house and carry in the planks. The full box of eight would have been too heavy, but I can manage four. I carry them to the back and lay them carefully at the doorway. The instructions on the box say to leave the planks in the space where they will be fitted for 48 hours before laying them in order to adjust to the temperature and atmosphere, but we ignore that. Ims will cut the planks to the exact length of the remaining section and then, on the bit he has just hammered together, my sister Adela and I will lie for a while like paperweights to hold them in place.

It is the biggest room in the house, built by my father and uncles for the four girls. Every weekend the men in the family and the ones we called 'uncle' even though they weren't, would come to help dig the foundations, then pour the cement, then slowly raise the walls. Now it had become my mother's bedroom, which she and her new husband, the Imam, will share.

The room is only emptied on big occasions like my father's funeral, or the day of my wedding, when I and the other women stood in the room next door, and heard Asief say the words that married us. Kabiltoen nikkahi … bien nafsie. Afterwards he whispered nervously, 'I didn't know if I married you, or the twenty-five men in the room with me'. Zugtie, who had driven him to the house from Kalk Bay, where we would be spending our honeymoon, told me Asief had been practising the Arabic words in his American accent all the way on the drive. He didn't stumble once during the ceremony.

For those occasions, the beds and tables are taken out and the red Persian carpet is rolled out and white sheets laid for people to sit on and, eventually, after the prayers, still other sheets are added for the food. But I'd never seen the room as empty as now. Even the shelves and the built-in desk along the side by the window are gone. Perhaps it hadn't been this empty since it had been built. Usually my mother's room is filled with things, her wardrobes always slightly spilling. Now, her baskets of knitting wool, my father's suit patterns he had inherited from his father, her bedside tables, the hundreds of paper, pamphlets and books from her Continuing Medical Education classes were all somewhere else. Standing at the door, I didn't know if I was looking at nothing, or the beginning of the next twenty years.

I haven't walked over the new floor yet. Adela has tried out the floor with her ballet shoes to see if it will scratch. It does, but I've told her to practice in a part of the room that will be hidden under the prayer mats. Each laminate consists of a plank 15 centimetres wide made of smaller five centimetre planks glued together. The smaller sections within the larger ones obscure the joints between the laminates themselves. The ruse works beautifully. The finished floor looks like an ice-rink or a lake – something smooth and untouched.

The changing of rooms after my father had died had also changed things more deeply – the solid geography of the house, the sense of where the children belonged, and the adults. Soon Mama and the Imam will come back from Australia where they were visiting Rafia, with whom I had bickered and whispered in the dark in this room for fifteen years.

The little bit at the door is all that remains undone. After that, the skirting will be fitted – maple too, but real maple this time, to seal the right angle between the floor and the wall. For the moment, the beautiful, false maple is edged with familiar blue and white books propped against the wall. Ims had inserted Adela's *Mills and Boon* love stories between the boards and the wall to ensure an even space for the skirting. The books are always the same thickness, their vision of love always precisely 210 pages long. Love gives its precision to the floor. Eventually, once the skirting replaces the *Mills and Boons*, they will go back to Adela's cupboard where she keeps her collection of love stories and Patricia Cornwell thrillers.

My father had built the cupboards in this room and, in fact, in all the rooms of the house, including the kitchen. I remember staring at the top of the cupboard in my parents' room when I was about seven. On the top shelf was a box of jewellery that contained a beautiful gold signet ring with my initial on it that I was only allowed to wear on special occasions. On the more ordinary days, I would look up and wish for the time when I would be able to reach the ring by myself. Making those cupboards, my father too went to Lansdowne Boards, stood still and made his choice.

When they first bought the house in 1972 with the advice of Imam Rashied at St Athans Road Mosque, the floors in the whole house were laid with teak, a dark parquet that was out of fashion in the 1970s, so in the kitchen and passage they lifted them and put down tiles instead. And the back room that they built onto the house never had any floor at all, just carpet laid on the cement.

My mother always looked at the kitchen and saw the things she didn't have. A spice rack against the wall by the stove, the cupboards whose top shelves she couldn't reach. Often in the afternoons, after she arrived home from Dr Abdurahman Day Hospital, Mama would call from the kitchen, 'Galiema, could you take down the cinnamon on the second shelf for me, please?' I think now about the way you know a house through the things that weren't there, the places you couldn't reach.

That night in the restaurant five years ago, we were there because of me. It was my parents' anniversary, but the family was really there to say goodbye because I was going to America on a fellowship. I was nervous but ready. I invited them to celebrate at a restaurant, even though my parents never ate out. It was an Indian place, halaal, and everyone had found something they liked. My friends Farah and Zugtie were there too, and had brought Ali, just sixteen months old. Farah was more like a sister, really.

That night, we chatted and joked and my father played finger games with Ali. After we'd all placed our orders, Farah and I went to the bathroom to change Ali. When we got back, the table had been pushed aside, my father was lying on the floor and a man from a nearby table was pumping his chest. My mother stood pale and silent. I remember trying to be efficient, phoning my aunts, paying the bill, driving home. I've never gone back to that restaurant nor, for a long time, to any restaurant.

Somehow we went back home that night, not to sleep, but to keep thinking about what we did not see, what we wouldn't from now on. In the house the rooms had changed, everything changed. I was wearing a red scarf. A wounded colour, the blood invisible, the heart not beating.

Now I am home for a while again. And the geography of home is being remade again. Rafia is having her second child, and Mama and her husband are there to help her adjust.

The big room is naked, but perhaps also waiting. I feel sorry for the Imam sometimes – we all have our ready-made stories but then, he has his too. New layers of memory will leave their traces on the floors. Being in the same place, we will all learn to adjust.

At Lansdowne Boards, nothing was hidden, after all. The painted cement floor at the back of the workshop was another way of dealing with traffic.

SEABOARDS

from A Writer's Diary (1997)

STEPHEN WATSON

2 March 1996
... Yesterday, for instance, I drove over the chain of Peninsula mountains to Scarborough, way down the Atlantic seaboard towards the southernmost tip of the Cape. On the pass over the Kalk Bay mountains I saw the coastal southeaster cloud pouring down the western slopes, the colour of those clouds close to the grey of mist. But there was also the astonishing salt-like whiteness of the sandstone scree on the slopes set against the grey of the fraying cloud, further highlighted by the clumps of pine, their trunks blackened by the pitch of noonday light.

I found myself more or less instinctively seeking out the textures, the tonalities in that landscape, devouring it so that I could re-make it. I had the happiness of knowing once again that this peninsula, these landscapes, were a kind of infinity which would never be exhausted and which would continue to elicit from me this passion. As I drove, I was already experimenting with the words that might reproduce the combination of southeaster cloud, white mountain stone, gale-force wind, and light-blackened pines. I knew myself to be saturated by this world; it was akin to the experience of physical love, that sense of being drenched by the reality of another's being.

Later, there was the view of the sea at Scarborough, the Sicilian blue of the icy water, the coastal milkwoods glittering green and black under the volleys of wind and light ...

8 October 1996
The view of Camps Bay in the rain of this endlessly prolonged winter: a late, milky light seeping through the clouded sunset, the greenish opalescence of a quiet sea, and the line of palm-trees along the shore road, collapsed like beach umbrellas, thinned out in the rain.

Behind the hotel the playing-fields of the local primary school as empty as the sea across the road. And then the sight of a pharmacy along the beachfront road – of its 1930s arcade and a Kodak logo, painted long before the days of disinvestment and sanctions, still dripping on its side-wall ...

17 December 1996
At Boulders.

Come summer, when the wind reverses itself, the heat carries the smell of salt, the presence of the ocean, back into the city streets. Each year we rediscover the sea.

And each time I enter this cove, to dive open-eyed down through the glassy surface, the smashed water effervescing around me, strata of coolness alternating with bands of cold as I descend, there is the memory: of the friend, long dead, who once told me that the sea had always been the deepest thing in him.

When the incoming tide brims the cove, it lifts one easily over rocks sharp with limpets, carries one with feet to spare over the beds of kelp, their heads anchored, floating upwards like thick ropes of hair.

But most of all I love to dive down ten feet, fifteen, past shoals of small fish swerving, darting, to clutch handfuls of clean sand off the sea-bed, and then to be carried to the surface by the body's full-lunged buoyancy, to break the surface, there to see the size of the mountains across the bay, the Hottentots Holland, huge from this level in the water.

18 December 1996
The dew on the coastal vegetation, sticky in the heat of dawn, the bushes salt-gnarled, grown dull-fleshed, off-green, in their resistance to the wind. The smell of the shore grass fed by sea-water, burnt by salt, the rock half-rusted by salt. And the sails of the yachts slatting as they go around Ark Rock.

Most of all I am at home with those who write books in which their love of the sea (for instance) shines through more powerfully than their love of books. It is hardly surprising that, in these pages, I should come back to Camus so often.

To return to Boulders is to be taken back to those earliest allegiances which no later love quite displaces. Even when, in the afternoon, the

wind gets up and heads the water with thin half-moons of foam; when
it manufactures its own belt of muddy cloud around the Muizenberg
mountains; when dune-sand is streaming across the coastal roads and
one senses a kind of blurring of the sky, blurring of the leaves under
all this air-blasting – all night long it will go on rushing the shacks
along the Cape south coast – this is no less a part of that allegiance.

from Return to Paradise (1993)

BREYTEN BREYTENBACH

We are staying in Paradise House, the summer cottage of the Fox family
out at Simon's Town. *'Simons Baay in de Baay Falso'* (Simon's Bay in
False Bay) was visited in 1687 by the Dutch Governor at the Cape of
Good Hope, Simon van der Stel. He recognized its excellent moorage,
protected from the worst winds, and ordered it settled. In 1743 Baron
van Imhof surveyed the town and it probably hasn't changed all that
much since. It is said that this safe natural harbour was one of the
main reasons why the British attacked and occupied the Cape. Over
centuries it became the most important naval base in the southern
Atlantic. Harbour and town now constitute the South African Navy's
headquarters; from here the oceans are scanned. A big part of the base
is buried in mountain bunkers behind the town.

Paradise House lies against the slope, screened off by tall trees and
fragrant bushes, a humble but magical dwelling, flat and whitewashed.
The front stoep overlooks the bay: first, the way a bird would see it falling
down the mountain wind (as they often do), the railway line and its station below from where we sometimes hear a clickety-clack. Then, to the
right, the town stacked in terraces of Victorian and Georgian buildings
and the harbour with piers and grey frigates; and to the left, hugging
the coast at the foot of the range, the road heading for Cape Town via
Fish Hoek and Muizenberg, white settlements sparkling in the sun. In
the lee of the harbour wall a host of yachts with, wallowing at anchor
like a swan among ducklings, the antiquated vessel used for laying and
repairing submarine cables (called *SA Cable Restorer*). Sometimes the
ominous black shape of a submarine surfaces on its way into base.

The water changes in humour and hue depending on the hour and the winds – from metallic grey to indigo to white-flecked emerald to the evening's silver and rust when the sun starts bleeding, and on to the liquid unsoundable black of night, sometimes crusted over by a glassiness of moonlight.

Clouds in the sky by day, an infinity of stars at night. Across the vast body of water, on a crisp day, one can see the white hem of sand running around to the Strand with above that again distant jagged peaks like the backs of a school of mythical dragons. At night loops of lights string jewels around the sea's throat.

Other people come with the house – a family of Xhosa squatters. Suzanne 'inherited' Bruman from a neighbour. In return for once a week raking the leaves and cutting the grass and looking out for the cobra who has taken up residence in the garden, Suzanne and Revel had a wooden hut built for Bruman on the terrain. His wife, Alice, arrived from the Transkei to see him right, and with her the children. Alice sometimes has a clay-whitened face. She is rumoured to be a *sangoma*.

I sit on my heels next to Bruman, who is cutting the lawn with a pair of shears. He wants to know where we come from. I explain about distant places, air travel over stretches of water, but he doesn't believe me. 'London?' he asks, and I give up and say 'Yes.' 'Factories?' he asks, and I agree, elaborating on cold reaches and foreign languages, but there are blacks there too. He shakes his head in disbelief. No, this man with the red shoes is a liar ...

The chirruping of birds, small wheeling clouds of swallows also preparing their departure; the ocean's deeper blue when the wind turns north; across the bay a luminous nearly white line as separation between water and mountain.

We have guests for lunch under the fig tree – [French ambassador] Joëlle and Olivier Bourgois, Jakes and Phoebe Gerwel. Yolande, being the best cook in the world, has prepared a selection of salads, rice, chicken, flavoured by her secrets. A blunt black shape surfaces in the bay to make its way to port – a South African submarine made in France. I fetch the binoculars; we take turns observing the vessel, and the French ambassador thinks I stage-managed this incident to embarrass her.

Lunch is nearly over, and we intoxicated with the beauty of the setting, when all hell breaks loose up the hill from the direction of the Xhosas. Alice comes charging down shouting furiously, clearly on the warpath. She grabs my arm to drag me towards the house. You must call the police immediately! We try to restrain her, at least to find out what it's all about.

The problem is a second woman, Pampata, who's been to visit them. We can't figure out the root of strife. I ask Jakes to calm Alice down; he is after all of the Party, should know how, and he offers a feeble conciliatory 'Sister' which she angrily brushes away. Up the hill we go.

There's a witches' concert of screeching and screaming. Bruman, who seems to have had a spot of bother with his fly, attempts to hold back a strikingly beautiful woman in a two-piece suit and beret. Pampata shakes off the arm and picks up a huge stone. Her natty suit, smeared with soil, shows the fight has already gone through an earlier physical stage. Alice stands her ground, arms akimbo, her kerchief knocked lopsided, her face a clay mask, spitting invective. Pampata moves in for the attack. Bruman is totally helpless; he fumblebuttons his fly and goes tut-tut-tut. I manage to wrest the rock from Pampata's hand but she picks up another. More threats and curses. More scraping of wings and scratching of dust.

Now Pampata takes my arm in an iron grip and frogmarches me down to the house; she orders me inside and on the telephone. I have no choice. Her employer must be called to testify – he's a naval doctor anyway. That 'country woman' up there (Alice) accuses her of having a snake between her legs! The doctor will bring the untruth to light.

I think I finally have a glimmer of understanding what this may be all about: two ladies spitting and spatting over one man (poor, placid Bruman), conflict between 'town girl' and 'country bumpkin', accusations of infidelity and man-theft, insults to clan and tribe?

The employer succeeds in soothing the feathers of the beautiful fury to the point where she relents her hold on my wrist (which is no snake). He also promises to alert the police. A policeman telephones to ask whaddabout de peepil, whether the trouble has been physical, is there blood, are there deads, and decides it's not worth coming out for. They must have numerous alarms every day.

We offer coffee to our slightly shaken guests under the fig tree. The wind has turned its nose, it is breathing stronger again. When they leave, chic Pampata and sturdy Alice are sitting with legs stretched flat on the ground on the incline below the hut, chatting amiably and sharing a bottle of tipsiness.

from Sea-Mountain, Fire City (2001)

MIKE NICOL

The moment we entered Muizenberg I could see that everything was not as it had been. For some years Muizenberg had been in decline, restaurants closed and rowdy bars opened, many of our neighbours fled to the suburbs as the slum landlords bought up property and the 'ghetto's' former quaintness took on the rough edge of what the sociologists call 'a transition phase'. I was surprised at just how much transition there'd been during our year away.

Our street was littered with broken bottles, half bricks, discarded shoes, the wrecks of cars. Men loitered in groups on the corners, music blared from windows. Babies crawled in the gutters, children played cricket in the middle of the road using tins as stumps. Women in curlers stood at their gates smoking. I groaned. I wasn't ready for this. I also knew I wouldn't ever be ready for this.

We reached our house.

For sixteen years, all through my thirties and into my forties, Muizenberg had meant a great deal to me. I had been infatuated with the place, intrigued by its characters, so at home that I thought I would only leave in a coffin. I had lived nowhere else longer than I'd lived in Muizenberg.

I went there because the houses were cheap and charming and the resort somewhat sleazy, but in a derelict rather than a nasty way. Even in those days it was a hard-drinking neighbourhood: on the stoeps imbibing cheap wine from tea cups sat a variety of Neanderthal types – men in vests and shorts, women in curlers and petticoats – who I later discovered existed from one disability pension payout to the next. Or more specifically from one bottle of brandy to the next. But to me they added a fascinating dimension. Far from being put off, I was enticed.

We moved into a house where we found unspeakable filth every-where and dead rats decaying beneath the floor boards. Undaunted, a lengthy process or renovation began.

Over the years converting the house, giving it a new dignity and making it our home became a dream on which we spent all our spare cash, not to mention a considerable amount of energy. And as a slow tarting-up started throughout the area we were content …

Muizenberg had been my home. I had felt as comfortable in its streets as I had in my living room. This sense of territory was gone now. The new inhabitants had usurped the streets.

Most of the new inhabitants were refugees, young men who'd fled the warring, hopeless regions of Africa. They rented mattress space from the slumlords and crowded twenty into unfurnished houses with one toilet, one bath, one basin between them. They took possession of the streets because there wasn't enough room in the houses. They spat, pissed, defecated, had sex before my eyes.

Hard-faced lowlifes had also moved in from Cape Town's other slum quarters. Graffiti appeared overnight on the walls: 'blood in, blood out' read one, ominous but at the same time incomprehensible and stupid. I was told of a crack house in the next street, a shebeen on the corner. I was told I could buy any drug going in the now misnamed Church Street. I no longer wanted to walk through the streets of Muizenberg. Not because they were dangerous but because I couldn't stand the filth, the noise, the sights. The beach, too, became a no-go zone. Too much litter, too many uncouth drunken people, too many full-volume car radios playing funk. Not the sort of beach for a leisurely afternoon swim.

Muizenberg no longer had anything to offer me. Which was when I should have reconciled the unease that had started in Berlin with my loss of Muizenberg and understood the message. But I didn't want to. I wasn't going to give up on Muizenberg that easily. I might feel alienated. I might abhor the misery and grime, but before it drove me crazy I should at least know something about the lives that contrib-uted to the misery and grime. Maybe empathy would help me adapt. I decided to find out about the refugees.

Down the street a hairdressing salon had opened recently. It was decked out in hairstyle fashion posters and the unsmiling glare of Tupac Shakur. Some product lines were haphazardly arranged on the shelves, and for some obscure reason two bales of hay served as window dressing. The salon was an instant success, it was also a social centre where impeccably dressed young men gathered in the afternoons to listen to music and talk. They played battered cassette tapes of much-loved singers in their home countries and they played them loudly. I couldn't understand how they managed to hear one another above the noise yet they always seemed to be engrossed in animated conversations. From the outside there was no visible grief in their lives.

One afternoon I went in and started talking with an Angolan who'd taken a job as a 'stylist' – his word – in the salon. He'd been in Muizenberg a few weeks and shared a room with three other men. His name was Robert Carlo. He was twenty years old. A small-boned, quiet man with a ready smile. During a break between clients, with reggae singer Lucky Dube at such volume on the boombox I could barely hear his soft-spoken story, Robert told me that he'd left Angola because it offered no future. We shared problems, I saw, although his were of a greater order. His English was halting but he knew enough to articulate his circumstances and, possibly because he had only a limited vocabulary, the details were all the more poignant.

'In my country there are many troubles,' he began. 'I know my country well, I know those people will not solve the problems. I can remember the bad times and I need a new life.'

For his first fifteen years Robert lived in Luanda. His father worked in the city as part of a Unita delegation negotiating with the MPLA government towards a peaceful settlement. Sometimes, if the talks broke down or the situation became tense, the Carlo family felt the repercussions. On one occasion, Robert came home from school to find their house gutted and his mother and sister wandering in shock among the smouldering ruins.

Shortly afterwards he was sent to relatives in a northern province where for the next four years he worked as a builder, learning the trade on the job. But this was not the life he wanted. He'd been trained as a hairdresser in Luanda and he missed city living. Then he heard about Cape Town: no wars, apartheid over, a modern thriving economy. Robert Carlo resolved to head south.

He returned to Luanda, acquired travel documents and said goodbye to his family. It took him a week, walking and hitching rides on trucks, to reach Namibia. It took him three days to travel through Namibia and another two before he arrived in Cape Town.

'I like this place,' he said to me finally, 'it is better.'

By now a group of seven or eight men had gathered around us. Some of them shook their heads at this last statement.

'He has only been here a few weeks,' said one of the men. 'Me, I have been here five years and now I am going to Holland. It is too dangerous for us here. If we walk alone in the townships they will kill us. The blacks don't like us.'

'Cape Town is not home for us,' added a dapper man in a double-breasted suit. He told me he was from the Congo but wouldn't give his name. 'The Xhosa don't like black foreigners,' he explained. 'They say, give me R5. And if you don't give it they will kill you. What is this? How can you kill someone for R5? We can't stay in Langa or Guguletu because they will kill us if they find us there. The people here they drink too much, they want to kill too quickly, they are lazy, they don't work. Things are going to be bad here, very bad. The whites don't care and the blacks are bad. When Mbeki is president then it will be even more difficult for us. So many of us are going to leave South Africa before the elections. When I see new people come here I tell them they are crazy. I say why have you come here? It is better to stay at home than come here.' ...

While I had every sympathy for the refugees, what I couldn't understand was why they turned their immediate surroundings into a slum. These well-dressed, well-groomed young men thought nothing about throwing litter out of the window into the street. Just as they thought nothing about pissing against our back wall. The houses they rented deteriorated daily simply because there were too many people sitting on the walls and leaning from the windows. They lived in appalling circumstances yet refused to improve their lot. Meanwhile they dragged down Muizenberg for all of us ...

Then, in the Saturday property section of the newspaper, I found plots of land for sale in a coastal suburb farther down the peninsula called Glencairn Heights. We decided to have a look.

It was a still, bright winter's day. The sea dazzled. The air had a brittle clarity. In the shadows were cold dewy patches. The mountains across the bay stood out in sharp relief. We drove round the headland into the narrow Glencairn valley. A small crescent of beach. A wetland with a river reaching back up the valley. The old Glencairn houses facing north on the farther side of the valley. The new Glencairn Heights opposite facing south.

We rode slowly past the vacant plots going higher and higher but began giving less attention to these than to the view. Not only the seascape but views back into the mountains at the head of the valley. Eventually I stopped the car. We got out, stunned. Silence. No disco music. Nobody hawking up. No bergie swearing. No one lying comatose on the pavement. No one begging. No broken bottles, used condoms, discarded plastic or tins. But breaking into the silence the calls of francolin and guineafowl. I noticed other mountain birds: bulbuls, robins, sunbirds, white eyes. Two francolins came out of the bush and crossed the road into a garden.

It was idyllic. Impossibly idyllic. So much light and air and space. There had to be a catch: why hadn't this suburb been bought up, built up? Why weren't people clamouring to live here?

We drove around marking the plots we thought had potential on a survey map supplied by an estate agent. There weren't many. Because the sea view was to the side some houses were built outwards on stilts in an effort to extend beyond their neighbour. As a result they completely blocked off this aspect for anyone who might try to build on the site alongside. Nevertheless there were two or three options.

And then we turned into a cul de sac. On the left-hand side the penultimate plot had a for sale notice. The map showed a strange five-sided erf with a narrow fifteen metre road frontage. Almost a panhandle. I stopped the car next to the for sale notice, facing down the hill. I could see the vlei, the beach, and farther along the peninsula, Boulders Beach and the rocks at Miller's Point. A little into the bay was Roman Rock lighthouse. Beyond that rose Cape Hangklip, where from the beginning of the eighteenth century until slavery was abolished in 1834 a community of runaways had lived, free of bondage but never able to return home. In the distance the sea seemed to rise into the sky.

I tried to break a path into the plot but it was so densely overgrown with fynbos and aliens that only a powerfully wielded machete would have made any inroads. To the side of the plot was a brown face-brick house shaped in a u with the two arms extending towards the sea.

At the end of the nearest arm was a bedroom, at the end of the other arm, a lounge. The connecting passage between the two arms was glass and slightly raised: from there the view was ideal. Nevertheless the house was intimidating, flat-roofed with a damp brick-paved court-yard between the arms. As it was empty we snooped around. From the lawn I was able to bundu-bash my way onto the panhandle plot. I discovered that after gently sloping down the handle the topography plunged quite steeply into the pan. I liked this instantly. Here we would be away from the street, entirely in our own world. I stood still. A striped field mouse rushed across a small patch of vacant sand. The air was filled with birdsong. I heard the crackle of the mouse in the bush. At that moment I was convinced this was where we would have to live …

Five months before we moved out of Muizenberg a nearby cottage was let to new tenants [the bywoners]. The previous tenants were a quiet, considerate, elderly couple who'd lived there for five years. In their stead came the original neighbours from hell. On the day they arrived there was no mistaking what bad news they would be: they revved their cars, they swore, they shouted, they played loud music, and that afternoon they drank brandy and coke on the pavement. 'Now everybody will know we're a party family,' shouted the mother, toasting the street in general …

In the sixteen years I lived in Muizenberg I had to call the police out half a dozen times. Three of those calls were in the last six months and they had to do with the bywoners. The last time was at three o'clock one Friday morning in November. We were woken by loud music. The bywoners had their door closed but the lights were on and the house rocked. The matriarch's cackle came rattling above the thump-ing. We wondered what to do. I wasn't going to confront them but we couldn't ignore this and go back to sleep. We called the police. Five minutes later the bywoners exploded on to the stoep. Now frustrated and angry, we both went out to remonstrate with them. They paid us no heed and we retreated saying we would call the police. The cops duly arrived and through the blinds we watched the ensuing fracas as the matriarch stood hands on hips in the doorway, swearing and shouting at the constables.

'Who are you?' she screamed. 'You're not the police from Muizenberg. I know the police from Muizenberg. So why don't you come with your casspirs and lock us up?'

She pushed at the cop. He swore at her and pushed her back. Why didn't he arrest her? But no, the slanging match and the pushing and shoving continued. The two policemen retreated to their van. The thug-like youth tried to square up to them. Then, enraged, he shook his fist at our house and shouted: 'You must watch out. Pasop. I'll get you. You wit naaiers.' The police drove away. The thug continued his litany against our house. 'Where's a stone? Pasop! Watch out! You wit naaiers!' He was restrained and the bywoners trooped inside, laughing that they had bested the cops. The street resumed its quiet but Jill and I went back to bed with real concerns about what retribution would follow.

As it happened there was no sequel. For the bywoners it was just another incident, nothing out of the ordinary. We might be trembling with trepidation but to them a confrontation with the police meant nothing and even the thuggish youth had forgotten his threats. The more I thought about the incident the more it clarified the violence of the bywoners' lives. Their response to challenge was instant aggression. For them the world was a wild place and the only way to survive in it was to fight everything. Also, although they were white, they understood that skin colour no longer gave them the edge in this battle. There was a certain irony in their lack of prejudice for they understood the politics of race and expressed it eloquently. That the thug had called me a 'wit naaier' meant he interpreted white in class terms, and identified himself with an underclass that in this instance was coloured.

It was, in many respects, a matter of them against the world. Certainly I marvelled that in such a crowded household there should be no infighting. Only once did the 'skivvy' break down and rail against the family. But he was drunk and despite threatening to leave, the next day he was fetching and carrying as usual. His was the only outburst I witnessed, and although the baby boys were verbally abused and frequently smacked, the family lived in remarkable harmony.

Their language was violent, but so debased that the words no longer carried meaning. Instead they were ugly guttural detonations of sound. One of the most frequently used words was 'poes'. The baby boys were both called poes, only the tone indicating when the term was endearing and when it was censorious. Similarly 'poes' could as easily be an exclamation of pleasure as an outburst of anger. The masculine woman in particular was adept at communicating using two words 'fok' and 'poes' in 'sentences' where the pauses between the words supplied the meaning. So, trying to dissuade one of the boys from eating bubble gum he had pulled off the pavement, she said: 'Fok poes poes. Poes. Poes. Fokpoes.' Loosely translated into a middle-class mum's language this could be rendered as: 'Poofy, darling, dirty. No. No. Awful.' …

More than a year has passed and the constant noise of the social issues that made Muizenberg compelling but an impossible place to live are memories. Whereas daily life there was determined by people – the voices of those rushing to catch early morning trains, followed by children heading for school, the mid-morning vegetable sellers, the postman, the fighting of the afternoon drunks – in Glencairn the pattern could not be more different. It is set by birds, the colour of the sea, the shift of the sun about the house, the screech of cicadas.

We wake to the piping of francolins picking through the garden and the squabbling of guinea fowl in the firebreak. During the day the birdsong is from prinias, bulbuls, bokmakieries, and the high-pitched twittering of sunbirds. Late most afternoons a southern boubou raucously dodges through the bushes after insects and in the evening four white-backed ravens come down the valley swooping over the roofs, heading for their roost in the quarry. The birds define the seasons too for in spring I often woke at night to nightjars calling across the mountain. By summer they were gone but then a pair of steppe buzzards perched on the black trees (the ghosts of the Storkwinkel tree) that I can see through the study window.

Each morning at breakfast we gaze enthralled over False Bay, having learnt to tell how the day will unfold by the blueness of the early morning sea. Last winter we watched long strings of cormorants pass low over the water and huge shoals of yellowtail stream across the bay in a frenzy. There have been schools of dolphins, and, of course, the whales …

The southeaster is a phenomenon we have been forced to take into our lives. Although we have lived with this wind for twenty years and know that it can topple buses and snatch off roofs, the narrow streets of Muizenberg were remarkably protected. The wind went over the top of the houses.

For our first few days in Glencairn the southeaster was down and then one afternoon a breeze went to gale force in a matter of hours. Being half way up a mountain, facing south east there was nothing to protect us. Hour after hour for five days the wind banged against the house. It screeched under the doors and through the rebates, it rattled in the ceiling. Gripped with anxiety I lay awake for most of the gale's first night imagining that at any moment the roof would be torn away. The wind was not a constant blast: what made it so frightening were pockets of stillness that could last as long as a minute. Suddenly the rushing noise would stop. Ordinary sounds would return: a dog barking across the valley, a distant car accelerating, the hum of the fridge. As the silence lengthened the tension became unbearable. When would it strike? Perhaps it was dying down? Then came a thrashing as the wind struck into the trees and barrelled up the valley until it boomed against our house. My chest would constrict, my heart thump; sometimes I buried my head beneath the pillow. After three days our nerves were raw. We began to wonder if we had made a dreadful mistake. We heard of people who had been defeated by the southeaster and retreated to the older suburbs where the wind was not a psychological condition. We were also told that we'd get used to it. So we bought ear plugs and set about accepting that at least half of the summer would be at gale force. If once I had been picked out for joking about living on a wind-blown peninsula, the joke was now on me.

But after another season of southeasters we have become acclimatised: not used to it, rather hardened against it. The wind still frays our nerves and after three days of a blow I can sense a tightening of the skin at my temples and a brittleness in our conversation. We are far out to sea on a roaring trade wind. We listen to the house, to its creaking and thumping the way sailors must have listened to the timber and rigging of their ships as they rounded the Cape. We listen with some dread, but know there will be calm days to come.

Side by Side, Far Apart (1997)

MICHAEL AV MORRIS

The Greeffs' house seems deserted but for a pair of outraged Rottweilers whose single ambition is finding a way through the solid brick and steel wall between us.

There's no need to ring the bell – the dogs have raised the alarm, and Mrs Greeff – Joey Greeff – emerges from the rear of the property.

There's an air of apprehension, of guardedness, about her, but she takes me in through the gate at the back, to an unexpected Eden, the shaded beginnings of a palm nursery. She turns the tap off and seems quite cheerful for a moment, standing among the dripping fronds. Soon, she says, they'll be ready for sale, but there's still much to be done, repotting, watering, nurturing the tough plants.

This is not the subject of my visit, though, and we go back to the dusty lane.

Ten metres away, less perhaps, is a dull grey vibracrete wall topped with a shaggy fringe of ripped plastic, snagged in the coils of barbed wire. It is less a garden wall than a border: Masiphumelele is just on the other side. By any standards, the contrast is striking.

On this side is an imposing, white double-storey house, the sort of home you'd expect at the leafy centre of an estate. On the other side, less than a stone's throw away, is a treeless, sandy expanse dotted with utilitarian toilet blocks and rows of shacks made of wood, iron and plastic.

With exasperation, I think, Joey Greeff actually laughs as she describes 'how terrible' it is, not because she thinks it's funny, just implausible. Joey and her husband, Willex, have lived here in Chasmay Road, for seven years. In this time, they have built their own house and laid out the garden.

Then, a few years ago, the bulldozers moved in and, later, the shack-dwellers. Mrs Greeff does not talk about race, though the temptation to cast her calumniously into a racist mould springs from the limited range of merely expedient concepts we invariably use to make sense of each other.

At any rate, if the colour of her neighbours matters, it matters less than other things. 'The smell, the fleas, the noise, the rubbish ... you cannot live like this,' she says without compromise.

'Who will buy this house?', she wonders bitterly, and provides the hopeless answer without pause: 'Nobody. Their bedrooms are right there, just metres away from the wall. The noise at the weekends is unbearable'.

There are two things the Greeffs want: a 50 metre wide roadway between their property and Masiphumelele, and houses, brick houses, where now there are shacks.

'You cannot tell me that with that government subsidy (R17 250) all you can do is put up a small toilet. We want houses here so that there's a buffer zone between us and the shacks.'

Mrs Greeff says that she feels 'so sorry for them (the Masiphumelele people), living under plastic and zinc in the wind and sand. And the fire threat is very real. Fifteen houses have already burned down. It is so grim (wreed) here.'

Almost as an afterthought, she adds: 'You cannot walk around at night. I have had to put up 16 mm thick burglar bars. My house is a prison.'

Not far off on the other side of the wall is plot 2667, with its peach toilet block, and the bare ribs of a makeshift boundary fence.

It is in the name of twenty-something Ndileka Gloria Ortman, mother, computer tutor, aspirant meat-vendor and long-time Noord-hoek resident. She is pleased to have her own place.

'I have lived in Noordhoek since 1973. My mother, Margaret, worked on a farm, then. Life was very hard. One day, after 18 years on the farm, they chased us away because my father didn't come to work on the Saturday.'

She has a tape recording of the family's history, which tells 'how we lived on the farm, and then at Khayelitsha, in tents. It was a terrible life'.

Ms Ortman did her schooling in Ocean View, but has continued learning new skills since. She earned enough from painting pottery to pay for part-time computer classes at Imhoff's Gift Farm, learning all the latest word-processing and windows programmes. She now uses these skills to teach others at Masiphumelele in a computer centre donated by Old Mutual. With three other teachers, she shares the R40 fee each pupil pays for a four-week course.

'We train people, men and women of all ages, so that they can do secretarial work.'

She has also done a course in helping abused women and children and wants to 'get active in this community'.

Responding to financial need, Ms Ortman ran her own meat business, until the repair bills for the car that was indispensable to the enterprise forced her to quit.

Now she wants to buy a bakkie to get the meat business going again.

'I started my business with R300, and it went well. But I did not manage to save anything because of the car problems. I used to go to Lynedoc near Stellenbosch every morning and buy offal and sheep's heads and bring it back and keep it in the fridge, then go out and sell from 4pm when people were coming back from work.'

She would sell upwards of R2 000 worth of meat a week, 'and I always worked in cash at Lynedoc'.

If Ndileka Ortman's new 'home' is still just an empty, sandy plot with a toilet block on it, the house she still lives in with her mother and other members of the family is pretty, comfortable and well-equipped.

Number 1657 – which is actually the plot number – in Mothopeng Street has walls of wood and board, covered with strips of floral wallpaper. There are four bedrooms, a pretty lounge with easy chairs, a couch and a television set. The kitchen has a stove, fridge, microwave and washing machine, as well as cupboards and table and chairs. The house has a telephone. Geraniums and irises bloom at the foot of a clipped hedge along the front of the modest property.

She will be moving out soon, filled with hope and ambition. She wants eventually to build a brick house. She also wants to launch aerobic classes. And get abused women working together.

Not least, she hopes to meet more of the white people living on the outside so that 'we can speak to each other, and so we can tell them that we can be together'.

It would be helpful, she feels, 'if the people outside accept us. I know there are some (Masiphumelele) people who are difficult, breaking into houses and things like that, but most of us are not like that, we would like to work with them (whites).

'What we do not like is that white people treat us like dogs. It is not all whites. We know that. There are some nice people, but most people living next to us are negative.'

Standing at her new plot, where she poses self-consciously for a photograph, the wind tears the sand off the plot and blasts it across the new neat kerb of the road. In an uncanny echo of Joey Greeff's sentiments, Ms Ortman says: 'The worst thing is the sand. And, in 10 years' time, I hope to see a lot of brick houses here because even with electricity, the wooden houses are still burning down.'

The Ndileka Ortmans of Masiphumelele are not helpless people. Their stamina in coping with the hostile or indecisive attitude – and, latterly, the limited capacity – of a succession of administrative authorities is matched by initiative, a measure of entrepreneurship and patience, even if the life has taken its toll, has bred alcoholism, abuse, despair.

Theirs are undeniably middle-class aspirations, and middle-class achievements too. It is the basis of a sufficient, if unexplored, common cause: what the 'outside' communities want is wanted on the inside too – better houses, better standards, better lives.

Even if the origin of the dilemma cannot be altered and the value systems are still at odds, there is at least shared self-interest. The key to a rapprochement is there – has probably always been there, if the communities would only reach out and find it.

What is also plain is that beyond meeting its basic obligations, the organs of state and civil authority have neither the resources nor perhaps even the mandate to make it work. If Noordhoek valley is to thrive, if its precious environment is to survive, and its disparate communities are to forge a common vision, it will be up to the Joey Greeffs and Ndileka Ortmans to help make it happen.

Either that, or an inconclusive fractiousness will continue to define an awkward divide between poor and better-off, and between white and black. It is as true of Noordhoek as it is of Hout Bay, and the Vrygronds and Marconi Beams of the present and the future.

It is, ultimately, the difficult, compelling truth of the new South Africa.

from Intricacy (2005)

MICHAEL COPE

Clifton was a different place when we came back. During the time that we had been away, the entire scene of our early childhood had been demolished and replaced with blocks of flats, which now loomed over the beach like some vast flattened Roman Colosseum.

I make a trip to Clifton forty-nine years after the events recorded in [his mother] Lesley's diary, hoping, if not to catch some glimpse of the earlier configuration, to capture an image of the actual place as it now exists, which I can compare with the old photographs. It is mid-morning on a perfect day, the 29th of February, the late summer sun bright in a blue and windless sky. We park on the road above Second Beach, opposite the block of flats called Heron Water. There is a curious tension for me in the buildings along Victoria Road, for they have each been gutted and remade many times since the 1950s, and each remake, while retaining some vague sense of the original shape, has moved successively in the direction which we call rich. It is as though I have arrived among a collection of ageing wives of wealthy men, all of whom I somehow know or ought to know, but who have had so many face-lifts, hair-transplants, lipo-suctions and the like, each dictated by ever-shifting tastes, that I can no longer claim with confidence to recognise them. The Clifton Hotel is no longer there, but a building consisting of several apartments still retains some semblance of its original shape. There is no public access and the periphery of the site is surrounded by formidable quantities of blade-wire. The pathway from Victoria Road to the top of the stairs leading down to the sand is still there, and it still looks as I remember it. But, like the former hotel, it is edged by a frill of blade-wire and the stakes, mesh and fencing to support it. The pathway is the same one which connected the stairs to the road before we left Clifton, but the stairs are not. These stairs, now much ground down by sandy feet, are the very ones which replaced the original wooden stairs during our absence in the Eastern Transvaal, and which appeared like a genie's palace on our return. The pathways remain the responsibility of the city and not of the extremely wealthy people who have come to own the land and houses that they connect, and that is no doubt why they have changed so little ...

The beach is almost deserted. One or two young people with unusually well-maintained bodies lie in the sun. Apart from our twins, there are no children at all. I climb over the rocks past Baby's Beach to Moses Beach. Among the rocks are pools with sandy anemones, seaweed and tiny fishes. The mussels are packed densely on the rocks, but all are younger than those that Jack [Cope] and Lesley would pluck to cook.

At Moses Beach, all of the structures above the left side of the beach have been broken down, and recently, for the workers are still busy, their vast cranes hovering over the cement-lined pit that has been excavated in the place where I had expected to see the residences of the Foxes, the Gillises, the Rabkins and many other families. Only the shoreline and ocean seem unchanged, the hard granite of the boulders having worn so little as to make no discernible difference.

I seek out one particular spot on the rock that we called 'red box rock' because of the life-saving box with its float and spool of rope. When I say 'spot', I mean it quite literally, but when I say that I 'seek', I am speaking figuratively: one of the older boys – someone of Raymond's generation, perhaps – had in 1959 found a small pot of sky-blue eye-shadow left behind by a sunbather, and with it had marked a thick greasy blue spot on the rock.

The mark made there before we left Clifton outlasted the bungalows. Its secret placement on the side of the red box rock (one had to climb onto a ledge to be able to see it) may have helped to preserve it, for it lasted many years, and I can remember climbing out onto the ledge to find it or its diminishing vestiges shortly after every arrival at Clifton. The spot of make-up has, of course, been gone for many years now, and the rock itself gives no clue as to its original situation. Does a memory that is accurate to within a metre or two count as accurate in any sense?

As I leave First Beach, I notice that at the bottom of the stairs are two steps and the ghost of a third leading into a blank wall. They were the first of about eight or nine steps which once led to our home …

When I tell people that I started my life at Clifton there is a noticeable shift in the way they regard me. 'Oh, well,' they say or think, 'you *have* been spoiled.' This is because they are reading the situation in terms of current demography. The smallest property there, even a bachelor apartment, now costs many millions, even in hard currencies; the Clifton Lifestyle is thus available only to the extremely wealthy.

When we lived there, however, this was not the case. The bungalows were, by and large, owned by the city and in poor repair. There were some wealthy people, but they tended to occupy the few freehold properties. The rest were middle-class or lower-middle class, bohemians and the like. Our neighbours were a council inspector, a motor mechanic, a clerk, and their wives, who were housewives. All of the residents at Clifton were, as the law required, white.

Trinity Hall, while not exactly a hovel, rose above that status only by having sewerage, running water and electricity. The roof leaked, the corrugated-iron walls at the back were rusty, the wooden planks at the front were rotten, and the embankment behind the house teetered on the verge of collapse. In big winter storms, the waves would breach the wall below and wash around the house, oozing in under the doors. The bungalow was freehold and was owned by one Billy Ray, as my mother's 1955 diary records. It had fallen, around that time, under the shadow of development, for the 1950s was the time when, all over the world, older buildings were torn down as if in an effort to match the depredations of the recent war, and blocks of self-similar flats were built to replace them.

Lesley's diary records that during that time, she and Jack discussed the possibility of renovating the place with Billy Ray, called in their friend Jack Barnett to draw up renovations, and had them approved, only to have the approval withdrawn as Ray wavered under the pressures of developers to sell. Some time after we left in 1958, but before we returned two years later, the bungalow was sold. Jack and Uys [Krige] together bought another bungalow, just two houses away, for, as I recall it, ten thousand pounds. They were still paying it off a decade later. After this, Raymond and I spent the long holidays, in winter and summer, with Jack and Uys: a total of nine weeks every year. The rest of the time was spent on the farm with Lesley.

Sea Girt, as the new house was called, was not much more up-market than Trinity Hall, and Jack, who was uncomfortable without some daily physical work, did such maintenance as he could, but the salt air attacked the corrugated-iron and all other metal continuously. The bathroom was slowly sliding downhill, the floor cracked and sloped. We had a lavatory with a pull-chain, and a telephone that rang an electric bell.

During the 1960s, wealth started to drift into Clifton as residents took advantage of the ability to sell their ninety-nine-year leases. Bungalows were refurbished and extended, had decks and picture-windows installed. By the mid-1960s, our bungalow was one of the more scruffy ones on the beach, and I still remember the shame I felt as my friends sang 'My name is Jack and I live in a shack,' after a popular song of the time ...

July holidays at Clifton were cold and rainy. The Atlantic ocean, churned by the north-west wind which came in winter in the form of cold wet low-pressure systems, threw up breakers which beat against the rocks, washed the sand from the beaches and out into the bay, and churned the water into a yellowish-white foam, which coated the surface for hundreds and hundreds of yards, like an ice floe, and which, when deposited on the rocks and the remaining sand, covered them with a wobbling, gleaming mass of tenacious bubbles that smelled of the sea and of the many tiny dying creatures who had given of their substance to make the foam. It dried and left streaks the colour of mustard on the white sand.

When the northwester piled the waves up high, they loomed like mountains, crossed the beach and sometimes even crossed the wall in front of our bungalow, so that it was a simple matter to imagine that Lion's Head, the mountain which rose behind us and dominated our skyline, was itself a wave and that it might at any moment break. Sometimes to this day, the waves and the mountain merge in my dreams and the rising water, whipped with foam, rises higher than the peaks and obliterates everything.

The Wrong Side of the Cape (2003)

RIAN MALAN

In the final analysis it was all the contessa's fault, she being my wife, a chic and glamorous Latina who grew up in Coral Gables, studied at Brandeis, left the USA in disgust during the Reagan era, and lived for many years in Paris only to wind up in Johannesburg, a vulgar city of new money, low culture, and rising crime. She learned Zulu and tolerated the city for a year or two but never quite saw the point of all the guns, guard dogs, and paranoia, the ugliness of the city in winter, the harshness of the light, the veld burned gray by frost and cold, and the houses on our street grimly disfigured by steel burglar bars and electric fences. When our neighbor was carjacked in his own driveway, she put her foot down. "I hate it here," she said. "It's this country or me."

She wanted to get out of Africa, but for me, leaving was unthinkable; my interests and obsessions are entirely African, and my roots in this country are more than three centuries deep. I love Africa, even love Johannesburg, in spite of its problems. On the other hand, I love my wife, too, so we drove down to Cape Town in search of a compromise.

And here I must confess that I was ashamed to tell friends I was even contemplating such a move. Cape Town may be the most beautiful city on the planet, but we Jo'burg dudes see it as something of a fool's paradise, a last refuge for white colonials driven out of black Africa by the winds of change. The first such settlers were rich Belgians displaced from their coffee estates in the Congo by the troubles of 1961. In their wake, as empires toppled, came white hunters from Tanganyika, tobacco barons from Southern Rhodesia, tea moguls from Nyasaland, and a band of aristocratic white Kenyans led by the Honorable Mrs. Patricia Cavendish O'Neill, daughter of the Countess of Kenmare, who set her beloved lions free on the Serengeti and retreated to an estate near Cape Town in the early seventies.

The trickle became a flood in 1980, when Robert Mugabe rose to power in neighboring Zimbabwe. The flood doubled after 1984, when Johannesburg and its surrounds were convulsed by a bloody anti-apartheid struggle, and doubled again in the early 1990's, when South Africa seemed to be sliding into a race war. We were spared that fate by Nelson Mandela and F. W. de Klerk, but their triumph precipitated a new influx of paradise hunters, lured this time by the perplexing (to outsiders) victory in our epochal 1994 elections of the conservative and mostly white-led National Party, which regained leadership in Cape Town and the Western Cape province.

For apprehensive whites, this was an amazing development: history seemed to be allowing whites to eat their cake and still have it, offering them the chance to practice democracy in Africa while continuing to live in a society where power was in the reassuring hands of "people like us." Thousands pulled up stakes in the hinterland and flocked to the Mother City. Immigrants arrived. Investments poured in. The economy boomed. Cape Town mutated almost overnight into one of the most stylish tourist destinations on the planet, thronged by aristocrats, film stars, and Eurotrash. Michael Jackson came shopping for real estate. Margaret Thatcher's son Mark settled here, as did Earl Spencer, brother of Princess Diana. By 2001 Cape Town had become, for me, a place where fools sat on sea-view terraces, sipping white wine and congratulating one another for finding a corner of Africa that was somehow immune to the chaos engulfing the rest of the continent. The contessa wanted to join them. I had reservations.

It's difficult to explain, but moving to Cape Town struck me as an admission of defeat. "This isn't really Africa, you know," Capetonians are always saying, and they're right, in a way. There are streets in downtown Cape Town that resemble New York or London, and in summer the city is overrun by camera crews shooting international TV commercials. The Atlantic seaboard is sometimes mistaken for the French Riviera. Out in the nearby Winelands, the oak groves and pastures are somehow European in their gentleness, and the arid west coast easily doubles for Spain. As for the better suburbs, frame your shot to exclude dramatic mountain backdrops and smoke from the shacks where poor blacks live, and you're in an upper-middle-class anywhere: Connecticut, Marin County, Surrey, or Neuilly.

Look at this, I told the contessa. It's totally unreal, a citadel of delusions, a generically Western whites-only moon base in Africa. No way, I said; my friends in Johannesburg will laugh at me. I wanted a log cabin in the wilderness near Cape Point, where we could live a simple life of spartan purity among trees tormented into strange shapes by howling gales, uncompromised by such bourgeois comforts as electricity and running water. You're nuts, she said, so we looked at Franschhoek, in my childhood a lovely valley of whitewashed cottages with plots out back where one could keep dogs and grow vegetables. Three decades on, it was still lovely, but it had somehow become more Provençal than even Provence. African farms had mutated into wine estates with names like L'Ormarins and Haute Cabrière, and the main road was lined with restaurants serving pretentious French cuisine.

The contessa was enchanted. This is even worse than the moon base, I sneered. Our marriage was apparently in deep trouble, but we were saved by St. James.

St. James is a suburb on the Indian Ocean side of the Cape Peninsula – the wrong side, in the estimation of real estate agents who kept trying to steer us to the Atlantic seaboard, where you pay millions for a water view. So what? Sea is sea, and on Cape Town's Atlantic side it's always freezing and thus of little use other than as a backdrop for parties on terraces. The sea at St. James was something else entirely, a giant horseshoe of sparkling blue, ringed by mountains, warm enough for swimming in summer and full of interesting sights besides. On the day we first came, the bay was full of whales. There were surfers on the reef at Danger Beach, swimmers in the breakers. There was a real fishing harbor nearby, with real fishermen, real fish stink, and real winos on the dilapidated boardwalk. There was even a slum, a once-grand holiday resort now running to seed and populated mostly by French-speaking Africans who had fled Zaire when the dictator Mobutu was toppled by rebels in 1997.

Intrigued, we returned the next day for a closer look, parking on the far side of Muizenberg, a mile north, and walking south along "millionaires' row." Here, capitalists with vast gold and diamond holdings once maintained stately summerhouses on a beach so huge and empty, you can still ride a horse for four hours in the direction of the sunrise and not come to the end of it. The great British imperialist Cecil John Rhodes established the vogue, buying a cottage here in 1899. He was followed by Williams and Rudd, his right-hand men. Then came Sir Ernest Oppenheimer, South Africa's richest man, soon to be joined by Sir Herbert Baker, a society architect whose houses of sandstone and Burma teak were all the rage among Johannesburg's smart set. Sir J. B. Robinson stayed with his daughter, Ida, the Countess Labia, who built a rococo palace next door to another mining magnate, Sir Abe Bailey. On a midsummer's day in the 1920's, the concentration of wealth in this mile of rock, sand, and mountainside would have rivaled anything outside the United States.

By the time we arrived, it had all vanished. The great capitalist dynasties had died out or moved their bases of operation to London. The grand houses along Beach Road had become sad Baptist seminaries and the like, and the waterfront hotels were slum tenements.

Also lost to time and emigration was the Jewish community that once thrived in the warren of crooked alleys and old stone houses away from the seashore. Bernard Bendix's electrical shop had become a speakeasy. Alf Rohm's kosher dairy stood empty, and the store next door was a Congolese barbershop, gaily painted in the French national colors and surmounted by the inscrutable slogan THE MOLOKAI IS ONE. Beyond Rhodes's cottage we came to St. James, a place from the time before cars, where Edwardian houses stood on terraces cut into the mountainside, reachable only by steep lanes overhung by rioting bougainvillea. In its day, St. James was to WASPS what Muizenberg was to Jews, a very English, very colonial outpost populated by merchants and bankers who would trip down the lanes of a morning in pin-striped suits and take the steam train into Cape Town, a journey of about 40 minutes. Their wives cultivated English gardens and croquet lawns, and were at pains to stress that they did not live in Kalk Bay, the enclave adjoining, because Kalk Bay had Creole or "Cape colored" people in it, once considered very dé-classé. Today, Kalk Bay is fashionable (at least among white bohemians) for much the same reason: it is one of the pitifully few racially mixed communities to have survived apartheid largely unscathed.

This was at least inadvertently the doing of a policeman named Tommy Carse, who came to Kalk Bay in 1940 to keep watch over the mostly Cape colored fishermen who lived there, working the bay in small wooden boats. Carse was white, but his heart was open. He started writing down old men's stories about disasters, miraculous rescues, whale hunts in open rowing boats, and the community's battle against storms and corporate trawlers. He eventually published a book that in turn became a state-sponsored documentary about a magical little village with cobblestoned alleys, where Cape colored fishermen lived simply but happily under the guardianship of their benevolent white superiors. It won awards at Cannes and Edinburgh and was seen by 80 million people worldwide.

Twenty years after Carse moved in, the mad scientists of apartheid arrived in Kalk Bay and were disturbed to find people of various races living in attached houses, and even, God forbid, intermarrying. Arguing that this was counter to the laws of nature, they decreed that all those with dark skin or curly hair were to be banished. The citizens of Kalk Bay took to the streets with protest placards, cut down the whites only signs on their beach, and threatened to let the whole world know that the community immortalized by Constable Carse was about to be destroyed by heartless racists. The government backed off, and the Cape colored fisherfolk of Kalk Bay lived on to be far more sorely threatened by gentrification, or more exactly, by people like me, yuppies who cringe at the thought of being mistaken for foolish colonials on the run from African reality.

I was not alone. The local real estate agent, Dalene, told us she had 27 buyers lined up with cash in hand, but there were no Kalk Bay properties for sale at any price. She did, however, have something in St. James, an ugly modern house high on the mountainside, with awe-inspiring views of mountains and sea. Standing on the veranda, we could see all the way from Cape Point northeast to the brooding peaks of Groot Drakenstein, almost 90 miles in the distance. The contessa thought a neighborhood so quaint could not fail to rebound again. I thought its charm lay in the fact that much of it was in decline, and thus mercifully free of delusion and vanity. We bought the place and saved our marriage.

Before we came to live here, I had always sensed something odd about Cape Town. For a visitor, the city is maddeningly difficult to come to grips with, a place of enclaves, each introverted and provincial in a different way, inhabited by people who seemed quietly abstracted and self-absorbed, as if their minds were on higher things. "Pretty place, stupid people," says my friend Adrian, who avoids Cape Town when possible – an astute summation, but not exactly right. After living a month or two in St. James, it dawned on me that the people among whom we had settled were less stupid than stupefied, so overwhelmed by beauty and so profoundly humbled by nature that displays of wit had come to seem superfluous.

Curious changes take place in your brain when you move to Cape Town. You get up in the morning, scurry out to make your fortune, and come face-to-face with an awesome sight – the sea, a storm, clouds streaming over mountain crags – that reminds you of your utter insignificance in the grand scheme of things. Your ambition starts flagging. You buy fewer and fewer newspapers, and grow less and less interested in what's happening across town, let alone in the larger world. In due course, visitors from more exciting cities start yawning at your dinner table, appalled by the banality of your conversation. The other night we spent hours analyzing the strange behavior of a great white shark that patrols our stretch of coast, nudging canoeists but never eating them. Then we moved on to another pressing issue: What are whales actually doing when they stand on their heads and wave their giant flukes in the air?

Our visitors rolled their eyes. You could see they felt sorry for us, but the feeling was mutual because they had no conception of the unbearable bliss of fine summer days when the water is warm and the figs are ripe and you are woken at dawn by a murderous sun rising over the peaks across the bay. The day begins with breakfast on the terrace and a plunge into the cool green depths of a rock pool at the foot of our mountain, followed perhaps by a cappuccino in one of Kalk Bay's sidewalk cafés. By now it's nine and time to work, often difficult on account of the ceaseless drama outside my windows: tides rising, whales blowing, birds diving, shoals of fish passing through, and in the early afternoon, the boats coming back to Kalk Bay.

We whistle up the dogs and walk down to meet the boats, joining a great convergence of gulls, seals, fishmongers, and housewives coming to witness the daily landing. Crewmen sling their catch onto the wharf; hawkers cry the prices; dealers step forward to bid and haggle. On a good day, there will be great piles of yellowtail, red roman, and Cape salmon, but these prize fish mostly vanish into the hands of the restaurant trade, leaving the rest of us to bargain for snoek, a barracuda-like predator that comes in huge runs, sometimes driving the price down to a dollar for a yard-long fish, and another 50 cents to the garrulous old fishwife who guts it and tosses the innards into the harbor, to be snatched up by boiling seals. By now we're hot, so it's time for another swim, then the climb back to our mountainside aerie, where we smear the fish with the juice of figs and lemons from our garden, set it to grill on an open fire, uncork a bottle of wine, and watch the moon rise over the bay.

The next day is much the same, and the day after, the heat-stricken rhythm of it broken only by furious southeast gales and the coming and going of visitors who want to see things and go places. We take them to Boulders Beach, to swim with African penguins, or to Perima's, a funky little restaurant where Gayla Naicker serves the best curries in Africa, but after a few days they too subside into bewilderment. Why travel to tourist attractions when you're in one already? In season, tour buses park on the road above our house, disgorging foreigners who gape at the view and then turn their binoculars on us, clearly wondering what entitles us to live in such a place.

As our first summer wore on, I began asking myself the same question. The contessa saw it as a Calvinist problem and suggested I seek therapy, but for me, it was like withdrawing from an addiction. I'd spent much of my life thinking and writing about the terrors and ecstasy of life in Africa, always half-convinced that we were heading for some sort of catastrophe: race war, revolution, economic collapse, famine, extinction by AIDS. I just didn't know how to live in a place where no one seemed particularly worried about anything, even when there was a real crisis to agonize over. "Our currency is plummeting, sir!" a wino called out as I passed the other day. "Could it be that some of it will fall my way?"

He was white, the grizzled bum beside him was not, but they seemed to get along fine. The school over yonder was integrated, as were the beaches and bars along the seafront. Sure, almost everyone is poorer than he'd like to be, and the eyes of Kalk Bay coloreds still grow hooded when they talk about the insults of apartheid, but memories are fading, and nobody's going to war about it. The only truly unhappy man in my little world is Bishop Kitenge, the glamorous *personne d'élégance* who runs the Congolese barbershop in Muizenberg, and his pain is rooted in frustrated ambition: he wants to go to America but can't get a visa. "I must be star," he says, struggling a bit with his English. "I must go to Miami, and open beautiful salon. I love America!"

And that's about it for the bad news from St. James, other than an isolated incident in which some kids broke into my pickup, and the night the contessa woke up screaming that a leopard was in the garden. I fetched a flashlight and probed the darkness, and there it was, a leopard-spotted feline eating our dog food. Turned out to be a genet rather than a leopard, but still – a wild creature from the mysterious mountain that looms above and behind our home.

In winter, when the bay turns gray and cold and the fishing harbor is stormbound for weeks on end, we turn away to the mountain, bundle up in scarves, boots, and waterproof jackets, and take the dogs along a footpath that leads onto a bleak, misty plateau, part of a national park that runs 50 miles from Table Mountain to Cape Point. You can walk and climb for hours up there, with absolutely no sense of being in a city. If a storm catches you, you might even get lost and wander in circles until you die. Some days, the clouds part, sun pours down, and we find ourselves suspended in light between two oceans, the slopes around us strewn with wildflowers, and snow on the peaks of Groot Drakenstein, 60 miles away. Then the weather closes in again and we turn back for home, where we huddle around a fire sipping Cape brandy while rain taps against our windows.

The contessa believes this is how the Cape will always be. I wonder. I lift binoculars to the barrier of mountains that separates us from the African hinterland and think of all the trouble out there – the grinding convulsions of what the *Economist* calls "the hopeless continent." It seems inconceivable that the Cape should remain untouched, but here we are, sun-drugged and stupefied. Summer has returned, and the snoek are back in the bay. We grilled one on the fire last night, and fell asleep to the sighing and gurgling of whales, happy fools in an improbable African paradise.

Prepare to Repel Boarders (2006)

TOM EATON

The little Dutch family was translucently white where it stood gazing out to sea from the Promenade. They had swaddled themselves in linen so as to look like albino Touareg nomads, and submerged the child in the pram in some sort of heliocidal balm, but still they squirmed under the African sun. The infant began to steam from its nostrils, and flapped peevishly with fingers like bleached chipolatas at the clogs and cheeses that dangled from its mobile, but its parents were distracted, enchanted by being able to see their partner's entire skeleton, shining a bloody blue through the skin, when he or she stood in front of the sun.

The few dozen spectators who sizzled on the seafront clapped telescopes to their eyes when a sharp bang echoed off the lighthouse; but it had merely been the Dutch baby exploding, launching out of its pram in an elegant smoking arc and sizzling into a distant rock pool. Out in the bay, the yachts were motionless. The Volvo Ocean Race, it seemed, had not yet started.

Half an hour after the scheduled start they still lolled, looming over the flotilla of pleasure boats that swarmed about their sides, launches and catamarans half a flute of Moët away from foundering. Far out to sea a navy corvette chugged about, those crewmen who had joined the service via APLA now locked away in the bilges lest they give in to their urges and empty the for'ard anti-aircraft gun into a particularly gilded motorboat. A flare drifted down in the windless, dazzling sky. A horn sounded. Still nothing.

An hour later one had to conclude that the race was underway, and in the absence of any actual forward motion on the part of the yachts, one resorted to a strong pair of binoculars in the hope of seeing some salty tars swarming about in the rigging, or a second mate with a Polynesian beauty tattooed on his chest, dancing a hornpipe. At the very least they might have presented their audience with a grim party gathered about a shirtless, defiant mutineer, the sea dog strapped to the titanium wheel getting fifty lashes with a bungee for bringing the sponsors' name into disrepute.

But what was most confounding was the dearth of women on board. Melbourne, the fleet's next port of call, is about 10,300 kilometres from Cape Town; and given that they covered 14 metres in two hours and were therefore travelling at about 168 metres per day, it is really not unreasonable to extrapolate that they'll be docking roughly 170 years from now. Tackling such a voyage without at least a dozen crates of women on board is folly, not only because one requires offspring (140-year-old lookouts apparently tend towards myopia) but because women know how to stop and ask for directions.

Lunch had come and gone unnoticed in the strain to see anything resembling a wake, and so it was time to retire to a trendy sushi restaurant across the road. The glare inside was insufferable: there was not a single black diner in the room. It soon became apparent why. Sitting at the bar, perusing the specials, sat Wouter Basson.

Eyes downcast, looking as debonair and at ease as most clandestine biological weapons experts do in crowded restaurants, he didn't want to be recognized. Fortunately the clientele around him didn't seem the newspaper-reading variety. Indeed, they barely seemed the menu-reading variety, moving their Botoxed lips as they battled through difficult foreign words like 'saki'. No, this was the demographic who employ Arts graduates to read the papers for them, with instructions to act out the funny or diverting bits, and to show them the picture from the back page. Dr Death might as well have been on the moon.

I was suddenly overcome by a terrible desire to introduce myself to him, to ask him for an autograph for my girlfriend Ann Thrax. But how does one break the ice with Wouter Basson? 'I've got this nasty ringworm in my armpit and nothing I've tried has killed it. Do you think you could take a look?' Is it polite to ask if he always wanted to be Dr Death, or whether perhaps he started more modestly, maybe as Dr Discomfort, fighting liberation armies by shrinking their fatigues and lacing their rations with Brooklax?

The questions lingered, and so the did the yachts. When we left Wouter to his raw fish, they had moved another yard.

An Ocean Apart (2004)

TOM EATON

To the west of the Cape Peninsula lies the great Atlantic Ocean stretching all the way to South America. To the east lies the great Atlantic Ocean, stretching all the way to Cape Hangklip, which is rather like South America but with fewer monkeys. It's the same ocean. And it's easy to distinguish which side is which. The eastern bit is full of sharks and sewerage. The western bit is full of Eurotrash.

Unfortunately the most southerly tip of Africa, where the Atlantic and Indian oceans really do meet at Cape Agulhas, looks like a disused dumping site for building rubble. There are some rocks, some smaller rocks, some dead seaweed and a sign. The Japanese find it terribly disappointing, and deprived of the chance to film the anticipated battles between giant squid and sperm whales they resort to photographing the tour bus.

The Peninsula, on the other hand, ends in a spike straight out of Mordor, without the impending sense of doom. It's the sort of thing young lovers jump off. It's also inspired generations of Capetonians to lie about the confluence of the two great oceans.

Capetonians lie about all sorts of things. That they don't mind the wind. That dassies don't bite. That they've been to Robben Island and wept. It's not surprising that they've allowed themselves to become complicit in all this ugliness.

Their corruption is in stark contrast to the athletes [of the Two Oceans Marathon]. Nothing keeps one honest like 28 kilometres into a south-easter, turning around, and finding that the wind has become a north-wester. It is here that runners draw on their interior reserves and often disappear into their heads. Either that or they disappear into cars, carefully camouflaged by the side of the road under palm-fronds or penguin-guano, and re-emerge near the finish replete with a dramatic buttock cramp and expertly applied sweat-stains.

The loneliness of the long-distance runner is well documented. He is lonely because he smells a bit and he's not holding up his end of the conversation. But what is he thinking as he pounds along, rushing towards a future of arthritic knees and malignant melanomas on his scalp? Where do you go to, my lovely, when you're alone on Chappies?

The odds are he's trying to remember if he switched off the oven that morning. He knows he put the box of fish fingers back in the freezer, because the mixed veg fell on his foot. Then he checked the clock, just before 3am. And then he opened the oven and took out the fish and … no, it's gone. A cyclist, terribly confused searching desperately for the rest of the Argus pack, swerves late and tumbles out of sight over the railing.

No, he definitely did. The oven light was off and the fan was going. But did that mean it was cooling off or heating up? Ten clicks to go. Look, a giant squid battling a sperm whale. Also, it was ticking, like it was cooling off. Five clicks to go. But …

PRISON

from Long Walk to Freedom (1994)

Minutes later we approached the outskirts of Cape Town. Soon, we could see the little matchbox houses of the Cape Flats, the gleaming towers of downtown, and the horizontal top of Table Mountain. Then, out in Table Bay, in the dark blue waters of the Atlantic, we could make out the misty outline of Robben Island.

We landed at an airstrip on one end of the island. It was a grim, overcast day, and when I stepped out of the plane, the cold winter wind whipped through our thin prison uniforms. We were met by guards with automatic weapons; the atmosphere was tense but quiet, unlike the boisterous reception I had received on my arrival on the island two years before.

We were driven to the old jail, an isolated stone building, where we were ordered to strip while standing outside. One of the ritual indignities of prison life is that when you are transferred from one prison to another, the first thing that happens is that you change from the garb of the old prison to that of the new. When we were undressed, we were thrown the plain khaki uniforms of Robben Island.

Apartheid's regulations extended even to clothing. All of us, except Kathy [Ahmed Kathrada], received short trousers, an insubstantial jersey and a canvas jacket. Kathy, the one Indian among us, was given long trousers. Normally Africans would receive sandals made from car tyres, but in this instance we were given shoes. Kathy, alone, received socks. Short trousers for Africans were meant to remind us that we were 'boys'. I put on the short trousers that day, but I vowed that I would not put up with them for long.

The warders pointed with their guns to where they wanted us to go, and barked their orders in simple one-word commands: 'Move!' 'Silence!' 'Halt!' They did not threaten us in the swaggering way that I recalled from my previous stay, and betrayed no emotion.

The old jail was only temporary quarters for us. The authorities were in the process of finishing an entirely separate maximum-security structure for political prisoners. While there, we were not permitted to go outside or have any contact with other prisoners.

The fourth morning we were handcuffed and taken in a covered truck to a prison within a prison. This new structure was a one-storey rectangular stone fortress with a flat cement courtyard in the centre, about one hundred feet by thirty feet. It had cells on three of the four sides. The fourth side was a twenty-foot-high wall with a catwalk patrolled by guards with German shepherds.

The three lines of cells were known as sections A, B and C, and we were put in section B, on the easternmost side of the quadrangle. We were each given individual cells on either side of a long corridor, with half the cells facing the courtyard. There were about thirty cells in all. The total number of prisoners in the single cells was usually about twenty-four. Each cell had one window, about a foot square, covered with iron bars. The cell had two doors: a metal gate or grille with iron bars on the inside and a thick wooden door outside that. During the day, only the grille was locked; at night, the wooden door was locked as well.

The cells had been constructed hurriedly, and the walls were perpetually damp. When I mentioned this to the commanding officer, he told me our bodies would absorb the moisture. We were each issued with three blankets so flimsy and worn they were practically transparent. Our bedding consisted of a single sisal or straw mat. Later we were given a felt mat, and one placed the felt mat on top of the sisal one to provide some softness. At that time of year, the cells were so cold and the blankets provided so little warmth that we always slept fully dressed.

I was assigned a cell at the head of the corridor. It overlooked the courtyard and had a small eye-level window. I could walk the length of my cell in three paces. When I lay down, I could feel the wall with my feet and my head grazed the concrete at the other side. The width was about six feet, and the walls were at least two feet thick. Each cell had a white card posted outside it with our name and our prison service number. Mine read, 'N. Mandela 466/64', which meant I was the 466th prisoner admitted to the island in 1964. I was forty-six years old, a political prisoner with a life sentence, and that small cramped space was to be my home for I knew not how long …

That first week we began the work that would occupy us for the next few months. Each morning, a load of stones about the size of volleyballs was dumped by the entrance to the courtyard. Using wheelbarrows, we moved the stones to the centre of the yard. We were given either four-pound hammers, or fourteen-pound hammers for the larger stones. Our job was to crush the stones into gravel. We were divided into four rows, about a yard-and-a-half apart, and sat cross-legged on the ground. We were each given a thick rubber ring, made from tyres, in which to place the stones. The ring was meant to catch flying chips of stone, but hardly ever did so. We wore makeshift wire masks to protect our eyes.

Warders walked among us to enforce the silence. During those first few weeks, warders from other sections and even other prisons came to stare at us as if we were a collection of rare caged animals. The work was tedious and difficult; it was not strenuous enough to keep us warm but demanding enough to make all our muscles ache.

June and July were the bleakest months on Robben Island. Winter was in the air, and the rains were just beginning. It never seemed to go above 40 degrees Fahrenheit. Even in the sun, I shivered in my light khaki shirt. It was then that I first understood the cliché of feeling the cold in one's bones. At noon we would break for lunch. That first week all we were given was soup, which stank horribly. In the afternoons we were permitted to exercise for half an hour under strict supervision. We walked briskly around the courtyard in single file.

On one of our first days pounding rocks, a warder commanded Kathy to take a wheelbarrow filled with gravel to the truck parked by the entrance. Kathy was a slender fellow unused to hard physical labour. He could not shift the wheelbarrow. The warders yelled: '*Laat daardie kruiwa loop!*' ('Make that wheelbarrow move!')

As Kathy managed to nudge it forward, the wheelbarrow looked as if it would tip over, and the warders began to laugh. Kathy, I could see, was determined not to give them cause for mirth. I knew how to manoeuvre the wheelbarrows, and I jumped up to help him. Before being ordered to sit down, I managed to tell Kathy to wheel it slowly, that it was a matter of balance not strength. He nodded and then carefully moved the wheelbarrow across the courtyard. The warders stopped smiling.

The next morning, the authorities placed an enormous skip in the courtyard and announced that it had to be half full by the end of the week. We worked hard, and succeeded. The following week, the warder in charge announced that we must now fill the skip three-quarters of the way. We worked with great diligence, and succeeded. The next week we were ordered to fill the skip to the top. We knew we could not tolerate this much longer, but said nothing. We even managed to fill the skip all the way, but the warders had provoked us. In stolen whispers we resolved on a policy: no quotas. The next week we initiated our first go-slow strike on the island: we would work at less than half the speed we had before to protest at the excessive and unfair demands. The guards immediately saw this and threatened us, but we would not increase our pace, and we continued this go-slow strategy for as long as we worked in the courtyard.

Robben Island had changed since I had been there for a fortnight in 1962. In 1962 there were few prisoners; the place seemed more like an experiment than a fully-fledged prison. Two years later, Robben Island was without question the harshest, most iron-fisted outpost in the South African penal system. It was a hardship station not only for the prisoners but for the prison staff. Gone were the Coloured warders who had supplied cigarettes and sympathy. The warders, now white and overwhelmingly Afrikaans-speaking, demanded a master-servant relationship. They ordered us to call them *baas*, which we refused to do. The racial divide on Robben Island was absolute: there were no black warders, and no white prisoners.

Moving from one prison to another always requires a period of adjustment. But journeying to Robben Island was like going to another country. Its isolation made it not simply another prison, but a world of its own, far removed from the one we had come from. The high spirits with which we left Pretoria had been snuffed out by its stern atmosphere; we were face to face with the realization that our life would be unredeemably grim. In Pretoria we felt connected to our supporters and our families; on the island we felt cut off, and indeed we were. We had the consolation of being with each other, but that was the only consolation. My dismay was quickly replaced by a sense that a new and different fight had begun.

From the first day, I had protested about being forced to wear short trousers. I demanded to see the head of the prison and made a list of complaints. The warders ignored my protests, but by the end of the second week, I found a pair of old khaki trousers unceremoniously dumped on the floor of my cell. No pin-striped three-piece suit has ever pleased me as much. But before putting them on I checked to see if my comrades had also been issued with trousers.

They had not, and I told the warder to take the trousers back. I insisted that all African prisoners must have long trousers. The warder grumbled, 'Mandela, you say you want long pants and then you don't want them when we give them to you.' The warder baulked at touching trousers worn by a black man, and finally the commanding officer himself came to my cell to pick them up. 'Very well, Mandela,' he said, 'you are going to have the same clothing as everyone else.' I replied that if he was willing to give me long trousers, why couldn't everyone else have them? He did not have an answer …

One morning in early January, as we lined up to be counted before beginning work in the courtyard, we were instead marched outside and ordered into a covered truck. It was the first time that we had left our compound. No announcement was made as to our destination, but I had an idea of where we were headed. A few minutes later we emerged from the truck in a place that I had first seen when I was on the island in 1962: the lime quarry.

The lime quarry looked like an enormous white crater cut into a rocky hillside. The cliffs and the base of the hillside were blindingly white. At the top of the quarry were grass and palm trees, and at the base was a clearing with a few old metal sheds.

We were met by the commanding officer, Colonel Wessels, a rather colourless fellow who cared only about strict adherence to prison regulations. We stood at attention as he told us that the work we would be doing would last six months and afterwards we would be given light tasks for the duration of our terms. His timing was considerably off. We remained at the quarry for the next thirteen years.

After the CO's speech, we were handed picks and shovels and given rudimentary instructions as to the mining of lime. Mining lime is not a simple task. That first day, we were clumsy with our new tools and extracted little. The lime itself, which is the soft, calcified residue of seashells and coral, is buried in layers of rock, and one had to break through to it with a pick, and then extract the seam of lime with a shovel. This was far more strenuous than the work in the courtyard, and after our first few days on the quarry we fell asleep immediately after our supper at 4.30 in the afternoon. We woke the next morning aching and still tired.

The authorities never explained why we had been taken from the courtyard to the quarry. They may simply have needed extra lime for the island's roads. But when we later discussed the transfer, we assumed it was another way of enforcing discipline, of showing us that we were no different from the general prisoners – who worked in the island's stone quarry – and that we had to pay for our crimes just as they did. It was an attempt to crush our spirits.

But those first few weeks at the quarry had the opposite effect on us. Despite blistered and bleeding hands, we were invigorated. I much preferred being outside in nature, being able to see grass and trees, to observe birds flitting overhead, to feel the wind blowing in from the sea. It felt good to use all one's muscles, with the sun at one's back, and there was simple gratification in building up mounds of stone and lime.

Within a few days we were walking to the quarry, rather than going by truck, and this too was a tonic. During our twenty-minute march we got a better sense of the island, and could see the dense brush and tall trees that covered our home, and smell the eucalyptus blossoms, spot the occasional springbok or kudu grazing in the distance. Although some of the men regarded the march as drudgery, I never did ...

After arriving in the morning, we would fetch our picks, shovels, hammers and wheelbarrows from a zinc shed at the top of the quarry. Then we would assemble along the quarry face, usually in groups of three or four. Warders with automatic weapons stood on raised platforms watching us. Unarmed warders walked among us, urging us to work harder. '*Gaan aan! Gaan aan!*' ('Go on! Go on!'), they would shout, as if we were oxen.

By eleven, when the sun was high in the sky, we would begin to flag. By that time I would already be drenched in sweat. The warders would then drive us even harder. '*Nee, man! Kom aan! Kom aan!*' (No, man! Come on! Come on!') they would shout. Just before noon, when we would break for lunch, we would pile the lime into wheelbarrows and cart it over to the truck that would take it away.

At midday, a whistle would blow, and we would make our way to the bottom of the hill. We sat on makeshift seats under a simple zinc shed shielding us from the sun. The warders ate at a larger shed with tables and benches. Drums of boiled mealies were delivered to us. Hundreds of seagulls, screaming and swooping, circled above us, as we ate, and a well-aimed dropping could sometimes spoil a man's lunch.

We worked until four, when we again carted the lime to the waiting truck. By the end of the day, our faces and bodies were caked with white dust. We looked like pale ghosts except where rivulets of sweat had washed away the lime. When we returned to our cells, we would scrub ourselves in the cold water, which never seemed to rinse away the dust completely.

Worse than the heat at the quarry was the light. Our backs were protected from the sun by our shirts, but the sun's rays would be reflected into our eyes by the lime itself. The glare hurt our eyes and, along with the dust, made it difficult to see. Our eyes streamed and our faces became fixed in a permanent squint. It would take a long time after each day's work for our eyes to adjust to the diminished light.

After our first few days at the quarry, we made an official request for sunglasses. The authorities refused. This was not unexpected, for we were then not even permitted reading glasses. I had previously pointed out to the commanding officer that it did not make sense to permit us to read books but not to permit us glasses to read them with.

During the following weeks and months we requested sunglasses again and again. But it was to take us almost three years before we were allowed to have them, and that was only after a sympathetic physician agreed that the glasses were necessary to preserve our eyesight. Even then, we had to purchase the glasses ourselves.

For us, such struggles – for sunglasses, long trousers, study privileges, equalized food – were corollaries to the struggle we waged outside prison. The campaign to improve conditions in prison was part of the apartheid struggle. It was, in that sense, all the same; we fought injustice wherever we found it, no matter how large or how small, and we fought injustice to preserve our own humanity.

from Memoirs (2004)

AHMED KATHRADA

One of the questions most frequently asked of Robben Islanders is whether any serious thought was ever given to escape. The answer is yes. During the eighteen years I spent there, at least four plans were made, and one of them reached a fairly advanced stage before it was abandoned.

Jeff Masemola and Sedick Isaacs, with the help of some common-law prisoners, spent hours modifying the door to the wood camp and turning it into a makeshift raft. They worked in stages, so as not to alert the warders, and Sedick went as far as studying the tides and currents in order to determine the most favourable time to launch the bid to reach the mainland.

But they never got the chance, as one of their collaborators alerted warders to the plan, earning Sedick an extended sentence and six lashes.

Mac Maharaj also devised a plan involving the mainland. On a visit to a Cape Town dentist, he noticed an open window in the surgery, which offered just a short drop to the street below.

Mac put the plan to Mandela, who readily agreed that it might work. In due course, they both applied to see the dentist and, as luck would have it, an appointment was also made for Wilton Mkwayi on the same day. With their handcuffs removed, Mac and Madiba were actually standing in front of the open window, looking out at the surprisingly deserted street below, when they suddenly realised it could be a trap and abandoned the plan. If their suspicions were correct, it would have been an ideal opportunity for the authorities to rid themselves of Mandela by shooting him while trying to escape.

The 'Daniels Plan', by far the most ambitious, was to be implemented on New Year's Day 1981, about two years after Eddie's release. Eddie had discussed it with Madiba and Walter, who both agreed, but told Eddie the plan had first to be approved by the ANC's External Mission.

The first day of the year, a pubic holiday, had been deliberately chosen, as only a skeleton staff would be on duty. While the prisoners were in the exercise yard that morning, a helicopter, with Eddie on board, would hover overhead and lower a basket, covered with the South African flag, to allay suspicion.

Madiba and Sisulu would clamber into the basket and be flown to the roof of the nearest foreign embassy, where they would ask for political asylum.

But the ANC's External Mission would not approve the idea, so it too was shelved …

Around 10 a.m. on Thursday 21 October 1982, I was called to the prison commander's office. 'Pack up,' he told me, 'you are leaving this afternoon.'

No one would tell me where I was going, and after eighteen years on Robben Island, I had less than four hours to pack my belongings and say goodbye to my friends. Amid the excitement of being moved and the trauma of leaving my colleagues, there was barely time to reflect on the supreme irony of some warders making me an unwitting accomplice to their illegal activities!

I had a number of cartons containing books and other effects, and the warders, unbeknown to me, had stuffed parcels of frozen crayfish – caught without the requisite permits – into boxes, which they placed among mine, telling me hastily that their counterparts on the mainland would take delivery of the cartons at the Cape Town harbour.

As the 2 p.m. deadline neared, there was time for no more than a quick handshake with my colleagues, and then it was through the main gate and onto the ferryboat.

Despite the fact that I was aiding and abetting, albeit unconsciously, their crayfish smuggling operation, none of my escorts would reveal my destination, but they couldn't resist a few last jibes. 'You'll never see Mandela again,' said one.

But, around 6.30 p.m., I *was* reunited with Mandela – as well as with Walter Sisulu, Raymond Mhlaba and Andrew Mhlangeni, at Pollsmoor Prison. It was wonderful to see them again, but none of us had any idea why I had suddenly been transferred.

When opposition leader Frederik van Zyl Slabbert asked the commissioner of prisons why I had been moved to Pollsmoor, he was evidently told: 'That coolie tried to be too big, he tried to take Mandela's place on the island, so we transferred him.'

On the day of my transfer I was given the very first letter written

to me on Robben Island in November 1964. It was from my brother
Solly, and had been withheld because of an 'offending' reference to
the outcome of the British election, which said: 'Harold Wilson and
the Labour Party are now in power.'

Not only was the letter held back, but the security police made
it impossible for Solly to visit me on the island by ensuring that he
was not issued with the permit needed by Indians to travel from one
province to another.

When I arrived at Pollsmoor I was also given an Eid card and a
photograph of a baby, captioned: 'The day I was exactly one year old.
With lots of love to my Daddy'. It was from Djamilla Cajee, whom I
had named some sixteen years before.

The move to Pollsmoor came in the middle of preparations for my
final examinations for a BA Hons degree in history, so it was not until
January that I really settled in.

For the first time since our arrests, five of us were sharing a communal cell. We were all early risers, but Mandela was up before anyone
else to do his exercises – running on the spot and a few laps around
the cell.

Living in such close proximity, we learnt a few other things about
Madiba as well. One very cold night, we were all kept from our sleep
by the loud chirping of a cricket. Eventually, Mandela left his bed and
captured the noisy insect by throwing a towel over it. He went into
the bathroom, and we naturally assumed he was going to flush the
insect down the toilet, but instead he opened the window and released
it into the dark.

Of course the cricket continued chirping throughout the night,
thanks to Madiba's concern for the preservation of all life. We should
have expected it – he wouldn't kill invading ants or hovering bees,
either …

I did not much care for Pollsmoor. Strange as it may seem, I missed
the island – not the prison or the pettiness of the warders, but the
'family' we had formed in B Section, and the setting.

As a descendant of peasants, I always was a rustic man at heart, and
I longed to see the grass and trees and flowers, the ostriches, tortoises
and buck that roamed the island.

Pollsmoor was a concrete edifice, cold and mean. One day, I saw a rainbow, and was quite overwhelmed by its beauty. I must have seen hundreds of rainbows in my life, but that is the one I remember.

On the credit side, our relatives no longer had to make the trip by ferryboat – often over rough and choppy seas – and since all the water at Pollsmoor was fresh, there were no more salty showers or stiff laundry!

The food at Pollsmoor was far superior in both quality and quantity to any other prison of our collective experience, but the diet still became monotonous. We were permitted to purchase a few additional groceries with our toiletries every month, and to receive food from outside at Eid.

On our first festival at Pollsmoor, Fatima Meer organised a veritable feast, flown to Cape Town from Durban. There were only five of us, but she sent enough food for fifty, hoping that the other prisoners might share our bounty. Other well-wishers followed suit, and eventually we had to appeal to them to cut back on the quantities, as no other prisoner was allowed anywhere near us.

Mindful of the pleasure our tiny patch of garden on the island had brought, Madiba decided to establish another one at Pollsmoor. In the absence of a suitable piece of ground, Madiba persuaded our jailers to provide a dozen or so oil drums, cut in half lengthwise, and fill them with soil. It was really his garden and he nurtured it almost obsessively, spending an inordinate amount of time and energy on his plants. Our contribution was largely confined to enjoying the end products.

When Mandela went to hospital, he left me in charge of the garden after writing out two pages of detailed instructions. Now, I knew absolutely nothing about gardening, but luck and nature combined to yield a first-class harvest of onions and a profusion of spinach. We also had a fair crop of leeks, a handful of beans and a few dozen berries. The beetroot and maize looked promising, but the tomatoes and cucumbers produced specimens that no self-respecting salad would publicly acknowledge as kin. Fortunately, my colleagues were not exactly gourmets, so my offerings were generally received with praise and appreciation.

Madiba paid almost as much attention to his physical appearance as to his plants, and his insistence on a certain brand of hair oil sparked what became known as 'The Pantene Crisis'. No substitute would do, and Christo Brand was instructed by the prison chiefs to scour the pharmacies of Cape Town on Mandela's behalf. I think he even took the matter up with Helen Suzman on one of her visits.

Brand finally managed to locate the last remaining stock of Pantene – possibly in the whole of South Africa! – and bought the few he managed to find. No one wanted to go through that particular 'mass action' again.

from The True Confessions of an Albino Terrorist (1984)

BREYTEN BREYTENBACH

It was quite late in the afternoon when I was finally processed through the books and handed clothes which had the number 4 stencilled on every item – meaning that they belong to Pollsmoor Prison, White Section. I also now belonged to Pollsmoor. I was further given a sheet, and pillowslip, a towel, a tube of toothpaste, a toothbrush and soap, and taken up three floors through many corridors and locked grilles to the section for White male prisoners and into my new cell, which was enormous compared to what I had been used to. Joy of joys – in one corner of the cell there was a large washbasin with hot and cold water and a shower and a toilet bowl. A low wall separated this area from the rest of the cell. (In due time I would spend time at night behind that low wall, pretending to stare vaguely at the door and the corridor where the *boere* patrolled, my knees half-bent with an open – illegal – newspaper balanced upon them: they couldn't see it, but I was avidly feeding the mind with politics and sports and small ads!) There were two tall, narrow, barred windows in the one wall actually giving on to the outside. I had a bed, I had a small table, a chair to go with it, and several lockers built into the walls of the cell. I had in reality quite enough room for my few possessions as the cell I was in normally held up to sixteen prisoners when White and maybe as many as thirty or exceptionally even more when Black.

But back to the window, Mr Investigator: I could actually see one part of a mountain! True, only the beginning slope, but it was something, a landmark, life outside uncontaminated by prison existence,

a limit to the void, to nothingness. I couldn't believe my eyes. It became dark and I imagined that with the dusk I could smell through
the windows (which I could open or close myself) the faint aroma of
magnolias or perhaps even gardenias. This was really the Cape then:
memories came flooding back of that other night when I had met
Paul somewhere in this same region and we'd gone walking through
a sleepy suburb, smelling the intimate gardens and hearing the wind
groaning in the oaks. Here from my cell I could surely, I thought, if I
really tried hard enough, get a whiff of the sea. My sleep must have
been filled with moonlight. This was paradise, Mr Investigator.

When I woke up seagulls were really flying over the prison, dropping their scissors-like squawks and screams in the concrete walled-in
courtyards. Indeed, when I pulled the table close to the window and
climbed on top of it I could just barely make out in the distance a
thin but unruly blue ribbon. The sea. The limitless ocean. Looking
at Antarctica.

Pollsmoor is situated in one of the most beautiful areas of No Man's
Land – perhaps of the world. It lies nestled in the shadows of the same
mountain chain which at one extremity is known as Table Mountain.
Here in this part of the peninsula it finally runs into the ocean with
the effect of creating a micro-climate. Wind there is enough of – the
so-called 'Cape Doctor'. It became a constant companion during the
months of the year – in fact it was a benchmark by which the progress of
the year could be measured. But that which particularly marked me and
made me was the mountain: my companion, my guide, my reference
point, my deity, my fire, my stultified flame, and finally – like a prehis-
toric receptacle – the mould of my mind, my eye, my very self.

The prison compound itself covers a large area which previously
used to be several farms and a race track. It is confined partly by walls
studded with watchtowers and partly by wire fences. These contain
four separate prisons consisting of a large building called Maximum
Security (which is where I now found myself), a series of single storey barracks-like constructions called Medium Prison, and two more
modern constructions called the Female Prison and the Observation
Station. A few years later the Female Prison would become Pollsmoor
White Males and the women were to take over Observation. (When
the day of moving came the White Males, each with his possessions
slung in a bundle over his back, were herded on foot to the new home

by warders with dogs and guns – all except me: I was taken there in a slow-moving closed conveyance. In the new place we found minutely scrawled graffiti of the most outrageous obscenity.) There are further-more the houses – with the well-watered gardens – and the blocks of flats for the warders and their families, the administrative buildings, the recreation halls and the club buildings for the staff, their rugby fields and their swimming pools, and quite extensive farmlands where vegetables are grown.

Immediately beyond the boundaries of the prison community and towards the mountain there were private farms, some with cows so that we could hear the lowing of the cattle, and some with vineyards. On one of the farms they must have had a donkey because for a long period I used to listen every night for the lonely braying of this animal. Somewhere not far off, towards the sea, there were suburbs leading eventually to Muizenberg, which is a popular seaside resort. Some houses were built very close to the walls separating us from the outside world. There were many trees both on the terrain and beyond it, including palm trees and a number of gigantic bluegums. An old prisoner later told me of how, in earlier years when only Medium existed, they had to clear the grounds so as to build the other jails from scratch, and how they had to take out these big bluegums 'car-rots an' all'.

I was now for the first time inserted in a prison community. I saw other prisoners trotting by my two little windows giving on to the pas-sage, one on either side of the door, and some of them actually stopped and talked to me – although it was forbidden. I was like a monkey that had been brought back to the jungle, Mr Interviewer, hanging on to the bars, trying to attract any passer-by's attention. Pollsmoor had (has) a normal prison population of 4,000–4,500 people of which maybe 200 at any given time would be White, or rather whitish – since we were now in the Cape where population groups merge into one another. (The intake would rise spectacularly when the bulldozers had been at their periodic dawn feast of shanties made of cartons and jute and tin, and hundreds of squatters would be swept off the Cape Flats and brought to prison in lorries.) The staff – warders and various tradesmen working either in the workshops or on the fields – add up to about 300. Usually there'd be also between twenty and twenty-six dogs with their dog handlers. These (the Alsations, not the *boere*) were kept in fenced kennels situated just behind the building I was in. Whereas the dominant or prevalent sound of Pretoria, particularly at night, was the constant who-hooting and huffing of trains being shunted around the station yard not far from Central, the Cape will always be marked for me by the insistent growling and yapping and barking of dogs at night. Whenever the siren sounded the dogs would take up the echo in a chorus of howling.

But one soon got used to that. We lived in a universe of sounds which became our allies – the sad night birds, early every morning the wild geese raucously on their way back from the marshes near the sea to the mountain, the wind, the dogs, the guinea-fowl living free among the cabbages and the radishes; and the manmade sounds: the hissing as of an ocean liner of the big boilers situated above the kitchens of each of the buildings, the 'cat' – as the siren is known – sometimes going off in the night to summon the staff back to the prison buildings because there had been an escape attempt or a murder or gang warfare in the cells, the footsteps and the jingling of keys, the clinking of those who were chained and who moved under escort through the corridors, and the whimpers, the whispers and cries and curses of prisoner and of keeper.

To this I now had added the vision, a real vision even if impaired, of the blue sky and the sun and the tree tops bending, of pigeons coming to perch on the water towers, of first light paling (impaling and embalming) the morning star, and always – at the turn of a corridor, dimly observed, or, when you were out in the yard like an enormous voice standing over you – the mountain. The mountain with its richness of clothes as the seasons came and went.

The very next day Brigadier Dupe, who had escorted me from Pirax, came to fetch me in my cell and took me three floors down, plus one more, until we were actually below ground level, to a large artificially lit area which was the General Stores. This was where I was going to be employed for the rest of my stay in prison ...

When I needed to go to the toilet I had to obtain permission from the officer in charge in the stores and I would then be accompanied by a *boer*, who had to have the rank of sergeant at least, deeper into the prison itself, where a special toilet was made available to me. Since this toilet was in fact in the Black section, I was daily exposed to their conditions. Over the years I was plunged, despite the most careful measures taken by the authorities, into the complete prison universe, populated both by Black and by White. Always there were teams of Black or Brown prisoners on their knees in the passages, moving rhythmically and in unison forwards or backwards over the gleaming cement. Each had a floor-brush and pads made of old blankets under the knees. A *voorsinger* (or choir leader) would be standing up front, improvising a song, and the group would repeat the refrain or the key words, or sometimes just hiss or say *ja-ja* or make funny little sobbing noises, and at the same time sway their shoulders and shuffle their knees. And so the group would proceed or retreat as one brushing body. The leader's song – if you listened carefully – would often be a running commentary on the conditions or the daily events. (*The foodsafree. Ja-ja. The sleepsafree. Ja-ja. The fucksa-free. Free-ja. So why-ja moan. Moan-ja. Here comesaboss. Boss-ja. Sobigbigboss. Isbig ja. So step aside. Ja-ja. Good morning basie. Ba-ja. Workashit. Sshit-ja.*) The activity is known as *gee pas*, to 'give the pace'.

Often warders with yelping dogs on leashes were rounding up groups of convicts. There would be bedlam – screaming and cursing. When it came to meal times the long lines of poorly clad prisoners (nearly always barefoot and moving in crouched positions with their hands clasped before them because of the chill in these corridors, even in summer) would fetch their plates – on which the rations had been dumped pell-mell – on the trot. Run, grab food, run. Up by the kitchen the dixies would have been set out nearly an hour beforehand. On meat days small chunks of pork would be floating in the watery or oily sauce covering everything. A White *boer*, Sergeant Nogood by name, was often on duty there, guarding the rations. And as often I saw him methodically going from plate to plate, fishing out and eating the morsels of meat. (Not out of spite. Maybe he considered it his privilege, as a perk. Maybe he was just hungry, or greedy. Certainly he would consider that the authorities were just spoiling the 'dogs' by letting them have meat.)

The smell in those nether regions was indescribable. There were always far too many people. The single cells would house three men each – one on the bed, one under the bed, and one on the available floor space – and they would have to use the toilet bowl for washing purposes. Once, after a ritual murder when the victim had been laboriously decapitated with tiny penknives and his head exhibited on the window sill for the night (to grin at the passing warder who kept on telling him to go to sleep), it came to light that the cell which normally had room for perhaps twenty people had held forty-seven convicts – and not *one* was willing to testify to having seen the execution! There were never enough warders to allow people to have showers. Everyone was involved in some physical labour – often hard and dirty work, as when spans of Blacks were used to unload and carry in lorry loads of flour – and always on the double. Clean clothes were issued only on Sundays, for inspection. Blacks were given one small tube of toothpaste a month and three or four squares of toilet paper a day. People awaiting trial had it even worse – no change of clothing, since they kept and wore the clothes they were arrested in until sentencing, which may be a year or more in the coming. The sections had to be fumigated regularly to combat lice and other vermin. Groups of juveniles, from six or seven years of age to fourteen (a 'fourteen' is a short-timer, someone doing less than eighteen months, just there 'to dirty the dixies'), would be using the same facilities as the men and being raped in the showers. So there was the pervasive stench of unwashed bodies, old half-clean clothes, stale food – 'lightened' from time to time by whiffs of the tear gas used to control a cell when there had been a riot or a gang fight. Germothol, a disinfectant, was highly prized: diluted with water, it would be sprinkled parsimoniously in the cells just before inspection to make them smell 'clean'.

A Holy and Unholy Place (1991)

SHAUN JOHNSON

The island is very flat. The boat comes upon it quite suddenly: there it is, through the fog and the towering swells of the Cape of Storms, an undistinguished stretch of green and brown which looks as if it might be submerged at any moment. There are no jagged cliffs, no impenetrable jungles, just waves washing kelp prettily up against the shoreline. This island is a legend not because of the doings of nature, but of man.

I went to Robben Island this week. I found there a place of some wildness and beauty. But most of all, I felt the haunting mystery of history. What a curious life this isolated oval slab of our land has led.

It has always been assumed by those in power to be a natural repository for South African outcasts of one kind or another. Van Riebeeck banished his troublesome Khoi interpreter 'Harry' there in 1658. Political prisoners have followed ever since. The Prince of Madura, a Muslim holy man, died on Robben Island in 1754. The Xhosa prophet Makana was ferried to non-existence across Table Bay in the 1800s. And there were lepers and lunatics too, through the centuries.

This hard history culminated in the 1960s, when the men who are now negotiating South Africa's future with a man much younger than they, President de Klerk, were banished to the island's maximum security prison for life. Their presence there has ensured that Robben Island will be a myth to conjure with for generations. It was the innards of this South African secret that I had really come to see.

The sprawling stone monolith of the prison is empty, the last eight political prisoners having been transferred to the mainland little more than a week ago. The ghosts are fresh. In some communal cells, tattered posters are still secreted behind locker doors, and Bibles (carefully inscribed: 'BJ Bogale', 'RB Mpondo', 'M Nyandeni') have been left behind in the rush. In the courtyards there are sculptures, lovingly painted by the prisoners. The main door is of steel, big and heavy. It shuts with the expected terrifying, echoing clang. The corridors, labyrinthine, are clean and insipid, the glossy paint of institutions the world over reflecting the harsh light of bare bulbs.

There is an office for 'Records' and one for the 'Censor'. The outer walls are thick – 45cm – and the window bars so sturdy that an adult's hand cannot easily close around them. In short, it is an old prison, like other old prisons. Except, as I say, for who has been inside it.

Nelson Mandela's cell, in 'Section B', is three paces wide and two-and-a-half paces long; a small space in which to spend nearly two decades. It has a wooden door on the outside, and a barred steel door inside. Its walls are cream and there is a small pine bookshelf above a steel bed. A high window looks on to a gigantic wall; if you stretch up on your toes you can see the exercise yard between. There is nothing in the cell to commemorate its occupant. A warder who knew him says he never hung things on the wall anyway, he just had some books around.

There are pigeons in the yard, and under an ersatz, home-made pergola, a bench for sitting and talking. Curiously, there is a chilli plant growing in the corner. Nearby, and offering a perversely spectacular and maddeningly enticing cross-water vista of the Cape peninsula, is the quarry in which Mandela and so many others broke rocks with pick-axes all those years ago. Only the gulls sing here now. The island is deeply affecting.

What will happen to this strange, holy and unholy place we have created? Visiting the prison felt like putting a hand into an open wound. As far as nature conservation and historical preservation are concerned, the government is doing admirable work. But surely it cannot decide alone on what to do with the prison. Just as much as Afrikanerdom has the right to decide what happens to, say, the sites of the Boer War's concentration camps, so the island jail's victims must choose its fate.

from The Number (2004)

JONNY STEINBERG

Pollsmoor is a journalist's paradise; it is an interminable labyrinth of pure story. You walk down a corridor, a journalist clutching a notebook, and you are assailed by a thousand groping hands. Everyone wants to stop you, to own you, to unload his tales into your notebook.

Our daily excursions through prison had to proceed at a snail's pace. In each communal cell we entered, prisoners would assemble to tell their stories like patients queuing before some special doctor who carries in his bag a rare and vital medicine. By the end of each day I was exhausted, countless threads of life stories tangled in a great knot in my head.

After you have heard a few tales, though, you realise that there is something wrong with them, but you can't put your finger on it. You are aware that something of the madness of the place has been transmitted into the narratives its inmates weave; but what, precisely?

About midway through our Pollsmoor tour, I sat up through the night reading *Cold Stone Jug*, the prison memoir of Herman Charles

Bosman, South Africa's most celebrated short story writer. In the late 1920s and early 1930s, Bosman spent eight years in Pretoria Central Prison, having been convicted for murdering his stepbrother. 'Touch a long-term prisoner anywhere,' he wrote in his memoir, 'and a story would flow from him like a wound. They were no longer human beings. They were no longer people, or living creatures in any ordinary sense of the word. They were merely battered receptacles of stories, tarnished and rusted containers out of which strange tales issued, like djinns out of magic bottles.'

Transcribing Bosman's words now, having spent some time observing the politics of Pollsmoor, I think I understand why I found prisoners' tales so unsettling during that first trip to the jail. It is not that the prisoners who told the stories were dead, or no longer human, as Bosman suggests, but that the stories themselves had died during their transmission from the jail to my notebook. By the time they were safely in my satchel, they had absolutely nothing to do with the world from which they were uttered. Indeed, they were a screen between us journalists and the prison.

I would come to learn that prison is a world nourished by stories. It would be no exaggeration to say that the master story – that of Nongoloza, the God of South African prisoners – organises life behind bars. A prisoner's capacity to imbibe and retell that tale is probably his most potent weapon.

But that is precisely the point. Stories in prison are weapons, tools, the stuff of action; they are insinuated into the exercise of power. Severed from their practical functions, regurgitated in the contextless context of a journalist and his interviewee, their meanings drain away.

It was only much later, when I came to understand something of the prison's internal world, of the ancient, elaborate and often violent game between captors and convicts which animates prison life, that the remarkable power of tales prisoners weave came home to me.

Back then, on my first trip to Pollsmoor, I got just an inkling of this internal world, second-hand, thanks to the insightful commentary of Andrew Bosch, one of the warders who shepherded us around the prison. At about noon one day we were passing the kitchen wedged between B section and D section. Jets of hot air carrying the acrid smell of overcooked vegetables and boiled meat hit our faces. The air was milky and humid, the vinyl beneath our feet wet. The Rastafarians had already come and gone, their plastic lunch boxes crammed with carrots and cabbages, and the food teams were milling about the doorway, waiting to distribute meals to every corner of the prison.

Bosch and I leaned against a wall in the corridor and watched.

'That's the nerve centre of the prison,' he murmured quietly in my ear. 'This is the point from where inmates exercise power.'

I looked at him and smiled at the drama of his announcement.

'All 3 300 prisoners must be fed every day,' he said. 'And all the food comes from the same place – the kitchen. It is the only place that connects every point of the prison with every other. So those trolleys,' he said, pointing to the food team waiting in the doorway, 'they don't just carry food. They are the prison's telephone lines; they carry information and instructions.'

'What sort of information?' I asked.

'There is a high-ranking position common to all three major prison gangs called the Glas,' he replied, not really answering the question. 'He has two imaginary tools: a pair of binoculars that hang from his neck, and a bunch of 16 keys tied to his waist. The binoculars mean he can see everything that happens in the prison. The keys mean he can go anywhere in the prison; he can open any door.

'What this really means,' Bosch continued, 'is that he controls access to the kitchen. His job is to see to it that the right gang member is appointed to the food team.'

'But warders appoint inmates to the food teams,' I said gingerly; I didn't know Bosch well enough to talk easily with him about corruption.

He stepped closer and put his mouth to my ear. 'You can't keep the gangsters off the food teams,' he said. 'If you cut off the ability of gangs in your section to communicate with other sections, they get nasty. We have the safety of our members to think about.'

I thought about this for a while. 'Seems to me it's a big game,' I said. 'Your job is meant to be to keep the prison closed, the sections separated from each other. Theirs is to keep the prison open. But if you won, if you really kept the prison closed, they would stab you. So you lose on purpose.'

He warmed to the provocation. 'It's actually not that simple. If we really lost, if the prison was really open, this place would be so danger-ous we would not have allowed you to come in. Weapons would pass between the sections every day, death sentences would pass between the sections. We would have to patrol the corridors with automatic weapons. It's about striking a balance. The sections must be mainly closed, but a little bit open.'

'Otherwise the gangsters will hurt you?'

'And each other. You see, prison gangs are paranoid, and if the prison is too closed, if they can't communicate with each other, there will be too much intrigue.'

'For example?'

'Take the 28s [a 'number' prison gang]. Something terrible happens on D section. Some 28 breaks a serious rule. Now, say there is only one 28 Judge in the prison, and he is on B section. He must be part of the decision, he must have the final say in handing down sentence. So, a message passes from D section, through the kitchen to B section, and the Judge is informed of the offence. He thinks about it, sends a message back, and the messages pass back and forth until the highest structure of the gang has met, via the messengers in the kitchen, and sentence is passed.

'Now, in this situation, you would say that our task is to keep the sections closed. If the judge can't pass sentence, it can't be carried out. But say the kitchen is closed, and D section makes a decision all on its own, and punishes the offender without the consent of the Judge. Rumours come to the Judge about what has happened, and he thinks some *laaitie* on D section has staged a coup, assumed the power of a Judge. Or the Judge hears a rumour that some upstart on D section has appointed himself treasurer and is hoarding all the money from the drug trade. Then the next thing that passes from B section, via the kitchen, is a knife, an order to kill.

'So, on the one hand you want to keep the sections closed, so the Judge can't order a stabbing. But then, you want to keep the sections open a little, otherwise the Judge will definitely order a stabbing.' He smiles at his paradox. 'It's difficult to know where the line should be drawn.'

*

The most interesting time of every day was lockup time, mid-afternoon. You needed neither a watch nor the use of your eyes to know when it was coming; were you to be blindfolded, sound and smell would inform you. If the staccato lyrics of American West Coast rap echoed from the cells around you, you were walking through territory dominated by the 26s and 27s. If you heard East Coast gangsta music, you were in 28 territory. I asked countless prisoners where this split in allegiance originated. They all laughed at me, as if I wanted access to a secret I had no right to know.

Accompanying the sound of the music, the sweet-sour fragrance of Mandrax fills your nose. It is a mid-afternoon smell; no warder is going to bust an inmate for smoking drugs after lockup. To find the master key, to open up the cell, to begin to search, takes too long. By the time the warder is in the cell the drugs are gone. So the odour of drugs tells you that you are on the seam separating night from day, lockup time from open time: the moment in the daily cycle when power shifts from warders to inmates.

Take off your blindfold, peer through the high barred window of a communal cell, and you see six men in the centre of the room talking in hushed tones. It is a daily meeting the gangs call the Valcross – two 26s, two 27s and two 28s: it inaugurates the end of the warders' day, the beginning of the gangsters' day. They are discussing how life is going to be organised for the next 15 hours.

The 28s are not allowed to talk directly to the 26s; the 27s mediate the flow of information. So, watching carefully, you notice that two of the six men remain in the centre of the room all the time. The other two couples step back and forth in turn, waiting patiently for their counterparts to finish.

What are they talking about? I asked many prisoners what life is like after lockup, and prisoners, being the compulsive story-tellers they are, told me many things. But nothing could substitute for being there …

At the end of that first tour of Pollsmoor … the head of the maximum security prison, Johnny Jansen, called us into his office to say goodbye. 'So,' he said, once we were all seated, 'I'm sure you've had a ball, wandering through my prison collecting horrible, sensationalist stories.'

Jansen was a heavy coloured man in his early fifties, a serious rugby player in his youth, and the residues of his once-powerful frame were still discernible beneath the layers of a sedentary middle age. Looking at his body, and the expression on his face, I was reminded that black and white South Africans share far more than they care to admit. His languid movements, his slow gestures, the patriarchal authority with which he carried himself, brought to mind the white Afrikaans *paterfamilias* of the suburbs. I could picture him at a Sunday braaivleis, a beer in one hand, a pair of barbecue tongs in the other, a coterie of other middle-aged men around him, talking rugby. Church on Sunday mornings and daughters home by nine.

The first time we met him, during our introduction to Pollsmoor, he had said something that made me wary.

'Many years ago,' he told us, 'I was called into this office by the head of the prison and I was racially abused. A white warder had called me a *hotnot* and I had given him a piece of my mind. You know what is a *hotnot*,' he said, for the benefit of our editor, who was European. 'It is a derogatory word for a coloured. It means you are a filthy little liar, that your dishonesty is in your blood. The head of the prison called me into this room, and all the senior managers were here. He told me I was a liar, that nobody had called me a *hotnot*. He said I must go back to my parents, because they had not brought me up properly.'

Jansen smiled to himself, then gestured round the room: 'Now I occupy this office. It's strange how things change, isn't it?'

At the time, Jansen's anecdote had unsettled me. He was among the first generation of black South African bureaucrats to run the post-apartheid administration. To my mind, the ones who were struggling, those who found themselves at the helm of a bureaucracy they could neither understand nor manage, they were the ones who told the kind of stories Jansen was telling us. They distracted themselves from their own drowning by incessantly rehearsing the grand narrative of their ascension to power.

So, throughout that two-week visit to Pollsmoor, I had this image in my head of a fumbling middle-aged man, charged with managing this inferno, collapsing under the burden. I imagined him sitting in his office steeped in memory, the story of how he came to run this place a heavy opiate transporting him away from the present.

I was wrong, very wrong. In the months to come, I was to discover that Jansen had begun an experiment of breathtaking audacity in Pollsmoor; he was one of those invisible heroes of the civil service, working his corner of the administration on home-grown wisdom and with little assistance, and performing small wonders.

When he took over Pollsmoor's maximum security prison in 1997, it was quite literally a battle zone. Warders patrolled the corridors armed with tear gas canisters and dogs. Gangsters, in turn, beat and sometimes killed any of their peers whom they suspected had spoken privately to a warder. It was an internecine war which had begun in the prisons of early-twentieth-century South Africa and had never abated.

Jansen, who had been recruited into the prisons service in the early 1970s as a lowly coloured employee, spent the dying years of apartheid organising coloured and African warders in open rebellion against the old guard. When he and his peers in the Pollsmoor prison complex finally came to office in the mid-1990s, the white men who had run the place for the past generation left in droves. Working-class men with little managerial experience, Jansen and his peers were administrators now, in charge of one of the most violent and chaotic institutions in the country.

He came armed with a philosophy as laudable as it was naïve: an evangelical belief that all men's souls are naturally gentle, that only the cruelty of history had made them bad. He identified with the gangsters behind the bars. The humiliations he had suffered as a coloured warder working in apartheid's jails were the same humiliations, he thought, that had turned many Cape Flats men into monsters. He believed that violence was born from self-loathing, that if he showed the Generals of the Number gangs how to respect themselves, their innate humanity would shine through.

A few months after he came to office, the dogs disappeared from Pollsmoor's corridors. And then the tear gas canisters too. For the first time in the institution's history, gang leaders watched warders walk into their cells unarmed.

In the awaiting-trial section of the prison, an anarchic place jam-packed with the soldiers and the generals of Cape Town's drug wars, Jansen identified the leaders of the Number gangs and walked into their cells to chat with them. They sat there aghast, wondering whether the new head was charmingly naïve or barking mad. He told them he needed their help in running the prison; he asked them to elect cell representatives to take complaints to warders, a representative to monitor the quality of food, and another to ensure that sick prisoners received adequate attention from the medical staff. He expressed his intention to start sports and recreations, and asked for the election of recreation officers. And then he spoke to the gang leaders about their lives on the outside, about being fathers and husbands. He asked them to describe their children and to volunteer their thoughts on what the Cape Flats would look like a generation from now.

Within a year of coming to office, Jansen had convened a forum of gang leaders and had invited several NGOs to run workshops. Motivational speakers talked of self-respect. There were workshops on aggression and on the nature of conflict. The forum's meeting room was host to bizarre scenes, awe-inspiring to the credulous, laughable to the cynical: a battle-scarred 26 dropping backwards off a table, caught inches from the ground by the hands of his foes in the 28s; hardened old assassins weeping hysterically for forgiveness.

THE FOREIGN VIEW

from Move Your Shadow (1986)

JOSEPH LELYVELD

On the other side of the subcontinent, near the Daniel F. Malan International Airport in Cape Town, the authorities in their gnomic and inscrutable deliberations have created an astonishing exposition of the racial caste system in operation. Of course, this was not really arranged for the convenience of foreign voyeurs on tight schedules, but it is now possible to fly in and absorb the whole bitter lesson in a couple of hours. There in a space of about five square miles roughly 200,000 browns and blacks have been distributed on a checkerboard of officially demarcated racial enclaves, each with the standards and regulations appropriate to the caste or subcaste licensed to inhabit it. Cape Town is the only metropolitan area in the country where blacks are in a minority. The largest population group there is not white but colored, yet it is a fundamental white aim to ensure that blacks will forever remain outnumbered in the western part of the Cape, the cradle of white "civilization" in Africa, whatever happens in the rest of the country. The reason is never stated, but it seems plain enough: Those who cannot abide the idea of black government can always imagine that they will be able to hold their original beachhead on the continent, if it ever becomes necessary to run the Great Trek in reverse. Because of the numerical predominance of the coloreds, Cape Town is more flexible on issues relating to the color bar than the rest of the country. But because of the official antipathy to black settlement there, it is also where the system of racial exclusion known as influx control is practiced most ruthlessly. The whites of Cape Town and even the Afrikaners of the *Boland*, the city's hinterland of orchards and vineyards, look down on the whites of the Transvaal as bloody-minded political primitives, but until 1984, when its special status was made less blatant in law, Cape Town was the only city where blacks couldn't even purchase the leaseholds on their homes. Half the blacks in Cape

Town are deemed to be "illegals" under the draconian administration of influx laws aimed at restricting the permanent black population to 20,000 families.

The result is an unending war of attrition between the authorities and the "illegals," the overwhelming majority of whom have origins in Transkei and are thus held to be foreigners even if they have lived and worked in Cape Town for years, married, and brought up children there. Usually it is the wives and children that the law seeks to expel in order to preserve the hierarchy of castes in the western part of Cape Province, which was officially proclaimed a "colored labor preference area," meaning that no black could have a job until white officials had certified that no colored was available to take it. Thus the same racial system that hunts coloreds like Cynthia Freeman on the fringes of the white areas in Johannesburg manages to claim solicitude for coloreds as its excuse for hunting blacks in Cape Town. This is not a procedural hunt with writs, affidavits, and other pieces of paper as the state's weapons; it is a hunt with riot police, dogs, and tear gas, usually in the middle of the night. With each major raid to flush the "illegals" out of the black townships, a squatter camp arises in scrubby bush on the sand flats near the airport. Pathetic little shelters, makeshift yurts, are created out of twigs, cardboard, and the sort of plastic sheeting that is used to make garbage bags. These become the targets of the police, who tear them down and set them aflame. Usually then there is an outcry, and sometimes – when enough families have been broken up, enough jobs lost, enough children hospitalized with pneumonia, and, crucially, enough TV footage broadcast in Europe and America – the authorities call a temporary cessation of hostilities. With each such truce a tiny new subcaste is created with something less than a right to remain but at least an ambiguous commitment that the dogs and police won't be set on it again for a period of uncertain duration while the authorities review its status. Hence the checkerboard.

You can start at the privileged end by driving to Mitchell's Plain, a segregated township for coloreds that was built as an apartheid showcase, mainly for coloreds who were bulldozed out of District Six, their old neighborhood in the heart of what they ought to be able to regard as their city. Tidy little town houses, landscaping, and floral beds near the main thoroughfares and shopping centers that look as if they belong in the suburbs of San Diego are supposed to help them forget what they lost. Then you can drive on to Nyanga, an established black township with unimproved matchbox houses and minimal facilities. Next to Nyanga is New Crossroads, a newer and much smaller subdivision for blacks that was meant to be a show-case but became frozen at an early stage of development when the authorities hatched a master plan for the 1990's that would involve rounding up all of Cape Town's blacks and depositing them in a new township called Khayalitsha ("new home") next to Mitchell's Plain. Meantime, there is still old Crossroads, a crowded warren of metal shanties that looks like a social disaster but is actually a triumph of black assertion, for it came into being without authorization and has been allowed to remain. Only half its population of about 40,000 can prove they were there when the authorities, under international pressure, called off the bulldozers that were about to raze this en-campment and relented in their plan to force its inhabitants back to Transkei; those who came to Crossroads later, in the hope of gaining legal status in Cape Town, are still deemed to be "illegals," but their cases are said to be under review.

Next to Crossroads, but separated from it by a sandy no-man's-land of less than 100 yards, are the remnants of later struggles with the police, divided and subdivided into further tiny enclaves. Some have official permission to build shanties; others are required to live in tents. The distinctions among the groups are arbitrary, governed only by the terms granted them for temporary relief from police dogs and mass arrests. Like rings on a tree or archaeological strata, these encampments chronicle a struggle for existence, and every eight months or so, when the authorities launch a new offensive against black "illegals" in Cape Town, another stratum is formed.

Everyone understands that the tidal movement of black population has its origins in the absolute poverty that exists in black rural areas. In their effort to resist it, the white officials are like the Irish king Cuchulain fighting the waves ("the invulnerable tide," wrote Yeats) or perhaps Dutchmen building dikes. Heartlessness and stubborn-ness are prime ingredients of their struggle, but they are matched by the obstinate courage of the hunted people who stand their ground out of desperation and a fundamental refusal to be designated as "il-legals" in their land. That courage can be very moving, suggesting words like "indomitable," but the truth is that heartlessness prevails.

The people in Mitchell's Plain do not make common cause with the people in Nyanga. The people in Nyanga and New Crossroads do not help the people in old Crossroads, where some of them first gained a foothold.

The people in the Crossroads camp are divided between those who are certified to be there and those who are seeking certification. And neither faction normally gives support to the people in the adjacent encampments on the sand flats, who give little or no help to each other. The system builds its dikes. It designates all blacks in Cape Town as foreigners, even those it accepts as "legals"; then it compartmentalizes the "illegals" into as many small, vulnerable groups as possible. Sometimes it retreats, but always it dominates.

It dominates, and yet the word "indomitable" still must be applied to its victims. If I mention several of the individual "squatters" and "illegals" I met over two years in the area near the airport in Cape Town, you will understand why.

Goodwill Zisiwe was trying to get warmth from a stinking, smoldering tire that had been thrown onto the dying embers of a fire at a bush camp near Nyanga when I encountered him on a cold, damp Saturday morning. He was a handsome young man of twenty-two, short and wiry, with a mild expression that reflected none of the tension and defiance that were inherent in his situation. The defiance was in his very presence at the bush camp, for he had been arrested at the same spot a couple of weeks earlier and thrown into Pollsmoor Prison, where he shared with twenty-one others a cell from which he had just emerged. The tension came from not only his general homelessness but his anxieties about his wife, Nofine. She had been in the final stages of pregnancy when she had been taken into custody. Some women who had been with her in the women's section of the prison told him that she had later been transferred to the prison hospital to give birth, but he had been unable to get information on her condition, the delivery, or the sex of his child. In the meantime, he had lost his job at a lumberyard. His white boss had been apologetic when he said he could no longer run the risk of employing a black whose papers were not in order.

I met Goodwill Zisiwe again nearly two weeks later, when I visited the bush camp at midnight. Nofine and their healthy new son were out of prison, he told me proudly, staying for the night in a church basement. There were roughly 600 persons in the camp that night, and the garbage-bag yurts had once more been erected. Small fires inside illuminated these flimsy shelters like Chinese lanterns, with long shadows flickering on their inflammable plastic surfaces as the huddled groups around the fires shifted positions.

"Dear little round house," a white woman who was there on a philanthropic errand cooed. "We very sorry," she said, speaking pidgin, or rather baby talk, to a self-possessed young black man, who sized her up with a long, cool stare.

"Why?" he asked.

"We sorry you not have house, permit, warm clothes like us. We *very* sorry."

It was an excruciating moment. The good woman had not really noticed anything about the man except his status as victim. For an instant it seemed to be touch-and-go whether he would respond to the decency of her sentiment or the condescension of her tone. He took a long drag on a cigarette, then split the difference, offering a neutral monosyllable. "Oh," he said mildly, a little dismissively but without apparent hostility. The white woman had now become the object of condescension, but she didn't seem to realize that either.

Another man went by, carrying a roll of plastic sheeting. "One man, one room," he quipped. A group around a fire that included Goodwill Zisiwe broke into laughter.

There were inspirational speeches and hymns in Xhosa for those who stayed up, and Goodwill Zisiwe was one of the speakers, holding forth in a manner that commanded respect. Then the group sang a hymn. I asked what it meant. "God's spirit is with me like a bird," I was told.

They were as dispossessed a group as I had ever seen, worse off in some obvious ways than the sidewalk dwellers of Calcutta, and yet they were singing about divine providence. I was inclined to the proposition that God's spirit had flown away, but I found myself powerfully moved. About six hours later, just at dawn, the police stormed into the camp and burned it down again. I had no way of knowing whether Goodwill Zisiwe had been re-arrested, but it was bound to happen. If the police missed him in that sweep, they would get him in another. And still, it was clear, he would return.

from In Search of Will Carling (1996)

CHARLES JACOBY

I woke up to complete silence in Cape Town. Walking down the hill from my mansion to the Dunkley Inn to watch the remains of the match, I was aware that South Africa had ceased to be. It was life, but not as I knew it. There was nobody on the streets, not even the drunk coloureds who lolled and yelled all day around the parks. There was quiet throughout the city. Yet, every few minutes, a curious groaning came from within every fifth or sixth house. It was as though the fog from James Herbert's nightmarish novel had passed through the city while I had been sleeping, and everyone had gone round to certain friends' houses, all over the city, for group sex.

'Yis!' chorussed a house as I passed. 'Yis! Yis! Yis! YIS! YIS! AAAAAAH, YIIIS! Yis-yis-yis!'

Everyone, but everyone, was indoors watching the match on the television. There was not a car moving anywhere.

I arrived at the Dunkley Inn in time for the last half of the second half. The bar was packed. There were a dozen people crowding below the television. They were all hooting and cheering at the screen high in the corner of the bar.

As well as the noise, there was a sense of intense concentration. Even Black, the coloured barman, was rapt. He would have ignored any orders for drinks, had anyone lapsed for long enough to ask for one. He was watching his idol, Chester Williams, the coloured Capetonian in the Springboks – in fact the only vaguely dusky player in the South African team.

Richard saw me come in. David held up a hand in greeting. Richard went off to fetch me breakfast – David and Richard, being English, were not so caught up by the wave the others were surfing, Roelf, Black, even Herman the German.

'YOU WON'T BEAT CHESTER, YOU WON'T BEAT CHESTER,' shouted Black. Chester had had a shove from a New Zealand player. He flashed a grin at the crowd to show he was not hurt. 'Look, he's smiling,' said Black.

'Brilliant!' boomed Herman.

'Brilliant,' echoed Louisa beside him.

This was the match of their lives.

The commentary switched to Xhosa: 'Eega fo rasi yebo gogo ee-preshaaah playaaar,' it streamed out. 'No for go la ti do ee-twentee-two-meetaaaars so ra mabokoboko ee-dead-ball-line.'

Garry Pagel came on for Balie Swart. 'Ooh,' went the crowd.

'Dess de guy we need now! Dess de guy!' shouted Black.

I had got there just in time to see South Africa at its most excitable. On the television, Morné du Plessis, the South African team manager, walked around looking anxious and chewing his tongue.

'Come on, guys,' roared Herman, banging the bar.

'Come on,' agreed Louisa.

Not many more minutes to go now. The Dunkley biker in leathers at the back of the bar jumped up and down, lit cigarette after cigarette, paced down and up, jogged on the spot. 'GO ON, GO ON, GO ON. DO IT, DO IT,' he exhorted. The score was 9–9. It was nearly the end.

New Zealand kicked for goal from the halfway line. 'Shit,' went the crowd. 'Shit, shit, shit. Aaaaah!' – scream – he'd got it. New Zealand 12, South Africa 9.

New Zealand kick for the tryline again. It bounces. Chester picks it up. 'RUUUUN, RUUUUN.' He passes it. It's a knock-on, and so close to the All Black line. 'That was a fucking try, man!' New Zealand still 12, South Africa still 9.

'I think the crowd are a bit partisan,' said David quietly. 'I haven't heard you shouting for New Zealand,' he added. 'I suppose you could always publish your book posthumously.'

'This is really energy-sapping stuff,' said the TV commentator, back in English again for the final few minutes. Those eyes not glued to the screen above the bar were sunk in their hands. 'It's a cat-and-mouse situation for both teams,' added the commentator.

Then a South African kick at the uprights. 'WOOOOOOOOOOO!' 12–12. The television shows a shot of Nelson in Bok cap and jersey, singing 'Shoshaloza' in the crowd. 'He's so sweet,' said a girl.

But it was not enough. There had to be more points for a winner. The referee had one eye on the clock, but he looked set to let the match go on until those points were scored. 'Give us a TRY,' implored Herman, one eye on the profit margin. 'Give us a TRY. Give us a TRY,' like a rally chant.

There was a scrum.

There was a tiny silence after the scrum. South Africa had possession.

'Stransky drop?' suggested a girl in a tight whisper.

He did.

'YEEEEEEEES, WOOOOOOOO.' The room went berserk. South Africa 15, New Zealand 12. They danced on the floor and on the bar, Black was up there with Roelf and the biker. Chairs and tables rattled and fell over. Herman thumped and thumped away. And they were snogging in the seats that stayed upright. Cape Town's reaction to world events is always oversexed. People were on bar stools, smelling victory. Richard and David beamed.

Just a minute to go. Penalty to South Africa. There is a bit of shoving on the pitch. 'Off! off! off!' – 'Do they know it's over?' – and at long last, at nine-months'-travel-and-very-long-last, the final whistle.

South Africa went up as a man, and national team captain François Pienaar was crying, and even Morné du Plessis permitted himself an anxious smile. Herman had two fist salutes to the air. 'Yes! Yes!' Olé, olé olé olé. Even Ella was excited. 'We are the power,' shouted a drunk coloured, stumbling around outside.

'Stransky, you beauty,' said Pienaar on national television. The crowd at Ellis Park in Johannesburg was on its feet. Nelson's cute face under his Bok baseball cap gave a cute smile. 'Papa, Papa,' the whites in Cape Town called him – high praise. 'Nelson, BAAAABY,' shouted Herman.

'This is the BIST game I've IVER seen in my WHOLE LIFE,' shouted Black.

Cape Town was white noise, bouncing and blasting off Table Mountain. Just as Rio de Janeiro is the party city of the world for southern Europeans, so is Cape Town for northern Europeans. The young came out for carnival in Cape Town. They roller-skated; motorbikes roared by; cars going up Long Street and Kloof Street hooted. All races drank and sang in the streets. The exuberance of black toytoy demonstration met the dancing hooliganism of whites having fun. Cars and *bakkies* were crammed with flag-wavers and shouters. Tramps white and black shook hands with yuppies black and white. People ran round and round Shortmarket Square with arms raised, screaming hoarsely.

Intelligent analysis of the game took place in the Gents of bars all over town, the only places you could hear yourself think.

'Thit was a disperate mitch,' said a man at a urinal.

'We fucked them good,' said a voice from behind a lav door.

'Close, hey,' said the urinal man.

'We rilly fucked them good,' emphasised the door, warming to his theme.

'Olé, olé olé olé,' added another door.

Outside, Table Mountain rang to the puberty of a new nation. 'SHOOO-SHA-LOOOOSA,' cried out the crowds. 'Shooooo-shoo-oooosa,' echoed back the cliffs. 'Shush,' whispered the trees, silhouetted on the top of Signal Hill. 'Shush, shush.'

from Swahili for the Broken-hearted (2003)

PETER MOORE

I knew I had been in Cape Town too long when people started asking *me* why the freeway overpass near the waterfront had never been finished. It stopped abruptly, just at the bottom of the City Bowl, as the city and inner suburbs are known, and didn't start again for another kilometre or so. It left an unsightly and dangerous drop of 30 metres at both ends, and for some reason I had taken a vague interest in why. Now – sadly – when visitors asked hostel managers about it, they were sent to me. In just ten days I had become the backpacker community's leading expert on Cape Town's unfinished freeways.

There were several theories. Some said it was because the city ran out of money before the freeway was finished. Others, in hushed tones because it reflected badly on South African engineering, spoke of a miscalculation that meant the two ends would never meet up. My favourite theory was that the overpass had been abandoned because it would have blocked the view of Table Mountain enjoyed by old retired seamen in the Salvation Army Hostel. But the really disturbing thing wasn't that there were so many different theories about the two ugly bookends of concrete and exposed metal reinforcement. It was that I knew them.

In retrospect, my decision to start my grand African adventure in Cape Town had not been a smart one. It is a stunning city of white beaches and tall leggy blondes bearing an uncanny resemblance to Charlize Theron. Beer is cheap and good and the parlous state of the rand meant that I could feast on rump steak as thick as a phone book for less than four bucks. Table Mountain provides a dramatic landmark – no matter where I went in the city it brooded, craggy and flat-topped, just to the south, or peeked out seductively from behind a building. And everywhere the good folk of Cape Town go about their business with an assurance that comes from living in one of the most beautiful cities in the world.

Nor did it help that I was dossing with Clive and Leanne in their flat in Gardens, a pretty suburb nestled at the base of Table Mountain. Clive and Leanne ran the southern Africa division of Worldwide Adventure Tours, an overland trucking company that specialised in taking travellers to Zimbabwe through Namibia and Botswana. Leanne, a determined blonde from Perth, made sure travellers got on the trucks. Clive, an English mechanic with a ginger beard that was a touch demonic, made sure the trucks were capable of making it there and back.

Clive and Leanne hardly knew me – it was a friend-of-a-friend doss – but that hadn't stopped them from telling me I could stay as long as I wanted. I had my own room (no long-term couch-related injuries). I had an immediate and lively social circle (they introduced me to their friends). I had unfettered use of a television and a sound system (including a selection of half-decent CDs). And the fridge was full of beer (including half a dozen bottles of prized Primus lager from the former Zaire). If I wasn't in dosser heaven, I was only a couple of clouds off.

It didn't take long for a daily routine to form. When Clive and Leanne left for work in the morning I'd still be in bed. And when they came home they'd find me sitting on the sofa, drinking beer and watching TV soaps …

My stay in Cape Town hadn't been all bizarre love triangles and Windhoek Lagers on a comfy couch. I had left the house. A number of times. It was just that they were short trips so I'd get back in time for my shows. It was unfortunate, too, that the time Clive and Leanne walked in after a hard day's work at the office coincided with the prime soapy slot.

For example: I'd caught the Rotair cable car to the top of Table

Mountain and marvelled at the spectacular view over the city to Signal Hill and towards Table Bay. Onboard entertainment was provided by a large Afrikaner who couldn't come to terms with the rotating floor, designed to spin slowly so that everyone could enjoy the view. He insisted on holding onto the rail no matter how many times it dragged him to the floor.

Then there was my day trip to the Cape of Good Hope Nature Reserve. Here I wandered along the sandstone cliffs, among the proteas and past the pounding surf, before spending an hour or so in the carpark watching a pack of baboons competing to see who could put the biggest dint in the roofs of the cars parked there. I finished the day at Hout Bay, eating fresh fish in a cafe overlooking the fish markets and the sheer slopes of Chapman's Peak.

Another day I visited the seaside town of Muizenberg to see the brightly coloured bathing sheds. I ate my lunch beside them and enjoyed a lively conversation with a coloured woman who told me a story about being busted by police while she was naked. 'I hope they like blue movies!' she kept muttering. Apparently the whole raid had been videotaped.

At other times you'd find me down at the Victoria and Albert Waterfront, wandering through the smart shops and restaurants, trying hard to convince myself that I wasn't back home at Darling Harbour in Sydney. Most days I'd sit on the docks, flicking food at the seagulls or watching them harass the Mandela huggers, as Clive called them, all clutching their battered copies of *Long Walk to Freedom* as they boarded boats for Robben Island.

I shouldn't have been surprised to find it difficult to leave Cape Town. It has always been a town that seduces visitors to stay a little bit longer than they had planned. In the days when Dutch trading vessels passed by on their way around the Cape of Good Hope, it was a refreshment station for the ships of the Dutch East Indies Company. It was an amiable halfway point where captains could stock up on fresh provisions before heading off for the Far East again.

That it was also known as the 'Tavern of the Seas' indicates the kind of 'refreshment' the sailors were indulging in. To them Cape Town was a place to have a few ales and wink at some wenches before hitting the lonely seas again. I suspect that, like me, a lot of those sailors would have quite happily stayed in Cape Town. But at least they had made a start on their journeys. I hadn't even begun my grand adventure to Cairo yet.

Before I left Cape Town though I wanted to visit a township. Not because I thought the shanty towns out on Cape Flats were the 'real' Cape Town (I've never understood how one facet of a city could be any more 'real' than another). But more out of interest in how things have changed since apartheid unravelled in the early nineties ...

Clive was even less impressed when I told him that I intended to catch a minivan, or taxi, as the locals preferred to call them. 'Taxi!' he spluttered. 'Do you want me to arrange your funeral now or should I wait until your body turns up in a ditch somewhere?'

Taxis in South Africa don't have the best of reputations. They are poorly maintained and often crash. I had visited a web site about Khayelitsha (even shanty towns have their own web sites these days) and it confirmed that they were death traps. It also hinted that bald tyres and dodgy brakes would be the least of my worries. 'Sometimes the drivers do not wash,' it warned. 'They just get up and smell awful. Sometimes, they are drunk.'

There was also an ongoing dispute over routes between the taxi drivers and the Golden Arrow Bus Company. The dispute had recently escalated into violence and the local papers were calling it a war. Passengers were being shot and bus drivers were wearing flak jackets, so I guess it was war. But I wanted to visit Khayelitsha and there was no other way of getting out there.

The minivan I caught to Khayelitsha came with standard side and forward safety cushioning in the form of African mammas heading back to their township homes after working in the city. They wore the uniforms of the cafes and supermarkets that employed them and sat chatting and gossiping with their friends. When I clambered in they shut up immediately and stared at me, stunned. 'What you do-ing going to Khayelitsha?' asked one after an interminable amount of time. 'Don't you know it's *dangerous*?'

I must have looked startled because she laughed and the other women in the van laughed that big infectious African laugh too. With that laugh the ice was broken. I spent the rest of the journey fielding questions about where I was from and where I was going and trying to convince them that not having any children did not necessarily mean I was impotent.

I steered the conversation towards more comfortable ground by showing the women the address for Vicki's B and B. They passed it among themselves and debated just exactly where I should get off. The consensus was that I should get off at the market in Section C and ask for directions from there …

Vicki was a large woman in a flowing kaftan and a scarf wrapped high around her head. The scarf was too high and hit the roof of the car, bending the same way Marge Simpson's hair does when she's driving the family car. Vicki told me it was traditional for married women to wear the scarf, but she didn't talk of her husband. I suspected that he had abandoned her – the practice seemed exceedingly common in South Africa – and this enterprise was her way of feeding her family, a family that not only included her four children, it turned out, but her sister and her two children as well.

It took twenty minutes to drive back to Vicki's shack. It was a modest building made from corrugated iron with two decorative swans at the door made from old tyres painted white. Inside it was surprisingly homey, with a feature wall made from interestingly shaped stones and shelves loaded with knick-knacks. Everything sat freshly dusted on doilies, and in the corner a television and a sound system had pride of place. The sound system was one of those smart all-in-one units with flashing LED lights. Not Japanese – Chinese, probably. But still, by township standards, Vicki was doing all right for herself.

There was no shower. Vicki would bring me a tub of cold water if I wanted to wash. And the toilet was a pit out the back that the whole neighbourhood used. I was given the kid's bedroom with a big soft bed that all four of them usually slept in. They didn't mind getting kicked out – it meant they would be sleeping with Mum – so I threw down my bag and lay on the bed, studying the school timetable written in pencil on the back of the door. Eventually, finally, I'd made it to my township B and B.

Dinner was served promptly at six o'clock on a small table that the whole family gathered around. We ate chicken stew and drank Coca-Cola that was poured from a 1.25 litre bottle placed on the table like a bottle of fine wine. As I ate the children reached across and tentatively stroked my hair …

I finished my stew and Vicki took me across the road to the local shebeen. It was called the Waterfront because it had a tap out the front. People came here from all over the neighbourhood to collect water, gossiping and discussing politics as they filled their jugs. Vicki said the owners were also having a sly dig at the upmarket bars at the Waterfront down town.

The shebeen was barely distinguishable from the other shacks, except maybe for the bare power cable illegally attached to the power line out the front to keep the beer fridge running. Vicki introduced me to a guy called Elvis and told him to bring me home when I was 'finished'.

Elvis was drinking with his friends at a table in the back corner of the bar. They looked like members of an LA hip-hop band who'd had all their jewellery stolen. Judging by the number of bottles on the table it looked like they'd been there all day.

'In the ghetto with Elvis,' I joked as I sat down. No one else seemed to get my oblique pop culture reference – I guess the King wasn't too big in these parts – so I let it slide.

'Two years ago you would have been dead by now,' said Elvis matter-of-factly. 'We'd have thought you were from the army and beaten you up, maybe even necklaced you.'

He poured me a beer and I smiled nervously, wondering if a little Fight Club action might not still be on the agenda.

'Now look!' he said, grinning, raising a chipped glass. 'Here we are in my shebeen, drinking beer.'

It seemed that drinking was all these guys did. Elvis told me that they couldn't get jobs, they didn't have homes and the money they used to buy beer came from mothers and girlfriends or 'other ways'. Most days – and nights – were spent here, in this shebeen, at this table ...

The next morning, after a delicious breakfast of hot porridge, Vicki took me on a walk around Khayelitsha. She showed me the schools and the hospitals and introduced me to Rose, a woman who single-handedly ran a soup kitchen. Another mother, abandoned and stuck with the kids, Rose got up at four o'clock every morning to serve over 600 meals a day.

Rose could have been forgiven for being tired and grumpy, but when I met her she was beaming. 'A food company just said they'd supply me with rice,' she said. 'That will make a *big* difference!'

At the end of the day Vicki walked me to the taxi stand where I had arrived the day before ... We stopped and chatted with women who were helping a friend move, by carrying chairs on their heads, and others who were selling bags of oranges that hung decoratively on the front wall of their shacks. I remember thinking about all the bad news stories we get out of Africa and wondering why we didn't hear more about women like Rose and Vicki. They were positive, vibrant women trying to make a difference. Maybe our attitude to the continent would be different if we heard about them instead of depressing stories about AIDS and corruption.

Vicki put me in a minivan heading into town and waved goodbye. It was full of sullen men going into town to get drunk or visit prostitutes. They didn't talk to me like the women had. They sat silently with their heads bowed, avoiding contact with me, sensing, perhaps, that I was judging them. I had met their women and seen the way they were trying to make a difference. The men sat around drinking beer, letting their children play among the bare electricity wires. Worse, they would bring AIDS into their homes, contracted, in all likelihood, on nights out like this. By the time I got back to Clive and Leanne's flat the optimism for Africa that Vicki and Rose had inspired in me had dimmed.

My mood was not improved when I discovered that I had missed the season finale of 'Isidingo'. As I had suspected there *had* been an explosion and *people were still trapped*! Clive took unseemly delight in relating the details (he had started watching 'Isidingo' too, just to see what I saw in it, he claimed) and in telling me that there had been a report on the news about plans to finally finish the freeway overpass.

There was nothing keeping me in Cape Town now. It was time to see the rest of Africa.

from In Transit (2003)

PAPA CHRIS

Three years ago, when I left my home country [Burundi], I never knew that I would find it impossible to go back. But, if God does not perform a miracle, I will never be able to go back as long as the Hutu and the Tutsis are not together. I will never go back as long as my country is divided into Hutu land and Tutsi land. I will never go back.

My life has completely changed now. I cannot trust anyone easily any more. I cannot easily believe what people tell me. I live in fear for my life. I tried to start a new life for myself and my family here but the trauma stays with us. I thought that coming to Cape Town, being so far away from home, would take the hurt away. But the reverse is true for me and for my wife especially.

When we arrived in Cape Town my wife was lodged at the Bonne Esperance, known as Philippi House, for refugee women and children, and the Cape Town Refugee Centre gave me shelter at Miami Tavern in Gugulethu. When my wife's period of six months free lodging expired we got accommodation in Hanover Park, in a Wendy house in the yard of an old man and brother from the church. We shared the toilet facilities with him. We settled in and I started looking for work which I finally got on the 3rd of September 1999, at Game Wynberg Branch as a trolley manager. Before this we had survived on the mercy of the community who gave us food and water.

A few months later complications began. My landlord stopped us from using the toilet because he said we wasted water in flushing and washed ourselves more than once a week. We had to resort to using the toilet at the Hanover Park taxi rank and at night we used plastic bags for toilets. He ordered us not to speak our mother tongue, Kirundi, in the back yard.

Twenty-four hours of this treatment resulted in my wife becoming seriously unhappy and depressed. She was admitted to Valkenberg hospital. She was discharged a week later but the conditions given us by the landlord remained the same, so I found another person's yard in Hanover Park where we moved to. But we did not stay there long either because my wife's situation got worse; she had started to develop mental problems. I took her to Valkenberg hospital and she was admitted again.

When I came home from the hospital all our belongings were outside. The landlady said she did not want to stay with people who were sick. I took our belongings and found another place to park my Wendy house thanks to the help of one of the sisters in the church. I paid R300 for the plot and we had stayed there for two weeks when we were told not to use the toilet when the landlord was at home. We had to wait for them to leave their home before we could use the toilet. It was difficult because she was always at home, so we had to move again to a new place where I paid R250 and on top of this I was supposed to pay for the groceries for that family as part of the rent. This was difficult as I did not earn a lot of money myself. On one occasion that landlady told my wife to give my four-year-old child urine to drink to save the tap water. All these bad experiences with landlords affected my wife negatively.

I then found a place in Retreat, in 3rd Avenue. The five-bedroomed house was occupied by twenty-two refugees all sharing one toilet and one kitchen. This place cost me R500 per month and because the living conditions were also very tough for us we moved again to another place in Retreat where I started paying R700 for the room.

Then one day my wife got caught in the middle of a gang fight. It brought back all the memories of the things she had seen at home. She could not stand it. She started asking me, "Why did you choose to come to South Africa? Do you find a big difference between this place and our home place?" I had no answer.

In January 2000 she got so depressed that I was obliged to take her to a psychiatric hospital. I took her to Groote Schuur and she was admitted to ward 23 where they treated her. All the time I had a big fear in me because I did not have the money to pay the bills and I was more worried about this than her survival.

When she was discharged we were not asked to pay. In February 2000, she was admitted to Valkenberg psychiatric hospital. The problem there was also about paying the bills. We were asked to pay but I never came up with enough money to settle those bills. Up till now I still owe them.

Her situation was very bad. She was crying, screaming, imitating gun shooting and singing the songs they used to sing when they came to kill people. The ambulance could not take her because she was fighting, imitating action back home. They brought the Philippi police to intervene to take her to the hospital.

She was admitted to ward 15 and after two weeks there she went to ward 3 and then ward 5. The doctors did everything in their power to assist me (may God bless them). They asked me to find a quiet place where she would not hear gunshots. I found a place in Retreat but it was the same there. It's impossible for me to find a place where she cannot hear gunshots. The quieter a place, the more expensive it is. I could not afford a quiet place.

After a short while we experienced the same problem. On the 23rd of May my wife witnessed another shooting. She became traumatised to the extent that life became utterly useless to her. One evening she attempted suicide.

She went to the railway line when the train was coming, the express train at peak hour. She lay down on the railway line, with my son on her chest, and slept there waiting for the train. Luckily, one of my friends phoned my pastor to come to witness the situation. They tried their best to pull her off the railway line. I thank them, may God bless them. It was very bad.

I took my wife to Valkenberg hospital. She asked me, "Papa Chris, why did you bring me here?" She seemed to be paralysed. All the horror, the things from back home, were in her mind.

I went to see her but it was not easy for me to speak to her because the only question she asked was, "Papa Chris, why did you bring me to South Africa? Did you think this was the best place to hide ourselves?" Then she would weep.

After two years of treatment the doctors concluded that she would never adjust to life in this country. My wife is in a poor state of health caused by the bad situation and harassment we have experienced since we escaped ethnic violence in our home country. My wife is suffering from chronic depression. She has been in and out of psychiatric hospitals because of the environment in which she is forced to live.

Today she needs counselling. The everyday shooting in Cape Town townships makes her live in fear and her situation is very complicated. No one has come to counsel her. No neighbours come to our place. We stay all alone.

from Diary of an Ex-Black Woman (2005)

JUDY KIBINGE

The first time I visited Cape Town I stayed at the Train Lodge, a place pleasantly described as a charming train-theme hotel a short walk away from the city centre. I'd been dying to go for years but could never afford it – Cape Town was always many Kenyan shillings away from Johannesburg.

Built from stationary train carriages, around a once functional platform, the Train Lodge came complete with a bunch of winos who by night made the train platform home – wrinkled teenagers and pock-marked men of indeterminate age wearing tortured expressions that betrayed generations of pain. Nobody seemed to have told them that this had long ceased to be a real station, so they happily congregated around the tiny green pool at the end of the platform, sucking warm beer through missing teeth and passing brown paper bags around in the darkness. On the inside of the door was me, sheet drawn to my chin, kept wide awake by the belching and braying, wondering if management had hired them to make the place feel authentic.

That first night, in a bunker of that stationery train carriage, bed draped with the contents of my suitcase, listening to the sounds emitted by the platform scavengers outside my door, I wondered which Cape Town I had come to, if perhaps there was another. But in the morning, when I awoke, I felt the shadow of Table Mountain draping over our little train village. It was so beautiful that my misgivings vanished. That was to be the first of the many contradictions Cape Town would offer me over this visit and the next.

I had arrived with other Kenyan filmmakers, all ready for Sithengi – it had announced itself to the world as Africa's biggest film market. Filmwise, there's not really much money available to buy what's being marketed, but this is a world where perception is reality, and by the sounds and sights that surround me at Artscape, most people have not tweaked on to the fact that they are wandering around a mirage. Or just pretend not to know. Everywhere, people dealing, meeting, lecturing, selling, posing, showing off and sweating in their designer suits. This is acting school 101 – we are all here on holiday but need to look busy. Different accents fill the air – American twangs, nasal Afrikaans, clipped British beats, Nigerian pidgin, Italian purrs ... but strangely, I can't hear or feel Zulu or Xhosa. But the Nigerians are making up for the absence of their Bantu brothers and sisters loudly and vigorously ...

I am bored. I'm bored by all the parties I go to every night, bored of the people I am meeting, bored of feeling like I am in jail, that someone is hiding something from me. Everywhere I turn, glittering people with glittering eyes who are so 'heppy to meet you'. I am reminded of that strangely bright, bleached smile aspiring actors waiting your tables in Los Angeles restaurants unleash. Where is Cape Town?

Tonight we are going to Observatory, or Obs as everyone calls it.

We are a mixture of Nigerians and Kenyans climbing into the bus. It's the first time I have gotten out of the city centre, which, by the way, is always eerily deserted, like London on Christmas Day. The tall Nigerian lawyer with the cane is disturbed by this and makes a large, loud, declaration as he climbs aboard: 'Dese treets are too empty oh! Cum to Nageria and I show you what a city is! I tell you, we are going to stat a bisness nah and bring Nagerians here by boat until we fill dese streets! Shah!'

The white bus driver taking him too seriously mumbles something about visas and emigration. The Nigerian lawyer is delighted to smell fear: 'Visa? Visa? You tink visa matta to a Nagerian? When did visa eva matta to Nagerian? We will pack dese streets till you no longer see de road because it's jammed with bodies!'

The ride to Obs is stunning but the light is fading fast. The houses we pass feel like California. They are built into the hills, around the hills, incorporating the landscape into their designs ... It's green, and as the sun sets orange then purple, I want to get off the bus, wander into someone's house and stay for the night. This life, up here, smells sweet and privileged. I press my nose against the window of the bus like an orphaned child and get a bump on the forehead for wanting what will never be mine. I think of a South African friend I haven't seen since college and for the umpteenth time feel a wave of guilt for not calling her. She has children now, and lives somewhere in Cape Town. I am reminded of her every time I reach for a sachet of sugar that bears her surname – she is from an immensely wealthy sugar family, and probably lives in one of these beautiful houses our Pan African bus is streaking past right now. I am afraid to meet her. Afraid the years will have made us too different. I am afraid that white South African fears will have seeped under her skin, that in our older ages I might remind her too much of the things she fears most. Or maybe I am afraid she will remind me of the things I am most afraid of.

There is mayhem at the bar. People waving chits and bits of paper that will entitle them to their tenth glass of wine. I wander about and meet the citizens of film that I have slowly come to know so well. We bump into each other at festivals across Africa: in Burkina Faso, in Zanzibar, here at Sithengi until slowly, slowly, one day you are family, with all the skeletons that this entails – love, jealousy, history and sibling rivalry. I spot François – he made a powerful documentary on gang members in the Cape Flats (a favourite topic among film-makers here it seems). I meet waves of other Capetonian film people who ooooh and aaaahh when I say I am a filmmaker from Nairobi. Anyone who says, 'fascinating!' as their eyes wander around for the next conversation invariably is pretending. I explain what I do a hundred times; they too explain for the hundredth time what they do. It's exhausting. So when I am waylaid by Richard, a Kenyan friend who lives in Cape Town, and he says he wants to drive me off to see something beautiful, I am gone in an instant.

We are standing on the top of a hill, looking down. To the left is Table Mountain. One side of her face is lit up by powerful spotlights so that she is blue and yellow and imposing. In front of us, like a thief's loot, sprawls Cape Town's jewellery, lights sparkling like a million tiny diamonds. The ocean is all around us. I see lights from boats, gliding to wherever people glide to on water at night. We stay there for a long while. I am trying hard to stamp this moment, this view in my mind forever. It's too much, too inflexibly beautiful – like a postcard or the backdrop of a city-wide film production. I want to study the left side for a night, then come back tomorrow and take in the right side. By day three I might just be able to absorb the front and on the fifth day I'll finally see and feel it all. Right now, its futile to look, it's much too much, like staring at the sun.

But I'm like a child about things – I hurt when I can't have some-thing I want. And I can't have all this beauty, can't own it, so what's the point? I want to go somewhere loud and raucous where they sell pleasure in a glass. I want to be obnoxious, loud and foolish tonight. I want to rub beautiful, unattainable Cape Town right out of my hair. I want the darker side.

Capetonians have disdainfully told me that Long Street is too touristy, but they seem to miss the point – we are tourists, damit. The smell of roasted herb floats across the street from The Lounge to our seats at the green-yellow-red veranda of Cool Runnings. Cool kids dressed in combat gear are skateboarding up and down the street at midnight. We walk across; climb the narrow stairs into The Lounge. The strip floors beneath our feet bounce as we walk, not just begging but assisting us to dance and so we do. In the front room, there is a TV set playing snow on the screen, the only light in the room. Once again we're the only black people in the whole place. By the bar is a white Rastafarian in glasses. Spotting my braids, he feels a connection that crosses race.

'Helloooooooo … sweet sistuh!'

I glare at him and he backs off but spends the remainder of the night casting me soulfully hopeful looks. On the veranda, there are all kinds of cool white kids rolling spliffs and smoking as though they are in *Cool Runnings*, the film. My friend Nash suggests we go to a strip club. We drive to three or four clubs but they are all closed or about to. Finally Richard says, 'there's one last place …' We drive until he announces, 'here we are'.

I look up and stifle a scream.

This is one of those joints that you see in American movies where tired old men with nothing to live for go to do their livers in once and for all as they watch bitter old strippers maliciously unveil flesh that ought to stay covered. There is a huge neon sign on the outside and it screams SEX!!! LIVE SHOWS!!! ADULTS ONLY!!! Tacky neon outlines of girls and cocktail glasses blink. The guys practically drag me out of the car. I'm protesting. But in we go, and I am ashamed to admit that I settle into it all quite quickly and in moments am thoroughly enjoying myself even more than they are. This is the tackiest place I have been to in a long time. But it has soul. Not nice angelic souls dressed in white floaty stuff, but the souls of untidy nights gone by stomping about at ceiling level colliding, heavy and regretful in the air. There's something very beautiful about damaged places drenched in tears – and this without a doubt is one of those. A deep brown carpet covers the floor, presumably purchased and placed to absorb stains of spilt drinks, blood and vomit. The cheapskate wood-panel-patterned wallpaper is peeling. I sit at the bar and order a double Jack, which for some reason – probably Hollywood inspired – feels right. Nash is busy talking to a shy, smiling girl. She does not look a day over seventeen. Her name is Anna and she is the first black Capetonian I have actually met since I arrived here. She's 21, delicate, fair skinned and has a long neck and the saddest eyes, like an antelope with a gun to its head. I feel for her, ask her why she is working here.

'Only for a year or two, then I'll have enough to go to college', she says.

I doubt. That's how it starts, life. And how it starts is more often than not how it ends. We can have a drink, she says, but the shows are over.

Nash begs and begs. He is cute and convincing. Coy, she goes to her boss – a swarthy, fat man in a dirty shirt behind the bar. She will put on a show – if we pay for it. Nash does. It's the last of his money but there's nothing he would rather spend it on. We enter the small dark room. There is a stage shaped like a T. The working girls are fascinated to see me in there. To keep the leering men off my case, I pretend I am married to Richard, which fascinates them even more.

'I can't believe your husband brought you here!' they screech. 'You are a very lucky woman!' I give a smile and the confident wife nod.

'If it makes him happy, I'm happy', I say. Clearly, my pal Jack D. is at work.

The show begins. Anna comes out making a poor show of emerging from behind the stage curtain to pretend she is collecting empty glasses. She pauses, unbuttoning her blouse: a tired, hot waitress. Off the top comes, right off. Then her skirt. Her bra. Her thong. Soon she is dancing away, on high heels which are stressing her, so that she keeps missing beats and wobbling to correct herself. Her breasts are a little floppy, her bum a little wobbly – all very surprising to me, who saw her as a picture-perfect young thing with clothes on. I am – I think – the only one who notices her imperfections. A group of young Indian men with wedding bands sit at the edge of the stage drinking their beer without breathing or taking their bulging eyes off her. An old white man sits in the shadows, alone and sighing – finally! Multicultural Cape Town revealed!

Anna is now steadier, moving faster and more fluidly, trying to assume a dangerous, sexy look on her face but not sure how to. An 'oriental', older, very sexy dancer joins. She has the moves, the body and the attitude that Anna is working herself up to. The Asian men are making sloppy, drunk grabs at her, bouncers pushing them off. Anna, upping the stakes, makes her way round to where we are. Nash's face lights up like a bulb. He is smiling so hard his molars can be seen, and his mouth is one black endless hole – the tunnel of love he wants to drag her into. She side-steps him, and before I've understood what's going on she has her legs on either side of mine, and is giving me a lap dance. Her face is close, really close, and her chewing gum breath washes over me. Richard forgets that he is not actually my husband and snaps angrily at her: 'that's enough!' She slides off me with a little shrug and a steamy backwards glance. I have never before wanted to kiss a woman but tonight, the thought crossed my mind. Is it Cape Town or is it me? Is this Cape Town anyway? Where am I? Who am I?

Outside, Nash tries to push his luck for Anna to come back to the lodge with him. Looking at me, past him, she says:

'I wish I could go with her. She's so sweet.'

It's definitely time to go. But not home. It takes us an hour to drive to a beachfront where we kick sand and dodge waves in the dark until the most fabulous sunrise paints us all orange.

from Dark Star Safari (2002)

PAUL THEROUX

The cold gusting wind, and the frothing sea, and the sunny dazzle on Table Mountain's vertiginous bulk looming behind it, made Cape Town seem the brightest and least corrupt city I had ever seen in my life. That was its appearance, not its reality. The high wind was unusual for the Africa I had traveled through but not for this coast, my first glimpse of the Atlantic. The wind was usually blowing twenty knots, and often gusting to forty, enough to tear the smaller limbs from trees and send them scraping along the pavement. The huge mountain and its precipitous cliffs made the city seem small and tame, and unlike Johannesburg which had a city center of dubious-looking people whose stare said *I can fox you*, Cape Town was provincial-seeming and orderly, the train station looked safe. I wanted to be near the sea, so I took a taxi and found a good hotel on the waterfront ...

What impressed me in Cape Town was its smallness, its sea glow, its fresh air; and every human face was different, everyone's story was original, no one really agreed on anything, except that Cape Town, for all its heightened contradiction, was the best place to live in South Africa. No sooner had I decided the place was harmonious and tranquil than I discovered the crime statistics – car hijackings, rapes, murders, and farm invasions ending in the disemboweling of the farmers. Some of the most distressed and dangerous squatter settlements of my entire trip I saw in South Africa, and without a doubt among the handsomest districts I had ever seen in my life – Constantia comes to mind, with its mansions and gardens – I also saw in this republic of miseries and splendors …

For a few days in Cape Town I did what tourists do. I took a day trip to the wine lands of Franschhoek and Paarl and Stellenbosch; looked at the vineyards and the cellars; went to wine tastings. I spent a morning at Constantia and an afternoon on the eastern slopes of Table Mountain, at the national botanical garden, Kirstenbosch, a lush repository of South African plants, filled with succulents and cycads and palms, as well as the fragrant varieties of low bush called *fynbos*, that was peculiar to the purple moorlands of the Cape. A boundary hedge, planted by Jan van Riebeeck in 1660, was still flourishing at the margin of Kirstenbosch.

One day intending to take the train to Simonstown I went to the station but got there too late for that. However, I was on time for another train, to Khayelitsha. I was in the mood for any train. Unable to find Khayelitsha on my map, I went to the information counter and inquired as to its whereabouts. The clerk, a young affable man of mixed race, showed me the place on the map.

Then he leaned across the counter and smiled and said, 'Don't go there.'

'Why not?'

'It's too dangerous,' he said. 'Don't go.'

'I'm just taking the train. How is that dangerous?'

'The train was stoned yesterday,' he said.

'How do you know it will be stoned today?'

He had a beautiful smile. He knew he was dealing with an ignorant alien. He said, 'The train is stoned every day.'

'Who does it? Young kids?'

He said, 'Young, old, lots of people. From the town. They're not playing. They're angry. And they do a lot of damage. How do I know? Because yesterday I was on the train to Khayelitsha. With my friend – he's the driver. We were in the driver's cab. When the stones came he was hit in the side of the face. He was all bloody. Listen, he's in the hospital. He's in rough shape. He was just doing his job.'

This convinced me. I decided not to go to Khayelitsha and told him so. The clerk's name was Andy. We talked a while longer. Khayelitsha in Xhosa meant 'Our New Home,' and there were 700,000 people there, most of them living in shacks, on the Cape Flats.

While we talked, another clerk sat rocking back in a chair, a big middle-aged African woman in a thick red sweater and a wool hat, with her feet propped against the counter, just out of earshot. She was staring straight ahead and fiddling absently with a scrap of paper.

'I'm not a racist,' Andy said. 'But the blacks in this country think they are being passed over for jobs. In places like Khayelitsha they have no jobs – no money. They thought that after apartheid they would get jobs. When it didn't happen they began to get wild.'

'I wanted to see a squatter camp.'

'No,' Andy said, smiling, shaking his head at the madness of it, and reminding me of all the times I had heard, *There are bad people there.* 'Don't go to a squatter camp. Don't go to a black township. You'll get robbed, or worse.'

The next day I went to a squatter camp. It was called New Rest, 1200 shacks that had been accumulating for a decade on the sandy infertile soil of Cape Flats beside the highway that led to the airport. The 8500 inhabitants lived mainly in squalor. It was dire but not unspeakable. There was no running water, there were no lights, nor any trees; there was only the cold wind. I never got to Cape Town International Airport, but I could just imagine travelers arriving and heading up the highway and looking at this grotesque settlement from the taxi window and saying to the driver, 'Do people actually live there?'

New Rest was adjacent to an equally squalid but older settlement, called Guguletu, a place of old low beat-up brick houses. Guguletu had achieved prominence in 1993 when a 26-year-old Californian, Amy Biehl, was killed here. She had been a Stanford graduate, living in South Africa as a volunteer in voter registration for the following year's free election, and had driven three African friends home to the township as a favor. Seeing her white face, a mob of African boys ('dozens') screamed in eagerness, for this was a black township and she was white prey. Her car was showered with stones and stopped, she was dragged from it. Her black women friends pleaded with the mob to spare her. 'She's a comrade!' Amy herself appealed to her assailants. She was harried viciously, beaten to the ground, her head smashed with a brick, and she was stabbed in the heart – killed like an animal.

A small cross at the roadside in Guguletu by a gas station marked the spot where she was murdered. It is a main road, there must have been many people around who could have helped her. But no one did. A crude sign board behind the cross was daubed *Amy Bihl's Last Home Section 3 Gugs* – misspelled and so crude as to be insulting.

Defying death threats, some women in Guguletu who had witnessed the crime came forward and named Amy's killers. Four young men were convicted of the murder and sentenced to 18 years in prison. But three years after their imprisonment these murderers appeared before the Truth and Reconciliation Commission. They had an explanation. 'Their motive was political and not racial.' They were members of the Pan-Africanist Congress, they said, and were only carrying out the program of the party; which regarded all whites as 'settlers.'

Their argument was ridiculous. How this murder could have been regarded as non-racial made no sense. Mandela was out of prison, elections were scheduled, the country had been all but turned over to the African majority. The mob was of course racially motivated, for they had singled her out. Still, the murderers 'regretted' what they had done; they claimed they had 'remorse.' They pleaded to be released under the terms of general amnesty. Everything they said seemed to me lame and without merit.

The murderers' freedom would have been impossible without the assent of Amy's parents, Peter and Linda Biehl, who attended those sessions of the Truth and Reconciliation Commission. Though the mother of one of the killers was so disgusted and ashamed by her son's description of what he had done to Amy that she could not face him, the Biehls embraced the killers. They said that their daughter would have wanted this show of mercy, as she was 'on the side of the people who killed her.' The Biehls would not stand in the way of an amnesty.

So the murderers waltzed away. Astonishingly, two of them, Ntombeko Peni and Easy Nofomela, were given jobs by the Biehls. They still worked in salaried positions for the Amy Biehl Foundation, a charity started by Amy's forgiving parents, in their daughter's memory. This foundation received almost $2 million from USAID in 1997, for being 'dedicated to empowering people who are oppressed.'

The details of this arrangement baffled me. As a father, the thought of losing my children this way was horrifying – I would rather die myself. What would I do in the same tragic circumstances? Well, I would want the murderers off the street; and if somehow they gained their freedom I doubt that I would give them a job. It would enrage me to hear them whining and making excuses. I would expect deeds from them. It would pain me to have to look into their faces. Amy's parents did not share my feelings.

Later, I asked a South African journalist what she thought of the Truth and Reconciliation Commission. She said, 'If it was not for the concept of forgiveness, which was a steering force of the Truth and Reconciliation Commission, I wonder where we would have been? Sometimes incredible things happened, an army general responsible for a bombing met a man blinded by the explosion and shook hands. A torturer was forced to relive his actions. Sometimes killers asked parents for forgiveness and were accepted or rejected. Many people felt the Truth and Reconciliation Commission was a sham, but I thought the process was remarkable when it worked.'

The extreme and unusual forgiveness shown by Amy Biehl's parents is often remarked upon – so often, provoking debate, that it almost seems that the incredible mercy they showed was provocative to a salutary degree. But much of what was said by the murderers and their supporters was just cant and empty words, for though no one in South Africa seems to remember it, at the time of the amnesty the Biehls challenged them by saying, 'Are you in South Africa prepared to do your part?'

Guguletu's grimness was its history as a workers' area – men's hostels and men's huts. Male workers in South Africa had always been easier to control if they were away from their families. For one thing, they could always be sent back to their village. The mines were notorious for the hostels that were regulated like prison blocks. The squatter colony of New Rest that grew up beside Guguletu after 1991 was composed mainly of women who wanted to be near their husbands and boyfriends. Because it had been just plopped down on forty acres of sand there were no utilities, and as a consequence it stank and looked terrible. The huts were sheds made of ill-fitting boards, scrap lumber, bits of tin, plastic sheeting. The gaps between the boards were blasted by the gritty wind.

'I get sand and dust in my bed,' said Thando, the man who showed me around.

But, unexpectedly – to me, at any rate – there was an upbeat spirit in the place, a vitality and even a sense of purpose among the squatters. No lights had been put in but there were shops that sold candles for a few cents and other goods were listed in scrawls on cardboard: *Oil, Teabag, Sugar, Salt* – the basics.

I had not gone to New Rest alone. I had been put in touch with a white couple who took interested foreigners there as a way of putting them in touch with life at the margins of Cape Town. The visitors, startled by the squalor, inevitably made contributions to a common fund. A crèche for the children of working mothers had been started with this money – probably the only clean and well-painted building in the place, where two kindly African women looked after thirty-five well-behaved children from the camp.

Most of the shacks were owned by women and more than half the women were employed somewhere in Cape Town, as domestics or cleaners or clerks. The shops in the camp were run by women, and so were the little bars – known as 'shebeens' throughout South Africa, an Irish word (originally meaning 'bad ale') that had percolated into the language from soldiers' slang. I went into several of these shebeens and saw drunken boys and men sitting hunched because of the low ceiling. They were nursing bottles of Castle Lager, and smoking and playing pool and pawing ineffectually at fat little prostitutes.

Life could get no grimmer than this, I thought – the urban shanty town, without foliage, too sandy to grow anything but scrawny geraniums and stubbly cactus; people having to draw water into plastic buckets from standpipes, and using candles in their huts; cold in winter, sweltering in summer, very dirty, lying athwart a main highway; what was worse? Rural poverty at least had the virtue of gardens and animals and the traditional house of reliable mud and thatch. Rural poverty had its pieties, too, as well as customs and courtesies.

Thando took me to meet the committee. This too was funded by contributions from the visitors. The committee was of course all men. But they were optimists.

'There are no drugs or gangs here,' one man said. 'This is a peaceful place. This is our home.'

The squatters were mostly people from the eastern Cape, the old so-called homelands of the Transkei and the Ciskei, as well as the slums of East London, Port Elizabeth and Grahamstown, industrial cities which were not faring well in the new economy.

The committee had aims. One was for roads to be made throughout the squatter colony; another was for piped water.

'We want to build houses here,' a committee member explained to me.

The scheme had been outlined and blueprinted by some volunteer urban planners at the University of Cape Town. Every shack had been numbered and its plot recorded. A census had been taken.

'In situ upgrade,' the committee spokesman said, rolling out the plan on the table in the committee room.

The idea of transforming a squatter camp into a viable subdivision by upgrading existing dwellings had been accomplished in Brazil and India but not so far in South Africa. This meant that in place of each miserable shack there would be a small house or hut. The driving force for this was the pride the people took in having found a safe place to live. The goodwill of foreign visitors also helped: they had contributed money for the crèche, for three brick-making machines, and for the establishment of a trust fund. The fund was administered on a *pro bono* basis by an otherwise outward-bound travel company, Wilderness Cape Safaris, which had put New Rest on its itinerary. Some children were sponsored by visitors who sent money regularly for their clothes and education. It was a strange hand-to-mouth arrangement, but the element of self-help in it made me a well-wisher.

I asked what had been here before the squatter camp and got an interesting answer. It had been low bush with the specific function of concealing initiates (*mkweta*) in circumcision ceremonies (*ukoluka*) performed by the local Xhosa people. The deed was done with the slice of a spear (*mkonto*) on boys – men, really – aged from seventeen to twenty-five. No one could explain why circumcision was left so late, but all agreed that it was a necessary rite of passage, essential for male bonding.

'Even these days they use it,' one of the committee members said. 'In June and December, we see them – sometimes many of them, hiding in the bush at the far side.'

Though it was not bush, but only scrub land that lay next to the highway and bordered large scruffy settlements, the area must have had some significance as a refuge in earlier times. Here the newly circumcised young men were rusticated for six weeks of healing, wearing only rough blankets, cooking over smoky fires, their faces painted in the white clay that designated them as initiates of the old ceremony. They remained in the background. In the foreground was

Guguletu and this camp. New Rest, the squatter camp, was filled with people so grateful, all they wished for was to make their shacks more permanent, so they could stay there for the rest of their lives ...

One hot Sunday morning, with reluctance, hating to signify the end of my safari, I set out on the last leg of my trip. It was a day of blue sky and brisk winds. I bought a ticket on the train to Simonstown. Though I had varied my journey with chicken buses and cattle trucks and overcrowded minivans and *matatus*, it was possible to travel by rail between Simonstown and Nairobi. Cecil Rhodes's plan had been to extend this line to Cairo. But he had always been something of a dreamer. Another Rhodes wish was for Great Britain to take back the United States, so that we would be ruled by the monarchy, the Union Jack flapping over Washington.

First Class and Third Class were clearly marked on the train, yet we all sat in First, in spite of our tickets, black, white and all the other racial variations that characterized Cape Town's people. The conductor was nowhere in sight; no one punched our tickets. We sat, no one speaking, on this sunny morning.

We stopped at every station – Rosebank, Newlands, Kenilworth, Plumstead, Heathfield – but in spite of the pretty names some looked prosperous and some poor, with bungalows surrounded by shaven lawns, or squatters' shacks blowing with plastic litter, graffiti everywhere. Some of these places were the addresses listed in the Adult Entertainment ads of that day's *Cape Times*. I knew who lived here – 'Amy Kinky to the Extreme,' and 'Nikki and Candy for Your Threesome' and 'Abigail – On My Own' and 'Candice – Come Bend My Fender,' and the anonymous but just as promising 'Bored Sexy Housewife.'

Dead silence in the swaying train, people reading the papers, children kicking the seats, the great yawning torpor of a hot Sunday morning. We stopped in the glare of roofless platforms and then carried on. Soon we were at the shore, passing the wind-driven waves at False Bay and Muizenberg, a very stiff southeasterly with wicked chop driving the greasy lengths of black kelp, so thick you'd take it for a chopped up ship's hawser. It was strewn in such profusion that it obstructed surfers from paddling out to the breaks.

Just after Fishhoek I saw a strange thing. Out the window about sixty feet from shore, sticking straight out of the sea was a great flapping whale's tail. It was so near, a swimmer could easily have slapped it. The tail was upright and symmetrical, like a big black rubber thing swaying above the water.

A whale standing on its head? I looked around. The adults were dozing and the children seemed to take it as a normal occurrence, a whale's headstand in shallow water, an enormous creature's vertical tail glistening in the sunlight, and remaining upright for so long it was still there after the train passed.

'They do that all the time,' a man in the next car said, when I noticed that he had seen the whale, and I asked him about it. 'That was a Southern Right Whale. It's known as "sailing." No one knows why they do it.'

At Simonstown, the end of the line, I walked out of the small white station into the high road. This could have been the high road of any English coastal town, with greengrocers and chemist shops and lime-washed bombproof-looking brick houses named 'Belmont' and 'Belvedere' and 'The Pines.' The arcades and shop terraces were dated 1901 and 1910, and even the coast itself looked English – Cornish to be exact, rocky and wind-flattened, as though Penzance might be just down the road.

The naval station was the reason for Simonstown's existence, so it was not odd to find fish and chip shops, and pubs advertising 'Traditional Roast Beef and Yorkshire Pud.' Captain Cook and Charles Darwin and Scott of the Antarctic and Rudyard Kipling and Mark Twain and many others who had rounded the Cape had stopped in this beautiful harbor. The funny old self-conscious timewarp, with cottages and villas and little chalets on the bluff above the road, even the bus shelters and the telephone kiosks, mimicked those in the blustery harbor villages of the kingdom by the sea.

I walked to Boulders Beach to see the colony of jackass penguins. Unperturbed by the nearness of bungalows and spectators, they were nesting on eggs, frolicking in the surf, and wobbling up the strand like perplexed nuns.

On the coast road at one of the Simonstown bus shelters I waited for a bus to Cape National Park. All the difficulty was behind me. I was just sitting on a bench, waiting to board a bus for the short ride to Cape Point, the end of my trip. A man sitting on a bench opposite was smoking a cigarette and reading a copy of that day's Johannesburg

222 · CAPE TOWN CALLING

Star. Some words caught my eye. Flagged on the front top of the paper was the teasing headline, 'PESSIMISTIC GLOBETROTTER WINS NOBEL PRIZE.'

'Looks like I've got the big one,' I murmured, and leaned closer, to give this stranger some news that would amaze him.

But he hadn't heard me speak, nor did he hear me sigh. The feeling came and went, like the overhead drone of one of those search and rescue planes that misses the castaway adrift in a rubber dinghy: just the briefest flutter of hope. But no one actually loses, because there is only one winner in the Swedish Lottery.

The man engrossed in the newspaper was fleeing his home in England, so he told me. I found it hard to concentrate after the vision I had just had. His name was Trevor. We sat together on the bus and he related his sad story. Trevor had been a crewman on a merchant vessel carrying ammo during the Falklands War. The ship had come under fire, days of shelling.

'The net result was the skipper lost it – went round the bend – wouldn't leave his cabin, had to be dragged on shore, was invalided out. But that wasn't the worst, was it?'

'What was the worst of it?' Still I saw the words, PESSIMISTIC GLOBETROTTER, but I took pleasure in the way Trevor, concentrating on his story, dealt with his newspaper by folding it in quarters and tucking it under his bottom, the teasing headline pressed under one buttock.

'Went ashore for the post, didn't I? Was a "Dear John" letter, wasn't it? And they thought I'd go mental like the skipper, so they discharged me before I could take a header off the ship. Called me wife, didn't I? She says, "There's nothing to discuss, Trevor" and "Why are you shouting?" And she bloody hangs up on me, doesn't she? So I went home and we split up. It was horrible. Now her boyfriend goes around saying, "Trevor refuses to have a drink with me."'

Trevor's story and the *Star* somewhat colored my view of the Cape Peninsula. We crossed a great empty herbaceous moorland of purply-blue *fynbos*, low bush shaking in the wind, as aromatic as the *maquis* in Corsica, miles of trembling herbs. Some wild things roamed here – eland and ostrich, children on school outings, baboons, tourists.

'*Tutta la famiglia!*' an Italian woman on the bus screeched, seeing some peevish baboons by the roadside baring their teeth at her.

When the bus stopped at this, the uttermost end of Africa, I got out. Trevor followed along. He lingered to buy a souvenir baseball cap lettered *Cape Point* on the crown. I kept walking, to the lookout, down to the sloping trail, to the narrow path in the bright afternoon, through the gusting wind. On my left, the cliff dropped away 200 feet to frothy ocean. I walked to Dias Point – Bartolomeo Dias was here in 1488 – and farther on, to Cape Point itself, jutting like the prow of a ship over the bright sea, until I reached the last of the warnings, *No Access Beyond this Point*, and *Do Not Throw Stones*, and *End of Trail*.

About the Authors

GABEBA BADEROON is the author of three poetry collections – *The Dream in the Next Body, The Museum of Ordinary Life* and *A Hundred Silences* – while her poems and short fiction have appeared in various anthologies. In 2005 she received the DaimlerChrysler Award for South African Poetry and held the Guest Writer Fellowship at the Nordic Africa Institute. Gabeba is also a scholar and has written for the *Sunday Independent, Mail & Guardian, Oprah* and *Real Simple* magazines.

BREYTEN BREYTENBACH is one of the leading poets of his generation and a gifted painter. He was a committed opponent of apartheid and left South Africa in 1960, settling in Paris. When he returned to the country with a false passport in 1975, he was charged with terrorism and jailed for seven years, a period captured in his prison memoir, *The True Confessions of an Albino Terrorist.* He currently divides his time between Europe, South Africa and the USA. He has exhibited his art in many countries and won numerous literary awards, including the Hertzog Prize (twice) and the CNA prize.

DARREL BRISTOW-BOVEY studied law at the University of Cape Town and completed a masters degree with distinction in English literature. He rose to prominence as a columnist on the *Sunday Independent* and went on to write for a number of magazines and newspapers. He has won numerous journalism and literary awards and has published two best-sellers: *I Moved Your Cheese* and *The Naked Bachelor.* He recently turned his hand to television screenwriting, acting as head writer for, amongst others, *Hard Copy* on SABC3. His most recent book, *Superzero,* won the 2006 Sanlam Prize for Youth Literature.

Multiple award winner EDWIN CAMERON studied at Stellenbosch, Oxford and Unisa before joining the Johannesburg Bar in 1983. He was appointed to the High Court in 1995 and served as an Acting Justice in the Constitutional Court before being appointed to the Supreme Court of Appeal. He has co-authored a number of books, including *Defiant Desire – Gay and Lesbian Lives in South Africa* and *Honoré's South African Law of Trusts.* His latest work, *Witness to AIDS,* is part memoir, part analysis, in which he grapples with the impact of HIV/AIDS on his own life and on society in general.

PAPA CHRIS was a teacher in Burundi who fled the troubles there in the mid-1990s to make a fresh start in Cape Town. Having a Hutu father and a Tutsi mother, he was persecuted by both sides in the ethnic conflict. Some of his family were killed before they were able to flee and he himself only narrowly escaped being burnt to death by a Tutsi mob. After suffering discrimination in various townships, his family have settled in Muizenberg. Chris has worked as a trolley control manager at Game and as a teacher.

Nobel Laureate and multiple award winner, J M COETZEE is the author of numerous critical works and novels, including the seminal *Waiting for the Barbarians* and *Life and Times of Michael K*. His novel *Disgrace* won the Booker Prize making him the first author to have won this award twice. Formerly Professor of General Literature at the University of Cape Town, he now lives in Australia.

MICHAEL COPE is the son of writer Jack Cope and artist Lesley. He has published two novels and two volumes of poetry. He is married to writer and academic Julia Martin and has three children. He lives in Muizenberg, where he works as a designer and goldsmith. His latest work, *Intricacy*, is a memoir that's been described as 'a magpie snapshot of one family's life in apartheid South Africa.'

TOM EATON grew up in Cape Town, completing his studies in English Literature and Creative Writing at the University of Cape Town. While finishing his Masters dissertation, a novel to be published by Penguin SA in 2007, he worked as a journalist for a leading sports website, a position he left in 2002 when he decided to go freelance. A year later he was offered a column by the *Mail & Guardian*, and he continues to write for that newspaper. His books include *Twelve Rows Back*, *The De Villiers Code* and *Texas*.

LINDA FORTUNE was born in the Bo-Kaap and grew up in District Six where she lived with her family until she was 22. After leaving Trafalgar High School, she worked as a secretary and office administrator until 1994, when she became education officer at the District Six Museum in Buitenkant Street. *The House in Tyne Street* recounts her childhood memories, presenting the vivid story of a place that is no more.

The English daughter of two Oxford dons, OLIVIA GORDON returned to her family's South African home when she was 17 and entered the rave scene of the late 1990s. *The Agony of Ecstasy* traces her experiences in the Cape's underground world of drugs and trance parties. After her time in Cape Town she returned to England to read English at Cambridge University. She now lives in London and writes for a number of newspapers and magazines.

CHARLES JACOBY is a British freelance journalist who won three young journalist of the year awards, co-adapted Graham Greene's *A Gun For Sale* for theatre, and co-wrote a comedy musical about water pollution called *Oogiligoogilidytes*. *In Search of Will Carling*, the story of an overland journey from London to Cape Town to see the 1995 Rugby World Cup, was his first book. He currently makes and presents television documentaries for, amongst others, the History Channel and the BBC.

ZUBEIDA JAFFER is an award-winning journalist, author, activist and mother. Working for the *Cape Times* and later with community newspapers, Jaffer played an important role in the resistance movement in the Western Cape and was a key organiser in the formation of the United Democratic Front. She headed the media department at the University of the Western Cape in the late 80s, after which she became a correspondent for South African and Canadian news agencies. Since 1997 she has worked as the group parliamentary editor of Independent Newspapers.

SHAUN JOHNSON was educated at Rhodes University and Oxford, where he was a Rhodes Scholar. A former newspaper editor and award-winning writer, he was previously Deputy Chief Executive of Independent News and Media. He is currently CEO of the Mandela Rhodes Foundation. Johnson has written for a number of international publications, been a political commentator for numerous television and radio stations and published works of fiction and non-fiction. *Strange Days Indeed* traces the last days of apartheid and the interregnum leading up to the first democratic elections in 1994. He recently published his first novel, *The Native Commissioner*.

JONATHAN KAPLAN studied medicine at the University of Cape Town before moving to the United Kingdom and then the USA to acquire specialist surgical qualifications. After ten years of clinical experience and research he left the secure career of hospital surgery to travel as a doctor, journalist, writer and documentary filmmaker. With *The Dressing Station* he won the Sunday Times Alan Paton Award for non-fiction. His latest book is entitled *Contact Wounds*.

AHMED KATHRADA was sentenced to life imprisonment for his involvement in the struggle against apartheid. He spend 25 years in Cape Town jails along with leaders such as Nelson Mandela and Walter Sisulu. After his release in 1989 he was elected as an MP and served as parliamentary counsellor in the office of the president. In 1997 he became chairperson of the Robben Island Council and, besides *Memoirs*, has written about Cape Town prison life in two other books.

JUDY KIBINGE is a Kenyan filmmaker who lives in Nairobi and describes herself as a Jack of All Trades. Having risen to the position of creative director of McCann Erickson advertising agency, she resigned in 2000 in order to make her own films and documentaries. Kibinge has written and directed a number of movies, as well as a television series untitled *Pumzika* (2005). 'Diary of an Ex-Black Woman' records her impressions of Cape Town during annual visits to the city's Sithengi film market.

JOSEPH LELYVELD worked at *The New York Times* for nearly four decades, some of the time spent as a correspondent in London, New Delhi, Hong Kong and Johannesburg. He also served as the paper's foreign editor, managing editor, and as its executive editor from 1994 to 2001. *Move Your Shadow* – the book about his time in South Africa – won the Pulitzer Prize for General Non-Fiction in 1986.

AL LOVEJOY was an international drug smuggler. His startling autobiography, *Acid Alex*, charts his experiences from orphanage to reformatory, from the District Six gangs to numerous prisons, from Angola at war to Stellenbosch during the Vöelvry movement. In the 1990s, Al set up a syndicate smuggling cannabis into Europe and ecstasy back to Africa, and he was arrested in Belgium, where he was imprisoned for two and a half years. He eventually had to face very hard realities and managed to break free from organised crime.

RIAN MALAN is an author, journalist and songwriter. He is best known for his memoir of growing up in apartheid South Africa, *My Traitor's Heart*, in which he explores his own family history and race relations through the lens of prominent murder cases. He has worked as a farm labourer, ridden freight trains across America, created screenplays for Mel Brooks and Mick Jagger, and served as a staff writer on *Esquire* and *Rolling Stone*. He currently writes for a host of local and international magazines and has brought out a CD of his brand of boeremusiek.

After 27 years in Cape Town jails, NELSON MANDELA emerged as South Africa's first democratically elected president and the nation's most admired son. Leading the country through a peaceful transition, his contribution to South Africa – and Cape Town – is unsurpassed. In *Long Walk to Freedom* Mandela recounts the experiences that helped shape his destiny.

PETER MOORE is an Australian travel writer whose young, alternative voice has found its way into a number of international travel magazines and newspapers in the UK and Australia. His innovative website and witty books on travel (such as *The Wrong Way Home* and *The Full Montezuma*) have made him one of the most popular new voices in the genre. In *Swahili for the Broken-hearted* he arrives in Cape Town for an epic journey from Cape to Cairo, but finds it extremely hard to leave the comforts of the Mother City.

MICHAEL AV MORRIS was born and brought up in Kimberley. He began his career in journalism at the *Diamond Fields Advertiser* in 1979, joining the *Cape Argus* four years later. He spent three years in London in the mid-1980s reporting for all titles in the Argus Group. Returning to Cape Town in 1988, he joined the group's team in parliament, becoming political correspondent for the *Cape Argus* in 1990. Morris has been a Special Writer on the paper since 1996. He is married to journalist Sharon Sorour-Morris, and has three children.

Following his tenure as Resident Scholar at the Ford Foundation's headquarters in New York, NJABULO NDEBELE became Vice Chancellor of the University of Cape Town in 2000. He is a writer with many years of teaching and research behind him and holds a number of honorary doctorates in literature. From 1993 to 1998 he was Vice Chancellor and Principal of the University of the North and previously served as Vice Rector of the University of the Western Cape. His book *'Fools' and Other Stories* – a chronicle of life in a black township under apartheid – was the joint winner of the Sanlam prize for outstanding fiction in 1986, and received the Noma award for the best book published in Africa in 1983.

NOMVUYO NGCELWANE grew up in the heart of District Six and today lives in the township of Khayelitsha. She is Circuit Manager of the Kuilsrivier area for the Western Cape Education Department. Her duties include assisting principals in Khayelitsha and Eersterivier with the management of their schools. *Sala Kahle, District Six* is a collection of her memories of growing up as a black woman in a predominantly coloured suburb of Cape Town.

MIKE NICOL works as a journalist and teaches creative writing part-time at the University of Cape Town. He has written novels, notably *The Powers That Be*, poetry and non-fiction, including *A Good-Looking Corpse* on the *Drum* journalists of the 1950s. His meditation on the Cape, *Sea-Mountain, Fire City*, resulted from a sojourn in Berlin and an attempt to find a sense of place in Cape Town, the city where he was born and has spent most of his life. His most recent work, *Out to Score* (written with Joanne Hitchens) is a Cape Town crime thriller.

SUREN PILLAY is a senior lecturer in the Department of Political Studies at the University of the Western Cape, where he teaches political theory and political philosophy. His research interests include the intersections of political identity and political violence, democratic theory, race and questions of coloniality and postcoloniality. He is also a visual artist.

MAMPHELA RAMPHELE is a medical doctor with a PhD in Social Anthropology (and numerous honorary degrees). She first rose to prominence in the 1970s as a founder member of the Black Consciousness Movement and later served as Vice Chancellor of the University of Cape Town before taking up the position of managing director of the World Bank in Washington DC. Ramphele was subsequently appointed as the executive chairperson of Circle Capital Ventures, a venture-capital black economic empowerment company. She has written a number of books, including *Uprooting Poverty: The South African Challenge*, for which she received the Noma Award for Publishing in Africa.

RICHARD RIVE grew up in District Six and studied at the University of Cape Town, Columbia and Oxford, where he received a doctorate in English and was later Junior Research Fellow at Magdalen College. He won many literary awards and his works have been translated into more than 15 languages. In *'Buckingham Palace', District Six* Rive recounts life in this community in the years leading up to the forced removals and demolition. Rive was murdered in 1989, a victim of the appalling level of crime in Cape Town.

The direct descendant of a Dutch East India Company soldier who arrived in Cape Town in 1696, WILLEM STEENKAMP grew up with an acute sense of Cape history. In the course of a varied career he has been an author, journalist, soldier, military-affairs commentator, scriptwriter, playwright, security advisor, specialist tour guide and producer of military tattoos. He has written 17 books in Afrikaans and English covering a variety of topics, and has been awarded three writing prizes and one journalism prize. One of his personal favourites is *Poor Man's Bioscope* which, he claims, has 'the last good title for a book about Cape Town' – he may be right.

JONNY STEINBERG was a Rhodes Scholar and received a doctorate in political theory from Oxford. He returned to South Africa in 1998 and worked for *Business Day*, reporting on the constitutional court and the police. He left the newspaper to write the best-selling *Midlands*, an investigation into the murder of a white farmer in KwaZulu-Natal. *Midlands* won the Sunday Times Alan Paton Award for non-fiction and the Booksellers' Choice Award. In *The Number* (which also won the Alan Paton prize) he looks at the world of Cape Town prison gangs seen through the eyes of an inmate in Pollsmoor.

PAUL THEROUX was born and educated in the United States after which he worked as a teacher and lecturer in, amongst others, Malawi and Uganda. During this time – the mid 1960s – he began writing articles, short stories and novels. He lived in England for 17 years before returning to the United States, but continues to travel widely. He has won numerous literary awards, including the Whitbread in 1978. His travel writing ranges over many continents; *Dark Star Safari* traces a journey from Cairo to Cape Town.

PIETER-DIRK UYS was born in Cape Town and has been in the theatre business since the 1960s. The creator of Evita Bezuidenhout, 'the most famous white woman in South Africa', he has an enormous following across the racial and political spectrum. His plays and revues are performed internationally and he is the author of a number of books, including the autobiographical *Between the Devil and the Deep*. He lives in Darling on the West Coast.

STEPHEN WATSON is a professor of English at the University of Cape Town and has published five volumes of poetry, including *Selected Essays* (1990), *A Writer's Diary* (1997), *The Other City: Selected Poems* (2000), as well as having edited several other books, most recently *Dante in South Africa* (2005) and *A City Imagined* (2006). A further collection of his poems is due out in 2007.

TONY WEAVER is a multi-award winning journalist and photographer, and a much published freelance writer. Between 1981 and 1992, he covered Namibia and South Africa's violent transitions to democracy for a range of outlets – initially for the *Rand Daily Mail* and *Cape Times*, and then for various radio stations. From 1989 until 1992 he was southern African correspondent for the Canadian Broadcasting Corporation's TV News. In late 1992, he and his wife – filmmaker Liz Fish – embarked on a two year, 65 000-kilometre journey through Africa. This led to a decade-long career as a travel and environment writer and photographer. He is currently news editor at the *Cape Times*.

Sources and copyright permissions

The compiler and the publishers are grateful for permission to reproduce copyrighted material. Every effort has been made to acknowledge all copyright owners and any inadvertent inaccuracies will be rectified at the earliest opportunity.

BADEROON, GABEBA 'High Traffic' in *Chimurenga* 7 (2005)

BREYTENBACH, BREYTEN *The True Confessions of an Albino Terrorist* (Taurus, Emmarentia, 1984)

———— *Return to Paradise* (David Philip, Cape Town, 1993)

BRISTOW-BOVEY, DARREL 'Operation Copulation' in *"But I Digress …"*: *A Selection of his Best Columns* (Zebra Press, Cape Town, 2003)

CAMERON, EDWIN *Witness to AIDS* (Tafelberg, Cape Town, 2005)

CHRIS, PAPA 'In Transit' in Shirley Gunn and Mary-Magdalene Tal (eds) *Torn Apart: Thirteen Refugees Tell Their Stories* (Human Rights Media Centre, Cape Town, 2003)

COETZEE, JM *Boyhood: Scenes from Provincial Life* (Secker & Warburg, London, 1997)

———— *Youth* (Secker & Warburg, London, 2002)

COPE, MICHAEL *Intricacy: A Meditation on Memory* (Double Storey, Cape Town, 2005)

EATON, TOM 'An Ocean Apart' in the *Mail & Guardian*, 7 April 2004

———— 'Prepare to Repel Boarders' in the *Mail & Guardian*, 3 January 2006

———— 'Merry Sport of Minstrelsy' in the *Mail & Guardian*, 3 January 2005

FORTUNE, LINDA *The House in Tyne Street: Childhood Memories of District Six* (Kwela Books, Cape Town, 1996)

GORDON, OLIVIA *The Agony of Ecstasy* (Continuum, London, 2004)

JACOBY, CHARLES *In Search of Will Carling: An Epic Journey Through Africa to the Rugby World Cup* (Simon & Schuster, London, 1996)

JAFFER, ZUBEIDA *Our Generation* (Kwela Books, Cape Town, 2003)

JOHNSON, SHAUN 'The Day Mandela Came Home' and 'A Holy and Unholy Place' in *Strange Days Indeed – Tales from the Old and the Nearly New South Africa* (Bantam Press, London, 1993; reprinted by permission of The Random House Group Ltd)

KAPLAN, JONATHAN *The Dressing Station: A Surgeon's Odyssey* (Macmillan, London, 2002)

KATHRADA, AHMED *Memoirs* (Zebra Press, Cape Town, 2004)

KIBINGE, JUDY 'Diary of an Ex-Black Woman' in *Chimurenga* 7 (2005)

LELYVELD, JOSEPH *Move Your Shadow: South Africa, Black and White* (London, Abacus, 1986; © 1987 by Joseph Lelyveld; reprinted with permission of The Wylie Agency, Inc.)

LOVEJOY, AL *Acid Alex* (Zebra Press, Cape Town, 2005)

MALAN, RIAN 'The Wrong Side of the Cape' in *Travel and Leisure*, February 2003

MANDELA, NELSON *Long Walk to Freedom: The Autobiography of Nelson Mandela* (Abacus, London, 1995)

MOORE, PETER *Swahili for the Broken-hearted: Cape Town to Cairo by Any Means Possible* (Bantam Press, London, 2003; reprinted by permission of The Random House Group Ltd)

MORRIS, MICHAEL AV 'Side by Side, Far Apart: The Valley's Great Divide' in the *Cape Argus*, 5 November 1997

—— 'A Suburb of Contrasts and Change', in the *Cape Argus*, 21 May 1998

NDEBELE, NJABULO S 'Elections, Mountains, and One Voter' in André Brink (ed) *SA 24 April 1994: An Authors' Diary* (Queillerie, Pretoria, 1994)

NGCELWANE, NOMVUYO *Sala Kahle District Six: An African Woman's Perspective* (Kwela Books, Cape Town,1998)

NICOL, MIKE *Sea-Mountain, Fire City: Living in Cape Town* (Kwela Books, Cape Town, 2001)

PILLAY, SUREN 'Notes on the Cape Town Skollie' in *Chimurenga* 7 (2005)

RAMPHELE, MAMPHELA *Steering by the Stars: Being Young in South Africa* (Tafelberg, Cape Town, 2002)

RIVE, RICHARD 'Buckingham Palace', District Six* (David Philip, Cape Town, 1987)

STEINBERG, JONNY *The Number: One Man's Search for Identity in the Cape Underworld and Prison Gangs* (Jonathan Ball, Johannesburg, 2004)

STEENKAMP, WILLEM *Poor Man's Bioscope: Cape Town – a Panorama of People Places and Events* (H Timmins, Sparta, New Jersey, 1979)

THEROUX, PAUL *Dark Star Safari: Overland from Cairo to Cape Town* (Penguin Books, London, 2002); © Cape Cod Scriveners Co., 2002

UYS, PIETER-DIRK *Between the Devil and the Deep: A Memoir of Acting and Reacting* (Zebra Press, Cape Town, 2005)

WATSON, STEPHEN *A Writer's Diary* (Queillerie, Cape Town, 1997)

WEAVER, TONY 'Poor No More' in *Living Africa*, July 1996

JUSTIN FOX is a travel writer and photographer for Ge*taway* magazine. He was a Rhodes Scholar and received a doctorate in English from Oxford University, after which he was a research fellow at the University of Cape Town, where he now teaches part time. His articles have appeared internationally in a number of publications and on a wide range of subjects, while his short stories and poems have appeared in various anthologies. He has written scripts and directed award-winning documentaries, and is a two-time Mondi journalism award winner (1999 and 2004). His most recent books are *With Both Hands Waving* (2002), *Just Add Dust* (2004) and *Under the Sway* (2007).